ISBN-13: 978-1-58023-082-7
ISBN-10: 1-58023-082-2

"A great resource for an~~y~~ ~~_ _~~ _ᴜᴜ
explore the connection between their faith
and caring for God's good creation,
our environment."

—PAUL GORMAN, executive director,
National Religious Partnership for the Environment

"Splendid.... Lively and compelling reflections
on taking care of the earth."

—*PUBLISHERS WEEKLY*

The ancient Israelites, like all our ancestors, depended on nature for their daily livelihood. Rain and crops determined their fate. Nature was an integral part of their lives and of their faith.

But what is our place in nature,
and what is nature's place in *our* spiritual lives?

In today's modern culture, we've become separated from the spiritual possibilities of the natural world. "Modern" religion often overlooks nature, focusing instead on history and human drama.

This book offers an alternative ... a different, eye- and soul-opening way of viewing religion: a perspective grounded in nature, and rich in insights for people of all faiths.

Respect for the holiness of Creation, our duty to protect the natural world, reverence for the land—a focus on nature is part of the fabric of Jewish thought. Here, innovators in Judaism and ecology lead us on an exploration of the concepts of sacred space, sacred time, and community. They bring us a richer understanding of the long-neglected themes of nature that are woven through the biblical creation story, ancient texts, traditional law, the holiday cycles, prayer, and *mitzvot* (good deeds).

Ecology & the Jewish Spirit is the first book in the emerging field of religion and the environment to reflect a Jewish ecological perspective. It describes the wisdom the Jewish tradition has to offer all of us, to help nature become a sacred, spiritual part of our own lives.

Ecology & the Jewish Spirit

WHERE NATURE AND THE SACRED MEET

Edited and with Introductions by
Ellen Bernstein

For People of All Faiths, All Backgrounds
JEWISH LIGHTS Publishing

Ecology & the Jewish Spirit: Where Nature and the Sacred Meet

2008 First Quality Paperback Edition, Second Printing
2000 First Quality Paperback Edition, First Printing

"New York Is a Girl" originally appeared in *Story* magazine; reprinted by per-mission of Robert Sand.

Library of Congress Cataloging-in-Publication Data

Ecology & the Jewish spirit : where nature and the sacred meet / edited and
    with introductions by Ellen Bernstein.
        p.cm.
Includes bibliographical references and index.
ISBN-13: 978-1-58023-082-7 (pbk.)
ISBN-13: 978-1-68336-040-7 (hc)

1. Human ecology—Religious aspects—Judaism. 2. Agricultural laws andlegislation (Jewish law) 3. Fasts and feasts—Judaism. I. Bernstein, Ellen, 1953–

2963'8—dc21

BM538.H85E36 1997   CIP
97-35828   r97

Manufactured in the United States of America

Cover art: *Phoenix Bird III.* Original Serigraph by Shraga Weil, 1987, Cat. #S-230. Published by Safrai Gallery, 19 King David St., Jerusalem, 94101 Israel. Fax: 972-2-6240387.

Book and cover designed by Chelsea Dippel

For People of All Faiths, All Backgrounds
Published by Jewish Lights Publishing
www.jewishlights.com

This book is lovingly dedicated to all the *shomrei adamah,*
the keepers of the earth whose work and caring continue to make
the earth such a beautiful place in which to live. May this book
be a blessing and a source of inspiration to you.

CONTENTS

Acknowledgments   9

Introduction   11

🍃 Sacred Place   15

1 *Adam, Adamah,* and *Adonai:* The Relationship between
   Humans, Nature, and God in the Bible
   JEFF SULTAR   19

2 Befriending the Desert Owl
   SHAMU FENYVESI   27

3 (Mis)reading Genesis: A Response to Environmentalist
   Critiques of Judaism
   NEAL JOSEPH LOEVINGER   32

4 Is There Only One Holy Land?
   BRADLEY SHAVIT ARTSON   41

5 How Wilderness Forms a Jew
   ELLEN BERNSTEIN   50

6 A Sentient Universe
   EVERETT GENDLER   57

7 Practical Kabbalah: A Family History
   CHARLES FENYVESI   69

8 Jewish Perspectives on Limiting Consumption
   ELIEZER DIAMOND   80

9 New York Is a Girl
   ROBERT SAND   88

🍂 Sacred Time   95

Cycles of the Jewish Year

10 The Sun, the Moon, and the Seasons:
   Ecological Implications of the Hebrew Calendar
   DEBRA J. ROBBINS   98

11 "In Your Goodness, You Renew Creation":
   The Creation Cycles of the Jewish Liturgy
   LAWRENCE TROSTER   107

12 Shabbat and the Sabbatical Year
   DAN FINK   112

13 The Land of Your Soul
   MARC SIRINSKY   121

The Holidays

14 Rain and the Calendar
   ELLEN COHN   127

15 Sukkot: Holiday of Joy
   ELLEN BERNSTEIN   133

16 Sukkot: Gathering the Boughs
   DAN FINK   137

17 A History of Tu B'Sh'vat
   ELLEN BERNSTEIN   139

18 The Tu B'Sh'vat Seder
   ELLEN BERNSTEIN   142

19 Purim Rivers and Revels
   DAN FINK   151

20 The Parsley versus the Potato: A Passover Reminiscence
   EVERETT GENDLER   153

21 Leaving Egypt
   DAN FINK   155

22 Grow Your Own—Barley, That Is!
EILEEN ABRAMS 157

23 Mountain Paths
DAN FINK 160

24 In Search of the Omer
ELLEN COHN 162

25 Of Dust, Ashes, Comets, and a Three-Year-Old
DAN FINK 167

🍃 **Sacred Community** 169

26 Cosmos and Chaos: Biblical Views of Creation
NEIL GILLMAN 172

27 Restoring a Blessing
SHAMU FENYVESI 180

28 What Is the Common Wealth?
DAVID EHRENFELD 185

29 Jewish Agricultural Law: Ethical First Principles
and Environmental Justice
VICTOR RABOY 190

30 The Blessings of Holiness
LAWRENCE TROSTER 200

31 Nature, Spirit, Body
SHIRA DICKER 207

32 Judaism's Environmental Laws
BARRY FREUNDEL 214

33 Business and Environment: A Case Study
PHILIP J. BENTLEY 225

34 Between Dust and Divinity: Maimonides
and Jewish Environmental Ethics
DAN FINK 230

35 What Does the Hour Demand?
    Environmentalism As Self-Realization
    DAVID GEDZELMAN   240

36 Living As If God Mattered:
    Heschel's View of Nature and Humanity
    MARC SWETLITZ   244

37 How Community Forms a Jew
    ELLEN BERNSTEIN   250

    Notes   257

    About the Contributors   269

    Index   273

Acknowledgments

My deepest gratitude to Henry and Edith Everett and Steven Rockefeller who provided the initial funding for this project. I began this book as a project of *Shomrei Adamah*—Keepers of the Earth in 1990 with Henry and Edith Everett's generous help. The original goal was to develop a manual on Judaism and ecology for the rabbis of New York. I soon realized that the project embodied an idea whose time had come and decided to develop the book for a broader audience. Steven Rockefeller provided additional funds to bring this work to fruition.

Special thanks to the original *Shomrei Adamah* Board: Rabbi Mordechai Liebling, Evie Berger, Mimi Schneirov, Rabbi Joseph B. Glaser *z"l*, Paul Growald, Pete Hoskins, and John Ruskay who provided much needed love, moral support, and sustenance over the course of this project.

A heartfelt thanks to Rabbi Dan Fink and Rabbi Everett Gendler who nurtured the soul of *Shomrei Adamah* since its inception. Thanks to all the authors who labored in love on this project and responded so generously to all of my requests.

Rabbi Lenny Gordon, Cecily Kihn, Mindy Shapiro, Peter Pitzele, Rachel Brodie, Ellen Frankel, Pam Bernstein, and Sandee Brawarsky read sections of the manuscript and offered helpful suggestions. Hannah Ashley provided early editing assistance. Harvey Blume taught me the art and joy of editing, worked on several essays with me, and provided constant friendship and humor through the winter of this project.

Many foundations generously supported *Shomrei Adamah*'s work over the years, providing me the opportunity to lay the foundation for this work. Thanks to Lynda and Carl Levinson and the Max and Anna Levinson Foundation, John Hunting and the Beldon Fund, and James Cummings, Ruth Sorenson Cummings, Rachel Cowan, Charlie Halpern, and the Nathan Cummings Foundation who took a risk on *Shomrei Adamah* and supported it through its infancy. Other foundations contributed to the growth and development of *Shomrei Adamah*. Thanks to Judith Ginsberg, Eli Evans and the Covenant Foundation, Hooper Brooks, Ed Skloot and the Surdna Foundation, and George Hess and the Joseph Meyerhoff Fund.

Thousands of individuals, synagogues, and Jewish institutions supported the work of *Shomrei Adamah* with their membership gifts and kindnesses for which I am forever grateful.

Finally, thanks to Stuart Matlins, Sandra Korinchak and the staff at Jewish Lights for being so sensitive to all my concerns and for producing such a beautiful volume, and to my editor Arthur Magida, who provided inspiration, laughter, and expert wordsmithing on the final leg of my journey.

Ellen Bernstein
Wissahickon Creek
Mt. Airy
Philadelphia, PA

Introduction

ELLEN BERNSTEIN

Twenty-five years ago, while studying at the University of California at Berkeley's environment program, one of the first in the country, I was troubled by the "problem" approach taken to the environment. This kind of orientation seemed to reduce the natural world into discrete segments and identified and attacked problems one by one. As fast as we could recognize and remedy one problem, a new one loomed on the horizon.

I believed there was something fundamentally wrong with this piecemeal approach, since the environmental crisis is, at its heart, a crisis in values. It begins when people objectify the natural world and treat nature as a resource to manipulate, rather than as an aspect of the Sacred to revere.

I concluded that part of what was at fault was an educational system that advances a reductionist and utilitarian world-view. I believed we must *learn* to value nature as an end in itself, not as a means to an end. We must educate for wholeness and joy, not utility. At that time, I decided to devote myself to teaching biology in a way that would inspire students about the mystery of life: I would rely on great nature writers and on the students' encounters with wilderness to help me with the teaching.

At the same time, I was on my own spiritual quest. After experimenting with many paths, I was ultimately drawn back to my own tradition. I began to study Jewish texts and found—to both my surprise and bewilderment—that Judaism was rich in spirit and wisdom concerning humanity's relationship with nature. The Creation story, Jewish law, the cycle of holidays, prayers, mitzvot (good deeds), and neighborly relations all reflect a reverence for land and a viable practice of stewardship. Judaism supported the values that I was teaching: that Creation is sacred

11

and humanity has the awesome and wonderful responsibility to guard and preserve it.

I believed I was tapping into a wellspring of Jewish culture that had been obscured by a generation whose world-view was molded by Israel and the Holocaust. I was disturbed that the precious wisdom of Judaism had never been made available to me; in fact, my early Jewish education left me spiritually empty and resentful. My experience was not dissimilar to many of my generation, who abandoned Judaism—never to return. I was convinced that the spiritual and ecological dimension that I discovered for myself had the potential to enrich Judaism and provide meaning for my generation and those to come. I hoped that someone would develop and promote this dimension of Judaism. At that time, no one did.

In 1988, with hospital syringes and other medical detritus washing up on the New Jersey shore and the threat of global warming becoming a reality, I founded *Shomrei Adamah*—Keepers of the Earth, the first organization dedicated to cultivating the ecological thinking and practices that are integral to Jewish life. With the input of many Jewish scholars, teachers, and rabbis around the country, *Shomrei Adamah* developed programs, publications, and curricula to illuminate Jewish ecological values and enhance Jewish spirituality.

As director of *Shomrei Adamah*, I believed that my most important contribution would be to synthesize a Jewish ecological perspective. So I targeted a group of colleagues who integrated an ecological orientation with their specific discipline, be it biblical studies, Jewish philosophy, Jewish law, anthropology, or agriculture, and who represented all walks of Jewish life, from Orthodox to Reform to secular, to work on pieces for a book.

Out of our discussions and work came *Ecology & the Jewish Spirit*, which for the first time, in one book, brings together the environmental understandings and practices implicit in ancient Jewish texts and makes them come alive for modern audiences.

Judaism's Hidden Message

It is important to address the fact that, up until now, Judaism's ecological message has remained hidden. There are at least three reasons for this:

- Biblical scholars and most modern Jews tend to focus on the historical dimension of Judaism. This tendency reflects the bias of our culture in general. Yet, the development of a civilization depends not only on history but also on nature. Until now, nature's role has remained hidden, the backdrop upon which the historical drama unfolds.

- Jewish texts are largely inaccessible to the unseasoned reader; the Talmud and Midrash invariably send the novice scurrying away. A beginner could not pick up a musical score and expect to play it immediately. So it is with classical Jewish texts, which are difficult and largely off-limits. Jewish texts are deep and rich, but most people will need a friend or teacher to help them navigate their way in the beginning.

- Moderns too often pose the wrong questions to religion. They ask what Judaism says about the "environmental crisis" or about "nature." *Nature* and *environment* are modern terms that have risen out of our separation from the natural world. Ancient Israelites depended on nature for their daily livelihood: rain and crops determined their fate, and nature was an integral part of their lives. In a culture where the wisdom and the force of nature were experienced each day and often each moment, terms like *environment* and *nature* have no meaning.

    Rather, Judaism's ecological message emerges when we observe what is sacred in Judaism. How are we to treat what is holy? And what is humanity's place amid the holiness? The Jewish understanding that the earth belongs to God attests to the fact that the earth and everything in it is holy, and this concept of holiness, *kedushah*, is the beginning of a unique Jewish environmental ethic.

Ecology & the Jewish Spirit explores this sense of *kedushah* in its many forms. The topics of the three sections, place, time, and community, are viewed in the context of holiness. The intention of such an approach is to offer the reader a vision of the whole: nature and environment as an integrated part of our lives, not separate from us.

The first section of the book, "Sacred Place," presents place as a religious principle at the heart of the Bible and examines the tension inherent in humanity's relationship to nature. It looks at the concept of place and our relationship to it from biblical, rabbinical, medieval, and contemporary perspectives.

Exploring place and our role in nature is familiar to many environmentalists. Exploring our relation to time, on the other hand, is an idea that few environmentalists consider. The second section of *Ecology & the Jewish Spirit* examines the dimensions of sacred time. Time is elusive and invisible; when we abuse it, place and community suffer. In Judaism, the temporal cycles are reflected in the seasonal holiday cycle, the monthly lunar cycle, the weekly Shabbat cycle, and the daily prayer cycle. These ritual markers encourage us to keep time in a way that is healthy for both people and planet.

The final section of *Ecology & the Jewish Spirit* examines the Jewish understanding of community and its implications for environment. While community is of concern for some environmentalists, it deserves a more prominent place on the environmental agenda. The early rabbis understood that humanity is inherently arrogant, and arrogance could lead people to destroy their neighbors, the natural world, and themselves. The rabbis devoted themselves to determining ways to ensure the survival of the Jewish community. Out of their discussions of individual rights versus responsibilities came not only an ethic of social responsibility but also an environmental practice that enables people to live with each other and the earth in a healthy and sustainable way.

In Jewish texts, we have a record of how a people managed both human destructiveness and human possibility over thousands of years. Through *Ecology & the Jewish Spirit*, their teachings can help meet the environmental challenges we face today.

Sacred Place

I have always been enchanted by place—by all kinds of places. My greatest pleasures come from exploring different environments. Gardens, overgrown corner lots, cemeteries, polluted rivers, and old, abandoned mills all find their way into my heart.

So it is no surprise that when I first began to explore the Bible for a spiritual direction, it was the places in it that spoke to me: the Garden of Eden, the Red Sea, the Sinai, the Jordan River, the Temple on Mount Zion, the waters of Babylon.

This view of Judaism was not particularly popular among the rabbis, theologians, and Jews I encountered in my youth. From them, I only heard about the historical events of the Jewish people: of the Exodus and God's rescue of the Jews, the salvation and redemption of the Jews. The mere mention of these words made me squeamish. Why did I need to be saved or redeemed? What did this have to do with me?

So I pursued my interests on my own, connecting to Judaism in my way. But not until I recently began studying at the Reconstructionist Rabbinical College did I recognize that I was not alone in my quest.

In my studies, I encountered the work of Jon Levenson, a professor of Jewish Studies at Harvard University, whose book *Sinai and Zion* explores the whole notion of "sacred place" in Judaism. So, too, Michael Fishbane, a professor of Jewish Studies at the University of Chicago, has explored in depth the notion of sacred center in Judaism. As it turns out, their work is partly a response to the generations of biblical scholars who emphasized the Deuteronomic morality tradition and the idea of a God who intervenes in history to save His people, to the exclusion of the idea of a Creator God and sacred place. When we also consider that throughout history, the rabbis were constantly defending themselves against pagan peoples who held a clearly defined sense of sacred place and therefore struggled to define Judaism according to its uniqueness—

its sacred history—then we get a greater understanding of why Jews tend to overlook the role of place and, with it, nature.

So, in fact, place *does* matter. To Levenson, understanding the role of the sacred center in Judaism can help us "acquire a sense of the lost dimension of spiritual experience." Levenson's work resonates with me. I have always felt that place most evokes my own spirituality, my connection with the Divine. Apparently, others feel the same way. When you ask someone where they have experienced the presence of God, they invariably say on a mountaintop or by water, rarely in a modern synagogue.

In the writings that follow, the authors explore the notion of place in Judaism, from the wilderness to the Land of Israel to New York City.

What is the Bible's view of the human place in nature? Does the text set humanity apart from nature and give us a mandate to control it? Or are we included in the natural order? To answer these questions, we need to examine the relationships between humanity, God, and nature.

Rabbi Jeff Sultar's close reading of the Bible identifies three clear attitudes toward humanity's role in nature. Genesis portrays humanity struggling with its God-given role as the keeper of the garden. Deuteronomy depicts a humanity that dominates nature. And the Wisdom literature (which includes Proverbs and Ecclesiastes) pictures a world in which nature predominates as humanity and God fade into the background.

Sultar's reading shows that the biblical text proposes no one solution, no fixed creed, no final dogma on the question of human place. On the contrary, the Bible honors the enduring complexity of the God-humanity-nature relationship by providing several frameworks within which humanity, now just as in biblical times, must find its way.

1

Adam, Adamah, and *Adonai:* The Relationship between Humans, Nature, and God in the Bible

JEFF SULTAR

According to the Bible, the first human was fashioned from the soil. That humans and soil are of one substance is expressed by the Hebrew words for each: *adam* for "human," *adamah* for "ground." Into this ground, God blew the breath of life and created a living being. Humans were still soil, but suddenly much more—both of and beyond the soil.

To provide companionship for Adam, God molded animals. While humans and animals are linked—both are conceived in *adamah*—no animal was a suitable partner for Adam, for though he was part of the rest of Creation, he was also distinct from it. Where then does this human belong? And what is humanity's role in nature?

Genesis: God Acts

The Bible's opening chapters tell the story of the newly formed humans seeking their place in their new world. Under God's tutelage, Adam and Eve experiment with the boundaries set for them. They totter back and forth, at first full of pride, then utterly humbled.

There are two different Creation stories in Genesis. In the first, humanity is the culmination of Creation. Day by day, the world is being prepared for the arrival of Adam. First, the elements are created: fire, water, air, and earth. Then plants, planets, water creatures, and winged and creeping creatures. And finally, Adam. Adam's job is to "have dominion" over the earth and all its creatures (Gen. 1:26). In the second version, humanity is the foundation of Creation. Adam is born directly of *adamah*; the shrubs and grasses depend on him for cultivation. Adam's job is "to work and to keep" the garden (Gen. 2:15).

The two stories reflect opposite poles of humankind: the domineering and the humble. They complement each other, yet point to the potential for tension in every individual. Given these two conflicting archetypes, the question arises again: What is the human place in the universe? To control and to master? Or to be part of the world while also caring for it? Or both?

Adam and Eve enjoyed an idyllic existence in the Garden of Eden, even with the responsibility God gave them to tend the garden. They lived securely, confident of their place. Only one thing was required of them: not to eat of "the Tree of Knowledge of Good and Bad" (Gen. 2:9). Just one rule—and they broke it. The punishment was banishment from paradise and loss of place, land, and security.

Humanity's expulsion from Eden is often interpreted as a curse, since it condemned all future peoples to obtain food through strenuous labor: "By the sweat of your brow shall you get bread to eat, until you *return* to the ground, for from it you were taken. For dust you are, and to dust you shall *return*." (Gen. 3:19). Yet twice in the Hebrew verse, the word *shuv,* or "return," appears. The implication is that humans are being *returned* to their proper relation to God. We can read the passage not as a curse but as a restoration of a proper relationship.[1] Service to the earth is an essential responsibility of humans, and eating the fruit of the Tree of Knowledge of Good and Evil threatened to rupture that relationship. Banishment from the Garden of Eden may be the means to ensure the proper relationship between humans and the ground. God puts Adam in his place, and that place was to work the earth.

This motif recurs often in Gen. 1–11, as the characters in the story try to advance closer and closer to God by moving further and further away from the ground. Each time, God puts them back in their place. Beginning with cultivation of the earth, civilization advances rapidly with the classification of animals, the division of labor, and the development of cities, metalwork, and art (Gen. 2:19, 4:2, 4:17, 4:21–22). When the Flood destroys the earth in the generation of Noah, all these advancements are wiped out, and the people must begin again. Similarly, the Tower of Babel represents the highest achievement of humanity, at least literally, and this effort, too, is thwarted, and the people are scattered by geography and language.

Humans rupture their relationship with the soil whenever they forget their roots. Following the Flood, the relationship between humanity and animals is also disrupted. God says that "the fear and the dread of you shall be upon all the beasts of the earth and upon all the birds of the sky" (Gen. 9:2). Yet, at the same time that humans and other animals enter into an adversarial relationship, God enters into an everlasting covenant with all the living creatures by stating, "Never again will I doom the earth because of man" (Gen. 8:21).

In these Creation stories, humanity is placed above the other animals but is limited by God's broader plans for Creation. Nature has a value all its own, independent of its relation to human beings.

Deuteronomy: The Covenant and Human Freedom

Following Creation, the Bible focuses on the life of Abraham and his descendants, the Israelites. The primary theme of the story is the Exo-

dus of the Israelites from Egypt, culminating at Mt. Sinai, where the
Jews receive the law and enter into a covenant with God.

Unlike Adam and Eve, who tested God in the Creation stories, no
experimenting with limits takes place here. God gives the law and establishes discrete boundaries for behavior. The people accept; a contract is
made. The laws are clear, unambiguous, absolute. The Israelites are simply expected to follow them.

Though the covenant is equally binding upon both parties, God,
being God, can be counted on to adhere to the divine side of the agree-
ment. Humans, on the other hand, must struggle to obey, and their
behavior is by no means guaranteed. God rewards and punishes the
Israelites for either following or breaking the commandments by controlling rain, the chief determinant of life and death in an agriculturally
based society: "If you follow my commandments, you will receive rain in
its season" (Deut. 11:13–14). Nature, then, becomes the intermediary
between the people and God, the means by which God metes out reward
and punishment, the indicator of human morality.

Rain is not the only element of nature that God uses to teach the
wayward Israelites. The land itself is defiled when the community
engages in murder, sexual misconduct, and idolatry. This pollution was
indelible, and nothing could be done to remove it. When the pollution
reached a certain threshold, the Israelites would simply be "vomited
out," and the land would remain vacant until it returned to its pristine
state.

This concept of spiritual pollution is a familiar one in the Bible. It
first appears in Genesis 3, when God says to Adam and Eve after they
eat from the tree, "Cursed be the ground because of you" (Gen. 3:17).
In the next chapter, Cain kills his brother Abel, and the land becomes
infertile. Again and again, the spiritual pollution of the land results in
the Israelites being spewed out. But as Leviticus warns after the people
have received the commandments, "You must keep My laws and My
rules, and you must not do any of those abhorrent things. . . . So let not
the land spew you out for defiling it, as it spewed out the nation that
came before you" (Lev. 18:26–28).

Here and in numerous other examples, the land collects pollution.
It serves as both a living memory of Israel's misdeeds and as a judge,

since the state of pollution determines the fate of Israel. And the land is victim of the Israelites' aberrant behavior, behavior that bears no direct relation to the land itself.

The workings of nature were a standing reply to the question posed by Israel: "How are we doing?" Nature was a line of communication between God and Israel and the way that God kept Israel in line.

This concept of God's relationship to the community and the land has intriguing implications. Since God acts only in *re-action* to human behavior, humanity is the free agent, the unpredictable element, the determinant of what God and nature must do. Although God is no longer creatively involved, God has not abandoned the system. God lives within it and is bound by it. Once the covenant is transacted, God holds tremendous power, yet with strict limitations. Here, Creation is flipped. Humans are the creative element, driving nature and history by their unpredictability and rebelliousness.[2]

The dynamics between God, humanity, and nature in Deuteronomy are very different than those in Genesis. In Deuteronomy, the fate of nature and history lay entirely in human hands. The catastrophes that befall Israel in the latter portions of its history are obvious signs that they have failed to meet the challenge of the covenant.

Israel could not have failed so utterly in the early chapters of Genesis because in the Creation stories, God personally oversaw human action, allowing people to make mistakes but also teaching and redirecting them as they did so. Human power was limited. The Creator had greater autonomy, and Creation itself carried more weight.

Wisdom Literature: Nature Teaches

After the destruction of the First Temple and the Babylonian Exile, Israel's sense of being protected by God was shattered.[3] It was under these conditions that the Wisdom literature flourished. In such writings as Proverbs, Job, and Ecclesiastes, the God who acts in history is no longer palpable. In Esther and the Song of Songs, God is not mentioned at all. Furthermore, the Wisdom literature is wary of humanity, since human arrogance has been the source of so much pain and ruin in the world. In Wisdom literature, themes of exodus, law, covenant, and history are noticeably absent, while nature, creation, and order are emphasized as a way to find meaning and purpose. An example of this perspective can be found in Prov. 6:6–9:

> Lazybones, go to the ant;
> Study its ways and learn.
> Without leaders, officers, or rulers,
> It lays up its stores during the summer,
> Gathers in its food at the harvest.
> How long will you lie there, lazybones;
> When will you wake from your sleep?

In other words, pay attention to the workings of nature to find wisdom and discover a proper livelihood. Wisdom replaces commandment; observation replaces revelation. Nature takes the foreground.

The prominent role of nature is also evident in Eccles. 1:4–7, where

> One generation goes, another comes,
> But the earth remains the same forever.
> The sun rises, and the sun sets—
> And glides back to where it rises.
> Southward blowing,
> Turning northward,
> Ever turning blows the wind;
> On its rounds the wind returns.
> All streams flow into the sea,
> Yet the sea is never full;
> To the place [from] which they flow
> The streams flow back again.

Here, as elsewhere, the enduring works of nature contrast with the fleeting character of human life.

In Job, the tension—indeed, the collision—between the covenantal understanding of God and the wisdom approach is made explicit. According to Deuteronomy's covenantal perspective, a perspective in which right behavior is rewarded and wrong behavior punished, Job does not deserve to suffer; he has done no wrong. When friends try to comfort him, they offer an explanation for his suffering that recalls this perspective: if Job suffers, it can only be that he deserves to. Job, who knows he is innocent, must find another way to understand the world; his vision (Job 12:7–9) reflects the wisdom perspective:

> But ask now the beasts, and they shall teach you;
> And the fowls of the air, and they shall teach you;
> Or speak to the earth, and it shall teach you;
> And the fishes of the sea, shall declare unto you;
> Who knoweth not among all these,
> That the hand of the Lord has wrought this?

Later, God is portrayed as delighting in a Creation in which humanity is not master: "Who causes rain to fall in a wilderness, where no man lives?" (Job 38:26). If the world revolves around humanity, why bring rain to the desert where no people live? In the next passage, God speaks of the wild ox as a beast that humans cannot tame (Job 39:9–12). Again, if the world exists solely for humanity—as implied in the covenantal understanding—why do animals exist that people cannot use?

God's dialogue with Job attacks human arrogance. As with much of Wisdom literature, it humbles humanity and underscores God's unconditional love for all Creation. It asserts that nature has meaning aside from human existence and that humans have much to learn from the natural world. In short, nature represents the pinnacle of Creation.

Finding Our Way through the Environmental Crisis

So what is the Bible's view of the relationship between humans, God, and nature? When one member of this triad dominates, it triggers a counterresponse in the others. To understand the human role in the world, we need to appreciate all three components, since God, nature, and humanity all influence one another.

In the early chapters of Genesis, God is central, nature has intrinsic value, and humans—powerful as they are—operate within strict limits monitored by God.

In the covenantal or historical vision expressed in Deuteronomy, humanity is predominant. God establishes a covenant with the Israelites that subjects God to human action. Nature is either the victim of human dominance or the indicator of human morality.

In Wisdom literature, nature is central. Humans are on equal footing with the rest of Creation. God has receded to a distant place, delighting in Creation but no longer actively participating in it.

What is crucial is not that these different sections of the Bible disagree with each other, but precisely that such divergent teachings are all contained in the Bible. The tension between these elements informs the questions we ask and the answers we seek. By refraining from offering simple, inflexible answers, Torah remains timely. Its complex web of possibilities, its different elements in tension and balance, mean that though Torah itself does not change, what it says to us can.

Today, we assume the environmental crisis exists outside and apart from us. We expect the specialists—scientists, lawyers, and environmentalists—to provide quick fixes to environmental problems. This attitude directs us away from our collective responsibility. Rather, today's environmental crisis must point us back to our problematic relations with God, the cosmos, and ourselves—the very relations that the Torah examines in depth.

Most people understand the Book of Job as a story about why bad things happen to good people. The story also places great value on nature, as does much of the rest of the Wisdom literature, including Proverbs and Ecclesiastes. Job experiences the mystery of God and gains an appreciation of nature. In this essay, Shamu Fenyvesi captures the deep ecological vision of this classic tale.

2

Befriending the Desert Owl

SHAMU FENYVESI

Draped in sackcloth, Job sat in the hot sand, unshielded by the shade of his limestone house. His black curls matted with dust, his arms and legs spotted with boils, Job mourned an inconceivable loss. To test Job's faith, God had allowed a vengeful angel to kill Job's ten children and scatter his flocks of camel, oxen, and donkey. Job saw nothing beyond his own suffering and a dark, dry world filled with injustice.

Three friends arrived to share his grief.

Job had been a wealthy and pious man, full of the faith of God. During the first six days of mourning, he remained silent, refusing to challenge God or even question his own awful fate.

On the seventh day of mourning, Job's humble piety slowly turned to rage. Finally, he stood up and raised an angry fist against the sky. He damned the day he was born and cursed the sun and the wind, the moon and the rain. His three friends were terrified and hid their fear behind a cloak of righteousness. Their compassion turned to anger, and their arguments spiraled into a crescendo of blame.

You Job, they shouted, must have sinned. Under God's knowing eyes, the righteous flourish like sheep under the strong hand of a good shepherd. Return to piety, and you will know that your house is protected and your fields are safe from harm, for God does not tolerate evil in His world. Although the lion may roar, its teeth are broken. The wolf is driven away, and the jackal roams the desert crying from hunger while the flocks of the righteous grow fat. God will protect his favorite children like a judge defends the innocent.

Their words did not touch Job's seething soul. He thought, What kind of a God would allow this suffering to befall me? If He is a judge, then let Him judge, for I have done no evil. Or perhaps God is not just. In his deep misery, Job cried out, I have been abandoned, forgotten, cursed; I am nothing but brother to the wild jackal, friend to the desert owl.

Job's plea for justice caught God's ear. And out of a whirlwind, God revealed to Job a startling vision of the universe.

Before Job's eyes, the skies opened. Planets and stars danced like raindrops on dry rock. Galaxies burst open like acacia blossoms tempted by the first drops of a storm. A winter rainstorm in the desert—the rain fell hard. The cracked clay beneath Job's feet turned to black mud. Far in the wilderness, he could see the desert burst into purple blossoms, the grasses joyfully shed their seeds, and the caper bushes drop fiery blossoms from the steep limestone cliffs onto wet sand.

The Jordan River poured through the valley, overflowing its banks. A crocodile thrashed through the rushes at the edge of the river. An angry hippopotamus, roused by the spears of hunters, broke the long bronze weapons like toothpicks in his fat jaws.

Two mounted hunters chased an ostrich across the plain. The bird's brilliant red neck bobbed on reptilian legs through the bushes like a puppet. As the riders approached for the kill, the ostrich, standing seven feet tall, raised a menacing foot with two huge clawed toes and tore at the air. Then he stretched his great white wings and ran, laughing a shrill cackle as he left the horse and rider in the dust.

On the cliffs, a vulture dug its hooked beak into a dead mountain goat, its bald pink head bright against the brown carcass. Warm gusts of wind brushed past Job as the vulture beat its magnificent wings toward a lone acacia. There, it lowered its bald head with a beak full of goat meat for its hungry young.

Job fell to the ground. He awoke from his vision as the sun dawned over the desert—a landscape revived by the rains that blew from the whirlwind of divine creation. The morning stars burst out singing, and the angels shouted for joy.

Job was awed and humbled. God had answered his angry appeal for justice with a tour of the universe, a vivid re-creation of the world. Although Job never left his home, the vision took him on a journey through the desert wilderness.

Sleeping beneath the Singing Stars

Job's ancestors had taken many such pilgrimages. Abel wandered the desert hills. Esau hunted hare and goat in these steep canyons. Moses shepherded the flocks of Midian in the wilderness. The whole Israelite community had traveled for three generations to be cleansed of slavery by the Sinai desert.

To sleep beneath the singing stars, the ancient Semite shepherds lived with only what they could carry on their backs. They depended on God and the desert wilderness and lived in a community that included the flying, crawling, and swimming of the earth.

Job mused: Was the vision a message to the generations that had grown distant from their ancestral wanderings? The clever merchants and ponderous scholars counted coins, not sheep. They preferred a world of their own creation—sanitized and safeguarded—to the wilderness that offered burning bushes, splitting seas, and manna from heaven. They knew neither the color of the desert flowers nor where the vulture made its nest. Job's generation found answers to questions of origins, purposes, and justice in books, not in the canyons, the stars, or the laugh of the ostrich.

To regain a sense of justice, balance, and order, Job could not be instructed by the wise men or by legal texts. He had to embark on a pilgrimage through the desert. Justice is bound up in the land. Birth and death, bud and flower, the daily creation of the world is itself justice, a justice far greater and more complex than anything he or his self-sure friends had imagined.

Gaining the perspective of the vulture, Job saw that his life, that indeed the entire drama of human society was no longer center stage. He celebrated his shared origin with all of Creation; he, too, was of the dust. Instead of clinging to the ideal of pastoral peace, he learned to accept predation, suffering, and death, a world he could not comprehend but must love. Job found solace in a joyful embrace of the wildness of the world.

He learned to give the soil rest and to leave portions of his harvest for the beasts and the poor. He distributed to the needy all of his flock except what he needed to subsist. He treated his horse and goats with a soft, knowing hand. He realized that his prideful anger had blinded him; now he was brother to the wild jackal and a friend to the desert owl.

Brother to the Jackal, Friend to the Owl

In the same limestone canyons that Abraham, Esau, and Job walked, I saw the torrent of a winter flood carry away the dusty landscape. The rain came in drops as large as pebbles. A cliff was transformed into an awesome waterfall. Chunks of limestone collapsed from the cliffs into the muddy river below.

In the days following the flood, the desert sang with purple blossoms, and the wind carried grass seeds and newly hatched insects. Though I heard no divine voice from the whirlwind, I experienced the desert in all its vibrancy and power, much as Job had before me.

At the top of V-shaped acacia, I saw the bleached and tattered remnants of a vulture's abandoned nest. Some years ago, God had shown Job such a vulture nesting in a tree like this. Today, only a handful of lappet-faced vultures soar over the Israeli desert. Neither in my wandering in the Arava and the Negev nor in my dreams have I ever seen such a bird. Only in a cage at a wildlife refuge, where they collect ailing animals to save them from extinction, did I see this sad bird sitting on an artificial perch awaiting a meal of frozen chicken. The folds of skin on its bald pink face that give the bird its name hung loose and limp.

I will never see the River Jordan as Job saw it: teeming with croco-

diles and hippopotamuses which offered the inspiration for the mythi-
cal biblical beasts Leviathan and Behemoth that we find in the Book of
Job. Now much of the Jordan is no more than a glorified irrigation ditch
enclosed by barbed wire, its polluted waters fought over by three nations.

Today's slogans of progress ring as hollow and dry as the dusty
phrases of Job's friends. Our society clings to the fallacy of unimpeded
and limitless economic growth, as Job's friends hid behind their comforting images of God, a tame world, and the godless jackal. We desperately try to subdue the wild world with dams, golf courses, and shopping
malls. We evoke the smug self-righteousness of Job's three friends by
praising the work of our hands and assuring each other that we are bringing justice and harmony. After all, on the sixth day of Creation, we were
granted dominion over the world and all its creatures.

We echo the angry Job's misconception by putting the human
drama on center stage. Our human-centeredness demands an impas-
sioned shout at the sky and begs for a vision like Job's: a pilgrimage
into the natural world to regain our sense of balance.

For generations, we have read the Book of Job and recognized it as
a riddle of divine justice, ignoring the messages of Job's wilderness
vision. We tend to pass over—without understanding—the poetic and
ecologically detailed depictions of the antelope and vulture, the desert
grasses and the ostrich, just as we overlook the inspired natural images of
the psalmist, discounting them as so many distant metaphors. However, our famous "dominion" cannot be understood without the laugh of
the ostrich and all the untamed life of the Book of Job. We need a collective wilderness journey like Job's to frighten us, integrate us, inspire
us, and remind us that we, too, are brother to the wild jackal, friend to
the desert owl.

All too often when problems develop in our personal lives or in the world, we look for someone else or some other community or ideology to blame. Placing blame can be cathartic and can provide us some immediate relief, but it never solves problems. It only avoids them.

In 1967, historian Lynn White published a controversial article that implicated the Judeo-Christian tradition in the environmental crisis. White contended that the Bible gave humanity a mandate to control nature, to use nature for human ends. His article generated a heated debate, which continues even today, among Christians, Jews, and environmentalists. In the following piece, Neal Loevinger critiques the critics of the Bible.

3

(Mis)reading Genesis:
A Response to Environmentalist Critiques of Judaism

NEAL JOSEPH LOEVINGER

One might think that the religious values of Western societies would counter those economic, cultural, and political forces that seem to permit people to abuse nature. However, many environmental historians and philosophers have harshly criticized Judaism and Christianity, claiming that elements of these traditions in fact *hinder* the development of a positive, caring relationship with the natural world. Many of these criticisms seem to be based on religious stereotypes and superficial understandings of the Bible. They demand a closer look from a Jewish perspective.

In 1967, Lynn White, a historian at the University of California at Los Angeles, set off the debate about the relationship of religion to environmental problems, which continues to this day. In his now famous essay, "The Historical Roots of Our Ecological Crisis," first published in *Science* magazine, White suggested that Western religious thinking, which developed from the Creation stories of the Book of Genesis, encouraged people to believe that nature was created solely to benefit human beings.[1] White's argument rested on the text of Gen. 1:27–28:

> And God created man in His image, in the image of God He created him; male and female He created them. God blessed them and God said to them: "Be fertile and increase, fill the earth and master it; and rule over the fish of the sea, the birds of the sky, and all the living things that creep upon the earth."

White claimed that this cultural/religious attitude, combined with the growing technological capabilities of medieval Europe, led to the ruthless exploitation of nature and to reckless pollution. He concluded that "since the roots of our trouble are so largely religious, the remedy must also be essentially religious, whether we call it that or not." He proposed that St. Francis be designated the new patron saint of ecology.

White's accusations stirred up a hornet's nest of controversy, as both Christians and Jews defended the Bible against the charges of environmental irresponsibility. Other environmentalists joined White's finger pointing at the Bible and the religions that revere it. Along the way, the subtlety of what he actually said seemed to be lost: that the Genesis story, *along with* new technologies and increased urbanization, had significantly shaped the Western view of nature and presumably still does. Most people, on both sides of the argument, seemed to react as if he'd written that the Bible is the *sole* cause of the environmental crisis.[2] For example, Ian McHarg, a prominent landscape design professor, who was then at the University of Pennsylvania, spelled this view out very clearly:

> Apparently, the literal interpretation of the Creation in Genesis is the text for Jews and Christians alike—man exclusively divine, man given dominion over all life and non-life, enjoined to subdue the earth. . . [This] view has become the Western posture of man versus nature.[3]

The core of this interpretation was that in Genesis, God had given the earth to human beings, who, with divine permission, have been tearing it apart ever since.

The Fallacies of Attacking Genesis

There are several problems with this argument from historical and religious perspectives. First, Western culture is not based solely on the Bible; it draws at least as much from Greek thought and philosophy.[4] Furthermore, White and his followers seem to assume that one or two verses of Genesis, taken literally, cancel out all the other verses in the Hebrew Bible that speak of the glories and wonders of God's Creation and of humanity's responsibility to preserve it. To offer just one example, God's commandment to the first humans to "fill the earth and master it" is balanced by the threat in Deuteronomy that the Israelites would be expelled from their land if they did not act in accordance with the divine will.[5] Surely, the Bible and rabbinic Judaism are just as concerned with the limits of human behavior as they are with glorifying our place in the cosmos.

One might even point out that the unprecedented exploitation of the earth's resources of the past few hundred years coincides with a real *decrease* in the power and influence of religion in public life, not to mention the emergence of runaway capitalism and empire building. Philosophers of science such as Francis Bacon and René Descartes deeply influenced how we think about the natural world, allowing us to think of nature as merely inanimate matter to be probed and dissected, rather than as a living whole of which we are part. All in all, the root causes of our seemingly callous cultural attitudes toward nature should probably be understood in the context of the entirety of Western civilization, of which religion, along with science, politics and economics, is only a part.

Extracting a few isolated verses from the Bible and interpreting them as representative of the "Judeo-Christian tradition" do little justice to a complex and important issue and may tell us more about the bias of the writer than about the verses in question. For example, the feminist environmentalist Elinor Gadon claims that the Genesis story "is no longer serving us well . . . [it] does not accord with our concept of either the universe or human dignity." To Gadon, the "Judeo-Christian world view" found in Genesis, which "undergirds Western culture," regards nature as merely dead matter for human use. It supplants mythology with "rational thinking." The mythic, she states, is "another kind of language which communicates more fully our inner knowing of self and of relationship to the world around us." For Gadon, the biblical Creation story is *not* mythic. Rather, she maintains, it is "linear, relentlessly moving onward." In her reading, the "patriarchal Creator God of the Bible . . . has become the model for authority," thus ensuring the ostensible iniquity of Western history in its ruthless, linear progression.[6]

These passages were chosen because they offer a particularly vivid example of a kind of thinking displayed by a whole school of environmentalists. Even Thomas Berry, a Catholic monk and prominent environmental thinker, sees the Bible as a key element of a Western ethic that allows for massive environmental destruction. The Bible, he says, encourages us to be "radically oriented *away* from the natural world." In a biblically inspired world-view, according to Berry, nature "has no rights; it exists for human utility."[7]

Clearly, there are several Jewish responses to these contentions. First, the phrase *Judeo-Christian tradition* not only obscures real and important historical and theological differences between the two traditions, but by subsuming *Judeo* into *Christian*, it revives the deeply held Christian notion that Judaism is merely unfulfilled Christianity. Moreover, it masks real differences in cultural, political, economic, and other forms of power that have developed over the last two millennia. Jews could not even *own* land in Europe and the Middle East for much of that time, yet the "Hebrew" influence is blamed for ruining it.

Equally important is a misunderstanding of how the Bible has been historically interpreted, especially by Jews. Ian McHarg, in the passage quoted earlier, claims that Genesis has been understood "literally." Yet Jewish and Christian teachers have always employed allegory, symbolism, and metaphor in their interpretations. For example, Maimonides wrote in the beginning of his massive code of Jewish practice and thought:

> . . . it is plainly stated in the Torah and the Prophets that God is bodiless, for it is written: "The Lord is God in the Heavens above and on the Earth beneath" (Deut. 4:39; Josh. 2:11). . . . In

view of this, what can be the meaning of the following expressions: "Under his feet" (Exod. 24:10), "inscribed with the finger of God" (Exod. 31:18) . . . and other such phrases? They are all adapted to human perceptions, apprehending only physical substances. The Torah speaks the language of human beings. Hence, all such expressions . . . are metaphorical. Has God a sword? Does He slay with a sword? It is a figure of speech; it is all figurative.[8]

Maimonides is saying that as humans, we must imagine divinity in familiar terms to make it comprehensible to human minds. This, in effect, is exactly what Gadon was talking about when she said that myth is "another kind of language," which lets the inexpressible become communicable. This is not to say that nothing in the Bible can be taken at face value, but rather that the meaning is not always easy to understand, given both its historical context and centuries of interpretation.

The Problem of Religious Stereotypes

Religion is a difficult topic to discuss objectively; everybody wants to make the best case for their own perspective, and it is hard see the merit of somebody else's beliefs. On the other hand, it is quite easy to ridicule and stereotype religious beliefs that threaten one's own. One example of this is the Christian description of Judaism as a religion of rote obedience and unassailable law in contrast with Christianity, the religion of love and grace. Christianity was often (and sometimes still is) understood by Christians as superseding Judaism and making it obsolete, since Christianity "perfected" older beliefs. This fails to understand Judaism in its own terms and sets up a paradigm in which anything Jewish is always compared unfavorably to its Christian counterpart. A classic example of Christian supersessionism is the very terminology employed for the Bible: "Old Testament" versus "New Testament." The latter is the fulfillment of the former and the source of perfect revelation.

This kind of cerebral anti-Judaism is sometimes found among environmentalists and intellectuals. One glaring example was the prominent British historian Arnold Toynbee, who wrote several articles on humanity's relationship to nature. At first, Toynbee echoed Lynn White: the opening chapter of Genesis "shattered the awe of nature" felt by ancient humankind and reads, in modern times, "like a license for the population explosion, and like both a license and an incentive for mechanization and pollution."[9] Because he thought that belief in nature spirits led to respect for natural places, Toynbee, like White, saw the displacement of pantheism by monotheism as a disaster for the environment.

Unlike White, however, Toynbee was far more lenient toward Christianity than Judaism, and this is where a careful reader might see signs of religious stereotyping. For example, he saw the Genesis story in terms of "Jewish monotheism," with its "crude" emphasis on "the exercise of power." On the other hand, he believed that the Christian Trinity stood for "love, benevolence and humanity," as did Buddhism and other "more perceptive and less aggressive" traditions. This classic false dichotomy between the religion of law (Judaism) and the religion of love (Christianity) so clouded Toynbee's thinking that he could not possibly understand that humility and self-restraint play a large role in Jewish spirituality. What does *halachah* (Jewish law) do, after all, if not train humans to curb their aggressions and desires? After all, the same Hebrew Bible that contains the Creation stories that Toynbee so dislikes also contains the commandment to cease our normal activities and observe Shabbat every seven days. Unfortunately, he could not see Judaism on its own terms and confused, rather than clarified, the role of religion in shaping environmental attitudes.

The Deep Ecology Position

While some environmentalists have critiqued the Hebrew Bible or specific religious teachings or traditions, others have gone much further, suggesting that all of Western religion stands in the way of a more balanced relationship with nature. One such school of thought has been the "Deep Ecology" movement, originally grounded in the writings of Arne Naess, George Sessions, and Bill Devall. The core idea of Deep Ecology is "biocentrism," which finds value in the biological web of life itself, not in humans as a special or unique species. Most versions of Deep Ecology grant an equal right to all species to flourish in their unique niche and abhor human interference with another species' well-being.

While conventional Western environmental ethics are usually grounded in such familiar ideas as personal responsibility and moral obligations, Deep Ecology sees itself as "transpersonal" and involving "self-realization."[10] Basically, these terms refer to an attempt to eliminate personal morality as a motivating factor in environmental change and focus instead on expanding our awareness of other organisms. This is the meaning of the phrase *self-realization:* by learning to see our personal self connected first with other humans and then with other species and even the whole biosphere, we will eventually understand that our individual well-being is inseparable from the well-being of everything else. According to this theory, complete self-realization will eradicate the need for ethics or morality. Instead, our motivation will arise from within; we will intuitively understand that by harming another species, we harm ourselves. Thus, we won't dump toxic waste into the river because we *are* the river, we are the fish that live in it, and they, in turn, are part of us. Our interests and those of the biosphere will inevitably become one and the same.

From a Jewish perspective, the biggest problem with this approach is that it obscures the real, everyday choices that people must make. People can do to other species what other species, generally, cannot do to us: an individual can wipe out a colony of mosquitoes in a pond, but the mosquitoes cannot do the same to the people who live in their habitat. Rather than being superfluous, the role of ethics is to make power differences explicit and to make past experience relevant to new situations. According to Jewish traditions, the capacity for ethical action is the blessing—and the curse—of being human. Jeremiah's wry comparison of the errant Israel with the more faithful birds makes this point explicit: "Even the stork in the sky knows her seasons, and the turtledove, swift, and crane keep the time of their coming; but My people show no heed to the law of the Lord" (Jer. 8:7). Animals are an absolutely vital part of Creation and have their own inherent worth regardless of their value to humans. Humans, on the other hand, are given both power and responsibility along with their free will and can tip the balance for the rest of the world. The most famous example is the Flood story, when humanity's cruelty, evil, and disrespect for natural boundaries eventually so maddened God that the earth was devastated (Gen. 6:5–13). Furthermore, it is precisely the special place of humans in the cosmos—created "in the image of God"—that inspires us to ever higher ideals of social justice and equality.

The advocates of Deep Ecology misunderstand the moral teachings of Judaism the same way Lynn White and those who picked up on his theories did: they do not see that there are many ways within the tradition to approach a problem as vast and complicated as the environmental crisis. White called for a new patron Saint of Ecology, St. Francis, as a model of humility and friendship with all that lives. Within Judaism, we can draw attention to those texts, such as Job and many of the psalms, that praise Creation and remind humans that we are only a small part of a much greater whole. Our tradition constantly reminds us that our possessions, even our lives, are not really ours but rather are entrusted to us. If, indeed, humanity is sometimes viewed as the "crown of Creation," this position is seen as a solemn responsibility and one that takes constant study and self-reflection to uphold.

Judaism Echoes the Environmental Message

In addition to encouraging an environmental ethic through its cultural and ideological orientation, Judaism also promotes environmental awareness by reminding us to examine the details of our everyday lives: what we eat, what we wear, what we say, what we buy and from whom. This attention to detail is particularly evident in Judaism's practice of distinguishing one kind of thing from another—kosher and not kosher, Shabbat time and weekday time, a fruit from the ground or a fruit from a tree, bread or unyeasted grains. Each act, often with its own appropriate blessing, evokes a moment of recognition of the world's splendid complexity and variety.

Deep Ecology often employs a language of rights, extending them to all creatures. But Judaism speaks also of responsibilities, of the individual and the community to each other, to Creation, to the Creator. We are responsible to each other for how we spend our time, how we spend our money, and how kindly we act toward each other. To Creation, we owe respect and restraint; such laws as *bal taschit* ("do not destroy") and *tsa'ar balei hayim* (compassion for animals) teach us that this world is all we have and that we must treat it as a treasure entrusted to us. To the Creator, whether experienced as a personal God or the deep Spirit within all life (or both), we owe gratitude for the beauty and pleasure of living on a world that so amply sustains us.

Although many environmentalists have made ill-informed and unfair critiques of Judaism and other religious traditions, ultimately what matters more than correcting the record is the sense of confidence Jews can feel when looking toward their tradition for spiritual and intellectual guidance when confronting seemingly intractable environmental problems. Judaism may not have one answer for everybody on, for example, watershed protection, but it can provide a broad framework in which to address the moral issues of modern environmentalism. That, in the end, is more important. For if there is one idea on which Jews, Christians, followers of Deep Ecology, and others can agree, it is that environmental problems are spiritual problems. No amount of scrubber technology on our smokestacks or research into the needs of endangered species will matter if we do not feel in our hearts that making changes in our lives and societies is the right thing to do, one that is part of a higher purpose. Choosing our everyday actions in the light of a higher purpose is the essence of both Judaism and environmentalism.

One danger of contemporary Zionism is that it can reinforce the impression that there is only one holy land or, rather, that only one land is holy. For some Jews living outside of Israel, this attitude can translate into indifference toward their own local environments. A number of American Jews, for example, feel such overriding concern for Israel that they abandon any attempt at creating a relationship with the land of America. Ignoring nature in their own communities and with no day-to-day relationship with the soil of Israel, these Jews achieve no genuine connection to nature and thus no possibility of global environmental awareness and practice.

In the following piece, Rabbi Bradley Artson shows how this attitude derives from an extremely limited reading of essential Jewish texts. Beginning with the Bible and moving on to the rabbinic expansion of biblical formulations, Artson shows that Jewish tradition fostered a conception of holy land that goes well beyond the notion of Israel as the one and only sacred place.

4

Is There Only One Holy Land?

BRADLEY SHAVIT ARTSON

Jewish tradition speaks at great length about the sacred qualities of the Land. Throughout the Bible, the Land is praised for its wondrous bounty. And while the Bible speaks mainly of Israel, later rabbinic writings expand the notion of Holy Land to include the whole earth. The rabbis do not deny the particular holiness of *Eretz Yisrael*, but their writings make the sanctification of all earth central to Jewish practice. For the rabbis, respecting the earth is a matter of religious duty.

On the one hand, the Bible recognizes the whole earth as holy:[1]

The earth is *Adonai*'s and all that it holds,
the world and its inhabitants.
For God founded it upon the ocean,
set it on the nether-streams. (Ps. 24:1–2)

How many are the things you have made, *Adonai*;
You have made them all with wisdom;
the earth is full of your Creations. (Ps. 104:24)

The Creation story itself focuses attention on the importance of the earth; the term for earth itself, *adamah*, lends its name to the first earthling, *adam*.[2] The Torah even directly proclaims the sanctity of a site outside of the Land of Israel. Moses, standing before the burning bush on Horeb, is commanded to "remove your sandals from your feet, for the place on which you stand is holy ground" (Exod. 3:5). This passage tells us that *land* is holy, not just *a* land. In Genesis, God is the Creator of the heavens and the earth; therefore, all lands are touched by God. Perhaps this appreciation that all the earth is God's place contributes to the age-old Israelite tradition that extols the wilderness as a place of holiness and of purity.[3]

Rabbinic writings, in part, continue this emphasis on the sanctity of the whole earth. For example, the central organizing categories for blessings over food are *p'ri* (fruit) and not-*p'ri* (everything else). The essential question is whether the food came from the soil or not. Other characteristics seem not to matter: "Over something that does not grow in or from the earth, one says *sh'hakol*."[4] ("Blessed are You, God . . . through Whose word everything came to be.") Once the food is identified as a type of *p'ri*, then further distinctions arise: Does the food emerge from the earth directly (*borei p'ri ha-adamah*)? Or does it grow on a vine (*borei p'ri ha-gafen*)? Or on a tree (*borei p'ri ha-etz*)?

These categories are so familiar to observant Jews that we may hardly think about them. But there is no intrinsic reason for the rabbis to distinguish between the nuances of various agricultural products while lumping together fish, meat, poultry, and dairy products. Why not a separate *berachah* for everything that comes from the sea or originates from a mountain or grows in the summer? By establishing the categories of *berachah* the way they did, the rabbis lent significance to the soil. What emerges from the ground, all ground, is uniquely sanctified, and the earth is recognized as a sacred and sustaining presence for humans.

This Soil Is Holier than That

Yet there remains a dichotomy at the core of the tradition's teachings about the sanctity of soil. While all the earth is sacred, there is one particular part of it in which inheres a special degree of holiness. That part is the Land of Israel. For example, while the Bible claims that Jews can observe the laws anywhere (Ps. 105:44–45), it simultaneously teaches that there is an uncleanness permeating the nations of the world beyond the borders of Israel. Thus, Hosea speaks of the Israelites who "shall eat unclean food in Assyria" (Hos. 9:3; see also Ezek. 4:13), and Amos speaks of the "unclean soil" to which Israel (the people) will be banished (Amos 7:17; see also Isa. 52:11). The Land of Israel is clearly the true focus of the Bible's passion for land.

Repeatedly, the Torah describes the Land of Israel as "a good land," one whose bounty springs from God's beneficence, rather than from any merit or labor on Israel's part (see Josh. 24:13). As biblical scholar Harry Orlinsky points out, the sanctity of *Eretz Yisrael* overrides the sanctity of all other places; it is only before the conquest of Canaan by Israel "that a site outside the Promised Land can be described as holy."[5] Only in this Land may sacrifices be offered to God, and only there is food considered ritually clean. The Land itself is a reward held out to Jews in the Bible: observe the mitzvot, God promises, and you will continue to dwell in the Land.

One may understand the distinction placed on the Land of Israel as one aspect of God's role as Creator. Though God "gave" the Land to the people Israel, God retains sovereignty over it, as over all Creation. As Leviticus 25:23 says: "The Land [of Israel] must not be sold beyond reclaim, for the land is Mine; you are but strangers resident with Me."

Leviticus makes clear that the ultimate owner of the Land of Israel is God and that the Jewish people have only "usufruct," which Webster's defines as "the right of enjoying all the advantages derivable from the use of something which belongs to another, as far as is compatible with . . . the thing not being destroyed."[6] The "another" in this case is God, who establishes the Land as holy and obliges us not to destroy it.

A series of agricultural laws—*peah*[7] (provision for the poor by leaving the corners of the fields); *orlah*[8] (abstention from the fruits of new trees); and *kilayim*,[9] *terumot*[10] and *bikkurim*[11] (tithes to the Temple and its clergy)—provide further evidence of God's ownership of the Land. If the human "owner" truly were full owner of the land, why the obligation to share the wealth of the land with the poor and the priests? Why must we not harvest a single fruit on a new tree for three years? Undergirding all the requirements is an assertion that the farmer is entitled only to "interest," whereas the ultimate proprietor of the "principal," of *Eretz Yisrael*, is God alone. The Jewish people are "borrowing" off the interest of God's assets and are obliged to use the loan well. In the words of the Talmud, "God acquired possession of the world and apportioned it to humankind, but God always remains the master of the world."[12]

One way to think about the biblical tension between all land being holy and the special holiness of Israel is to look at various perspectives on holiness that the Torah teaches. In the Creation story, the Torah's perspective is universalistic, and "all" land is considered holy. As the focus of the story shifts to a particular people, the Israelites, the focus of holiness also shifts to the land of the Israelites, that is, *Eretz Yisrael*.

The Rabbinic Revolution

Reversing the biblical thesis, rabbinic law and legend begin with the centrality of *Eretz Yisrael* and, through innovation and interpretation, establish the sanctity of the entire world, or at least of any place inhabited by *Am Yisrael*, the people Israel.

In the words of the Mishnah, "The Land of Israel is holier than all lands."[13] Fully one-third of the Mishnah is devoted to the agricultural laws of tithing, far beyond any proportional length provided by Scripture.[14] Tithing laws, with three exceptions,[15] were obligatory only inside the borders of the Land; the purity system, too, was fully applicable only within the Land.[16] Therefore, the notion of the impurity of the other lands, which has roots in the Bible, continued into rabbinic thought as well.[17]

When the Mishnah was written, most of the people Israel lived within the Land of Israel. Today, the opposite is true: the majority of Jews live outside the borders of the Land. However, even during mishnaic times, the Diaspora had begun; significant Jewish populations were living in Syria, Egypt, and Babylon while large numbers of non-Jews were living inside the Land. How did Diaspora change the notion of a single Holy Land "owned" by God?

While the ideal remained the intersection of the Jewish people with their sacred Land, *Am Yisrael b'Eretz Yisrael*, the rabbis kept pace with the facts of the postbiblical world. They acknowledged diversity of practice and spirituality. Gentiles living in the Land are exempt from the requirement of *shevi'it* (refraining from agricultural work during the seventh year), *hallah* (offering a tithe of dough to the *kohanim*), and *terumah* (tithing produce for the *kohanim*). Jews outside of the Land are also exempt from most of the agricultural laws. On the other hand, Jews living outside the Land are still obliged to take *hallah*; they are also mandated to say the *birkat ha-mazon*, the grace after meals. Grains exported from the Land of Israel do not require taking *hallah*, however, at least according to Rabbi Akiva. Even though the grain is grown on Jewish land, it will be eaten by other peoples with their own laws and customs. "The entire world potentially is sacred space," scholar Richard S. Sarason interprets Akiva's ruling. "Different areas are subject to different standards, different rules. People in the Land and outside the Land alike have their own special roles to play. . . . Mishnah's rabbis clearly wish to do justice to both principles—both Holy Land and Holy People—without fully embracing the one over the other."[18]

Broadening the notion of sanctity to other lands exercised a profound effect on rabbinic Judaism, making holiness "portable." Jews could bring their laws, or at least most of them, wherever they went. And therefore, Jews would make any land in which they lived holy. It says in Scripture, for example, "They shall be carried to Babylonia, and there they shall be, until the day that I remember them, says the Lord." Rabbi

Yehudah, commenting on this passage, goes so far as to equate living in Babylonia with living in Israel because remaining in Babylonia would fulfill a holy imperative.[19] All lands, in the right circumstances, are holy.

This view implies that the rabbis of the mishnaic and talmudic eras wished to align Jewish religion to the reality of Jewish settlement beyond the borders of Israel. Without ever abandoning their commitment to the mitzvah of *yishuv ha-aretz* (dwelling in the Land), the sages transferred their ideal from living on the Land to observing the law. Whereas the Torah celebrates living in Israel as a *reward* for pious observance, the rabbis invert that celebration, valuing living in Israel because it *allows* for greater observance:

> Rabbi Simlai expounded, "Why did Moses, Our Rabbi, yearn to enter the Land of Israel? Did he want to eat of its fruit or satisfy himself from its bounty? . . . [T]hus spoke Moses, 'Many commandments were commanded to Israel which can be fulfilled only in the Land of Israel. I wish to enter the Land so they may all be fulfilled by me.'"[20]

Rather than embodying the goal, the Land becomes the means. The implications of this revolution are staggering. While maintaining the centrality of the Land, since certain mitzvot could only be performed there, the revaluation of the Land's meaning now placed the weight of Jewish piety on the observance of deeds that could be performed anywhere. As opposed to making Israel the treasure at the end of the hunt, the rabbis made the hunt for piety the treasure and the Land a sacred tool for finding one's way.

The liturgy of the calendar reflects this shift from living in the Holy Land to keeping the law.[21] Authority over the calendar—long a source of contention between the Jewish sages in Israel and those in Babylonia—was finally taken by the leaders of Babylonian Jewry, and Babylonian seasonal cycles, not those of Israel, were the ones that were marked.[22] So even our notion of time, which became so important after the destruction of the Temple, was no longer defined by the sun and the moon as seen from the borders of *Eretz Yisrael*.

In the aftermath of the destruction and with the rise of the local synagogue, rabbinic Judaism adopted an attitude of expansive holiness, though supposedly a temporary one: a willingness to roam the world until the messianic age restored the nexus between Land and people. In the words of talmudic scholar Jacob Neusner:

> What Mishnah does by representing this cult, laying out its measurements, describing its rite, and specifying its rules, is to permit Israel, [through] the words of the Mishnah, to experience—anywhere and anytime—that cosmic center of the world. . . .[23]

Holiness, previously found only within the Land of Israel, became portable. Israel, the holy people, could encounter holiness anywhere and everywhere. The entire earth offered an encounter with God and godliness.

The Earth Is the Lord's: Blessings for Food

A revisitation of rabbinic blessings for food reveals the effort to recognize the sanctity of the entire world and yet to maintain the special status of the Land of Israel. The biblical instruction to praise God for food specifies that this obligation applies only within the Land of Israel itself: "For the Lord your God is bringing you into a good land . . . a land where you may eat food without stint. . . . When you have eaten your fill, give thanks to the Lord your God for the good land which God has given you" (Deut. 8:7–10). The Land possesses a special holiness, and the Landedness of the Jews justly elicits a unique gratitude. (It is interesting to note, however, that nowhere in the Bible, from Abraham to Aaron, is this instruction to give thanks actually implemented.)

In opposition to the Torah, however, the rabbis assume that blessings are appropriate both in and out of the Land. They place no limitation on the location of the meal or the source of the produce to be consumed. "Our rabbis taught: It is forbidden to enjoy anything of this world without a *berachah*."[24] Whereas the Torah prescribes gratitude to God because God is sovereign of Israel, the rabbis extend that recognition of sovereignty to the entire earth.

However, characteristic of their ability to mediate a dual agenda, the rabbis still reinforce the notion of *kedushat ha-aretz*, the particular holiness of the Land. They insert blessings in the *birkat ha-mazon* that distinguish between produce characteristic of the Land and all other produce. Yet, they again contradict the notion of one "Holy Land" because the actual source of the grains, fruit, or vegetables is irrelevant; they could have grown anywhere. What matters is whether they are a type reminiscent of *Eretz Yisrael*. The "cosmic center" can be invoked anywhere, as long as the words and the ingredients are holy.

Responsibility for Our "Place"

After examining biblical and early rabbinic attitudes toward land and its sanctity, we can now address issues concerning land from a Jewish standpoint. Our tradition becomes a guide.

We begin by noting the shift from the biblical assertion that a particular place—*Eretz Yisrael*—is intrinsically holy, and therefore a reward for good living, to the rabbinic inversion that a place—any place—is made holy by the fidelity and piety of its inhabitants. In fact, land can be "soiled"; it can react with revulsion to the greed, rebelliousness, or violence of humanity. Well-known are the many passages warning that the price of spurning the mitzvot is expulsion from the Land.[25] The theologian W. D. Davies wrote, "That observance and non-observance of the commandments have geographic, territorial, and cosmic consequences points to the truth that ecology is indissoluble from morality, land and law being mutually dependent, and that a people is ultimately responsible for the maintenance of its 'place.'"[26] In short, human relationship to the earth, specifically between Jews and *Eretz Yisrael*, is one of covenant, of *brit*.

As Jews, our loyalty begins with *Eretz Yisrael*. But we are not only Jews. As human beings, we also owe fealty and love to the entire planet, as well as to that particular corner of it on which we make our home. The same kind of claim that the Land of Israel makes on our Jewish commitments, the world claims as well.

The early rabbis established precedents for broadening the notion of holiness to include the whole world. Through focusing the blessings for food on "fruit of the ground," by adding liturgical petitions on behalf of the weather outside of the Land of Israel, by providing for multiple models of land sanctity, the Mishnah and the Talmud establish a claim for the holiness of the whole earth, without relinquishing a special Jewish estimation for Israel itself.

The path of the Bible and the early rabbinic tradition is one of expanding concentric circles, decentralizing the notion of holiness into a provisional portability that permits a relationship with the sacred anywhere and anytime. That schema sanctifies all the earth, summoning us, as Jews and as humans, to enter into a relationship of love and piety with our beleaguered planet. It is incumbent upon us to make of this earth a place where *Shechina*, God's presence, can inhabit, so that the whole world becomes a holy dwelling place, a *mishkan*.

Wilderness plays a tremendous role in the story told in the Bible, but somehow when I was growing up, no one taught me that the wilderness experience was so fundamental to my tradition. If they had, I would have been much more enthusiastic about being Jewish from an early age. Instead I had to "back into" Judaism. My life experiences, my values, my sense of spirituality sent me, unwittingly, in a Jewish direction.

5

How Wilderness Forms a Jew

ELLEN BERNSTEIN

What I learned there . . . seemed to confirm the conjecture I had toyed with for so long that Natural Selection has designed us—from the structure of our brain-cells to the structure of our big toe—for a career of seasonal journeys on foot through the blistering land of thornscrub or desert. —BRUCE CHATWIN, *The Songlines*

Since my youth, adventuring in the "great outdoors" has been as basic to my survival as eating and breathing. Growing up, I paddled, biked, skied, and meandered through the New England countryside. This penchant for the outdoors and the need to journey determined many of the choices I would make throughout my life.

My first extended wilderness journey was in the Trinity Alps in northern California when I was 19. My Free Clinic comrades Marc and George and I had planned a two-week hiking trek. I remember our lengthy days of food preparation: determining to the ounce the size of our portions, filling film containers with a variety of savory herbs, and squeezing peanut butter into plastic push tubes. I was preparing psychologically as well: psyching up to see bear, fox, wolves, coyotes. I was eager to be scared.

When we finally arrived in the Trinity Wilderness area, I recognized, somewhat sadly, there was nothing to be afraid of. Whatever big mammals were left in the American Northwest would not venture forth in the presence of people. Luckily Marc and George had lugged along an eight-pound hardcover book by Philip Munz, *A California Flora*. They knew that if it was wildlife we were after, there was a much better chance of finding it in the flowers.

Aside from wildlife, there was something else I would find in the wilderness that I didn't know I was looking for. Late one afternoon, having spent the entire day climbing, we reached a summit ridge. As evening descended, the three of us walked silently on a gentle trail, each absorbed in our own thoughts. I had been hiking for at least ten hours but wasn't tired. Even with a 50-pound pack, my steps were light and effortless. I was mesmerized by the panorama of oceanic mountains that surrounded me and propelled by the rhythm of my feet touching the ground. The soft golden light of the setting sun cast the forest in an emerald glow. I was captivated by the moment and felt lifted and humbled. Every breath inspired me. I had discovered the meaning of worship.

It was then that I began to take my wanderlust more seriously. I recognized that my adventuring resembled a religious quest. It was my chance to encounter life's mystery. It would usually take several days on the trail to leave behind the weight of my ego, my self-consciousness and all that is familiar and routine, and free my mind. In these moments, the world opened up to me; I felt an intimacy with the earth, I was more aware of the plants' special habits, I laughed easily and was eager to chat with strangers. I felt a profound generosity toward the world that comes too infrequently in my daily life.

Wilderness journeys also provided me a doorway to inspiration, to my vision and self-awareness. Usually, my mind is too cluttered for inspiration to find a way in. Yet in the state of deep relaxation I experienced on my journeys, my mind seemed to open up to new ways of thinking and new possibilities. I would come home from these journeys refreshed and with greater self-understanding. It is interesting to me that mystics use the *repetition* of particular words or the focus on the flow of breath in and out of the body over an extended period of time to attain a tranquilizing effect on the mind. Perhaps it was the constant *repetitive* motion of walking or paddling over a prolonged period that allowed my mind to relax and expand.

It is this sense of uplift and farsightedness that I recognize I craved on all those youthful journeys. My experience led me to believe that adventure—or something similar—must be a vital component of healthy identity development.

Wilderness as Pilgrimage

I did not recognize any connection between my newly identified spirituality and the religion of my family—Judaism. As a youth, I had rebelled against what seemed to be a hypocritical, archaic, and dead tradition, and I gravitated toward the universal spirituality of my New England forebears, the Transcendentalists.

My observations about Jewish culture at that time concerned Jews, not Judaism. I found it curious that, although I was surrounded by Jews in social and academic settings, my fellow wilderness travelers—particularly the men—were almost all *not* Jewish. Wilderness adventure did not seem to be part of the repertoire of activities of the Jewish men that I knew. Rather, having chosen the fast-paced career track, they were weighted down by mortgages and too much ambition. Many seemed dispirited. I was curious about their lack of wanderlust and wondered if they might be substituting something less healthy (and perhaps addictive) to achieve the deep relaxation and inspiration I thought were necessary for life.

Given the off-putting Jewish experiences I had had while growing up, the last place I expected to find models for the spiritual journey was in Judaism. Yet, once I was able to drop my intolerance toward my heritage and yield to it, I recognized that my tradition embodied the most profound teachings about wandering. For, if anything, being a Jew is being a wanderer. Somehow what appears so obvious now took years for me to notice.

Many of our ancestors took to the wilderness. Abraham, Jacob, and Moses were all called to forsake their settled lives, their homes, and their communities to endure a period of uncertainty and unfamiliarity in the desert. It was only in the unknown that true self-knowledge could be obtained. There they would meet God, discover their sense of purpose, and become Jews.

Not just the biblical heroes, but the entire congregation of Israel embarked on a spiritual journey. Sinai, where our people received wisdom, the Torah, and became partners with God, was just a two-month trek from Egypt. Upon reaching it, the Israelites should have been able to proceed the short distance into the land of Israel and settle there. But Israel was promised to a free people, and this people was still in bondage. Although they had left Egypt, they carried their slavery—in the form of perceptions and behaviors—deep inside of them. It was the only way of life they knew.

It would take 40 years of traversing back and forth across the same wilderness for the Israelites to become free: to take responsibility for their own destiny, to believe in themselves, and to dream again. Only then would they be sufficiently prepared to receive the gift of the land. For these Jews, wandering was not an avocation; it was an occupation. It was a necessary initiation rite—part of the making of a Jew. Even one early name for the Hebrew people, *hapiru*, comes from a Semitic word for "wanderer."[1] Wandering was an essential component in the development of Jewish identity.

There were obvious differences between the pilgrimages that my ancestors made and my own. I had the luxury to choose my journeys; I arranged my trips so they would come when the weather was auspicious; I planned my route meticulously before leaving, knowing where I would camp every night; I prepared all the food and clothing I would need before setting out; I made sure to bring enough fuel for emergencies. My ancestors, on the other hand, did not know where they were going. They did not how they were going to get there, how long it would take, or if the journey would ever end. Often, they did not carry food or fuel. Although our circumstances were different, one thing remains the same: the heart of the journey was a voyage toward the soul.

The Inspiration of Wandering

In the nineteenth century, Samson Raphael Hirsch, an Orthodox rabbi, wrote that God took us into the wilderness so that we could deal with our anxiety.[2] Hirsch suggested that anxiety was the true slavery; it is a condition that we perpetuate in ourselves by not claiming full responsibility for our lives. Anxiety results when we are dependent on others for our sense of our selves, when we blame others for the situations in which we find ourselves. I was charmed by Hirsch's reading of slavery and his understanding that a sojourn in wilderness could provide the context necessary for spiritual growth.

Hirsch wrote:

> The desert was the ideal venue for the revelation of His Torah because it was virgin soil, unpolluted as yet by egoism and ambition, undefiled by the pursuit of vanity. He chose the desert far from the cities, far from society and inhabited lands, far from an already corrupt society . . . .

I have often noticed how my own perceptions and values change when I take to the wilderness. In the city, I am aware of myself and my individuality: my looks, my clothes, my car, my house, and all my possessions. In wilderness, my self-consciousness and inhibitions dissolve, and I am more conscious of the whole. In the city, I hurry through my chores joylessly so I can engage in more *important* things, like work. In wilderness, I find the greatest pleasure in fixing dinner, fetching wood, and bathing in an alpine lake. In the city, I always need *something*. My pleasure seems to derive in part from the goods I have acquired. In wilderness, I am content with what I have: the company of friends, the beauty of the place, the pleasure of walking. I am not aware of wanting anything. Being resourceful and making do with what I have are part of the adventure.

In *The Songlines*, Bruce Chatwin connected the wandering life with inspiration and the settled life with resignation, boredom, and the accumulation of goods. He suggested that Cain and Abel were archetypes of these two contrasting character types: "The names of the brothers are a matched pair of opposites. . . ." Abel wandered the mountains, tending his sheep. His name comes "from the Hebrew 'hebel,' meaning breath or vapour: Anything that lives or moves and is transient." Cain was settled; he was associated with the development of city life. "The root of 'Cain' appears to be the verb *'kanah'*: To acquire, get, own property."[3]

My point is not that the life of wandering is necessarily good and a more settled life is necessarily bad. Too much wandering can lead to problems just as too much settling can. I am arguing that a sojourn in the wilderness can fill a basic spiritual need that we all have. If our need goes unfulfilled, we will find other ways to satisfy it. Cain's way—the accumulation of possessions—has dominated our culture for generations. We have become heavy with the weight of owning things, and the spirit has too often been wrung out of us. It is time to bring the spirit of Abel back to feed our souls. It is time to take inspiration seriously.

The experience of wilderness was not just about the Israelites' relationship with the Divine. It was about their relationship with each other. Stripped of their physical baggage, their class and financial status, the Israelites had to get down to the bare essentials: the survival and development of the community.

Rarely are we so close to our neighbors for so long that we can even begin to imagine what spending 40 years homeless in the desert with thousands of other people must have must have been like. Living in such close quarters surely exacerbated tensions. Day in and day out, people were hungry, cranky, tired, sick; kids were crying for attention; mothers were giving birth; and old people were dying.

Under desert conditions, community can be forged because people are forced to rely on each other through boredom, fear, anger, depression, and pain. Today, we take pride in keeping our problems to ourselves. We build walls to keep the world out. But for the desert Israelites, there were no opportunities to get away from each other. The wilderness was the ultimate test of the sustainability of the community.

As in any community, the Israelites had a system of law to ensure order for its people. Jewish law developed to deal with the multitude of concerns that arose between neighbors. Confronted with the unknown in every moment, the law could provide some comfort and some code with which to ensure justice and harmony. Given that the Israelite people spent their lives walking, it is little wonder that *halachah*, the word for "law" in Hebrew, is linked to *holech*, the word for "walk." They both derive from the same three-letter root H-L-K. *Halachah* literally teaches us the art of walking. It teaches the boundaries of the path and lets us know when we have trespassed; it conveys the stance we should adopt for different occasions. It is the tool we were given to help us build community.

The experience of wilderness promises two of life's primary lessons: we find out who we are and where we belong, and we learn to live in community with other people. In the process, we have the opportunity to see our slavery for what it is, to purify ourselves, to receive a vision, to become proactive, to develop intimacy with each other and the land, and to participate in the process of community building.

Today, many people tend to view the biblical wilderness experience as a metaphor for the journey we must all take to confront the unknown side of our soul and gain self-knowledge. Given that almost the entire biblical story takes place in the context of the desert wandering, I am convinced that the experience of wilderness is more than a metaphor.

I have always thought that our relationship to nature was a lost part of Jewish culture. So, too, the experience of wandering and wilderness and the spiritual journey. Today, the term "Jewish identity" is a buzzword in many Jewish circles, but most people are still loathe to attach identity to a relation with God, to self-discovery, to a deep personal journey, especially one that occurs in wilderness. We must recognize that we truly don't have any identity until we find ourselves. In Jewish tradition, a spiritual journey is the way.

Jewish practice affords us the opportunity to integrate the wilderness sojourn into our lives three times a year. The regular pilgrimage festivals that mark the Jewish year—Pesach, Shavuot, and Sukkot—provide us with the chance to regain our bearings and find our direction in every season, to leave behind our certainty and our arrogance for an experience with the unknown. It is no coincidence that these three harvest festivals, on which our ancestors traveled hundreds of miles from all over Israel to bring offerings to the Temple in Jerusalem, were collectively called the *shalosh regalim*, literally the three "on foot" days. Pilgrimage was a routine and necessary part of the yearly cycle. It would take weeks, even months for many of the Israelites to arrive and weeks to return home. I have to believe that the process of getting there was as important as the holiday itself.

The idea that the earth is alive has existed for thousands of years. The ancient Greeks called the earth "Gaia" *and* thought of her as a living entity—Mother Earth. In 1785, James Hutton was the first scientist to articulate a belief in a living earth, claiming that the cycling of elements in the environment could best be compared with the circulation of the blood and that the earth could be understood through the study of physiology.

In recent years, the scientist James Lovelock coined the phrase "the Gaia theory" to refer to the earth as a living system, a "self-regulating entity" with the capacity to remain healthy "by controlling the chemical and physical environment" (*Gaia: A New Look at Life on Earth*). But Lovelock and other scientists draw a strict distinction between a universe that can control itself chemically and a universe that feels, that is sentient.

This distinction becomes nebulous when viewed from a religious perspective. When one subscribes to the great mystery—God—at the root of all life, then the question of a "living" earth, a sentient earth, becomes all the more compelling.

To adopt the view of a "living" earth could change us. How do we act if we know the whole world is alive? If our perceptions mold who we are—if we are what we think—then cultivating a world-view that knows the earth is alive could be the most important step in becoming environmental citizens. In this piece, Rabbi Everett Gendler examines a strand of Jewish thought that presupposes a living universe.

6

A Sentient Universe

EVERETT GENDLER

It is taught: R. Jose says:
Alas for creatures who see but know not what they see,
who stand but know not upon what they stand.

—TALMUD, HAGIGAH 12B

Moses saw the Divine face to face. Still, God had to remind him, "Remove the sandals from your feet, for the place on which you stand is holy ground" (Exod. 3:5). Considering that Moses, the greatest of all prophets, did not fully comprehend the nature of the ground upon which he stood, it is not surprising that we, too, remain oblivious to the underlying mystery of nature.

A tree stands in front of us; it appears solid. But the molecular physicist, examining it with utmost scrutiny, observes that there is more open space than substance in the tree. What else might we miss upon first observation? This tree is clearly alive, but by ordinary human measure, it is without will, desire, emotion, or spirit. Perhaps we lack adequate senses to perceive the nature of the tree's inner life. Does the tree "feel" as we do? Consider the grass beneath our feet, the sand, the soil, the stones. Consider the stars overhead. Does sentience or panpsychism, in any sense, characterize the rest of the universe?

These terms need not alarm us. *Sentient*, though solemn sounding, simply means "sensing, feeling, having some degree of awareness." And as for *panpsychism*, which is a near synonym for *sentience*, it is neither a New Age notion nor an ancient Greek practice connected with the god Pan. It is simply the idea "that the basic physical constituents of the universe have mental properties, whether or not they are parts of living organisms."[1] In other words, every "material" particle, however small, is not only "matter" but to some degree "mind," even if it remains forever beyond our experience.

Genesis 9: The Covenant with Earth

Everyone knows that the Bible does not claim that independent, distinct spirits or souls are found in nature. In this way, Judaism differed from other faiths of its time. This does not mean, however, that Judaism understands nature as lifeless and lacking all spirit or feeling. After all, one can have spirit without spirits. In the biblical account of Creation, God, while connected with nature, is not entirely limited to it. The Divine is, in some significant way, more than nature. Yet, this does not necessarily mean that Creation is lacking in spirit or mind. In fact, a fresh look at Gen. 9:8–17 will quickly confirm that the Bible itself presupposes some degree of sentience in Creation, even in the earth itself (italics added):

> And God said to Noah and to his sons with him, "I now establish My *covenant* with you and your offspring to come, and with every living thing that is with you—birds, cattle, and every wild beast as well—all that have come out of the ark, every living thing on earth. I will maintain My *covenant* with you: never again shall all flesh be cut off by the waters of a flood, and never again shall there be a flood to destroy the earth."

> God added, "This is the *sign* that I set for the *covenant* between Me and you, and every living creature with you, for all ages to come. I have set my bow in the clouds, and it shall serve as a *sign* of the *covenant* between Me and the earth. When I bring clouds over the earth, and the bow appears in the clouds, I will remember My *covenant* between Me and you and every living creature among all flesh, so that the waters shall never again become a flood to destroy all flesh. When the bow is in the clouds, I will see it and remember the everlasting *covenant* that I have established between Me and all flesh that is on earth." Then God said to Noah, "This is the *sign* of the *covenant* which I have established between me and all flesh that is upon the earth."

In this passage, both the terms *brit*, "covenant," and *ot*, "sign," apply to all living creatures and to earth, not only to humans. Upon first consideration, the reader, who tends toward rationalism, is likely to dismiss the wording as a mere figure of speech. Yet, the sevenfold repetition of *brit* and the three-fold repetition of *ot* prevent easy dismissal. (Seven and three are, in many traditions, sacred numbers.) Their repeated use and their specific references to living creatures and the earth imply that the notion of divine covenant in relation to earth and its life must be taken seriously. While the covenantal references do in four instances specify human beings, in those same four instances the other living creatures are included as well. Two covenantal references pertain generally to all living creatures, while the seventh speaks exclusively of God's covenant with the earth.

To accept seriously God's covenant with other living creatures as well as with the earth itself raises questions that are disconcerting, yet exciting. A covenant is reciprocal. It involves an exchange of responsibilities and duties. What does this imply about the status of earth and its living creatures? If the earth can participate in a covenant, then the earth has some of the qualities of a living being. Johannes Pedersen, one of the twentieth century's greatest biblical scholars, argues that

> . . . the Israelites do not acknowledge the distinction between the psychic and the corporeal. Earth and stones are alive, imbued with a soul, therefore able to receive mental subject-matter and bear the impress of it. The relation between the earth and its owner . . . is a covenant-relation, a psychic community, and the owner does not solely prevail in the relation. The earth has its nature, which makes itself felt and demands respect.[2]

Therefore, according to Pedersen, the important thing is to "deal kindly with the earth, to uphold its blessing and then take what it yields on its own accord."[3]

When Pedersen uses the term *soul*, he does not mean something immaterial and unrelated to the physical composition of an object or person; he means the collection of innate tendencies or inclinations of that entity, or what we would call its nature or character. "Earth and stones are alive" concludes Pedersen. They are "able to receive mental subject-matter."[4] In this perspective, some element of the mental or spiritual characterizes all Creation.

Similarly, Professor Monford Harris, a philosophy professor at Spertus College, argues that the natural world was alive for the ancient

Hebrews. It could be used, it could be appropriated, but it could not be violated. "Man has covenantal relationship, community, with the natural world,"[5] writes Harris, adding that in the terms of Martin Buber, an "I-Thou" approach to the natural world must complement and constrain our more ordinary, more instrumental "I-It" approach.

Psalm 148: The Sound of Nature's Symphony

The fact that earth and all living beings are bound by covenant to God implies that Judaism takes universal sentience for granted: all of Creation must be alive with feeling. Yet rarely do we think of the Bible as making such a claim. Why is this? How did we come to see all the world—except our species—as essentially inert, lifeless, and lacking sentience? We are not lonely soloists in this world, the only ones capable of experiencing and expressing. There is a vast symphony singing, if we could only hear. Grasses whisper and animals sing the praises of God. The Bible tells us this again and again.[6]

Psalm 148, which is included in the daily morning service of the Hebrew prayer book, is particularly rich in this regard. Observant Jews recite it 365 times a year.

> Praise God, sun and moon;
> praise God, all you shining stars!
> Praise God, you highest heavens,
> and you waters above the heavens! . . .

> Praise the Lord from the earth,
> you sea monsters and all deeps;
> fire and hail, snow and frost,
> stormy wind fulfilling God's command!

> Mountains and all hills,
> fruit trees and cedars!
> Wild animals and all cattle,
> creeping things and flying birds!

> Kings of the earth and all peoples,
> princes and all rulers of the earth!

Young men and women alike,
old and young together!

Let them praise the name of the Lord . . .

Among those summoned to "praise the Lord" are sea monsters and
the deeps of the oceans, fire and hail, snow and frost, and stormy wind.
So, too, are mountains and hills, fruit trees and cedars, wild animals
and cattle, creeping things and flying birds—together with kings, peoples, princes, rulers, men, and women. The wording of the psalm is clear:
the same praise asked of humans is asked of the other natural elements.

Yet, rarely do these words touch our hearts. Rather, we defend ourselves from the fantastic possibilities suggested here. First, we tell ourselves that the psalms are not referring to *literal* praise. Instead, the
authors are implying that the orderly functioning of nature is itself a
kind of praise for the Creator. What could be more of a hymn to God than
the dance of crackling fire? Doesn't a hummingbird hail the Creator simply by hovering near a flower? Surely, nothing more than this is meant
by the repeated phrase, "praise God." Alternatively, we reason that to
"praise God" is simply a figure of speech and need not be taken literally.

If we think about it, however, we might well ask: Why do we overlook what is written? Isn't such a denial of the simple meaning of the text
illogical? In fact, such a reading is contrary to the principles of Jewish
scriptural interpretation.

If orderly functioning is all that the term "praise" implies, then it
is superfluous to ask for such praise; it *already* exists. In Ps. 19:2-5, for
example, the alternations of day and night, the regularity of the sun's cir-
cuit, and the patterns of the heavens are deemed sufficient praise of their
Creator, without words to embellish them:

The heavens are telling the glory of God;
    and the firmament proclaims His handiwork.
Day to day pours forth speech,
    and night to night declares knowledge.
There is no speech, nor are there words;
    their voice is not heard;
yet their voice goes out through all the earth,
    and their words to the end of the world.

But Psalm 148 demands more. It asks for *intentional* praise of the Creator not only from humans but from all realms of nature. It asks for praise *beyond* simple existence. The psalm presupposes a response from nature. Why ask for praise from something that is not capable of giving it?

As for the second way we defend ourselves from feeling the wonder of the psalmist, we dismiss the praises of nature as metaphorical. It is disappointing that even so distinguished a scholar as Nahum Sarna, the preeminent biblical commentator, avoids the issue of sentience by using precisely this device. Commenting on Psalm 19, in which "the poetic notion of nature's constituents [extol] their Maker," he cites Psalm 148 and Job 38:7. He admits that in Psalm 148 all heavenly beings and objects are called upon to "rhapsodize God" and that in Job "we are told that at the creation of the world, 'The morning stars chanted in unison, and all divine beings shouted for joy.'" Sarna then blunts the sharpness of the language by declaring, "We are dealing, of course, with figurative language."[7]

"Of course" is hardly a compelling argument. It is, in fact, no argument at all, but circular reasoning, an appeal to commonly held beliefs. Confident that the psalmist or Job was either in error or carried away by human emotion upon contact with "the timeless magnificence of the celestial scene," Sarna seeks to explain the dynamics underlying the figurative language. Obviously sensitive to "the inward, spiritual experience" that the starry skies can evoke in us, Sarna can only suggest that the psalmist "projects this situation onto the heavens and the heavenly bodies, which are now all personified."[8] Thus Sarna, like many other commentators, succumbs to the post-Cartesian intellectual fashion that asserts the radical distinction, the total difference, between minds and matter.[9]

In fact, Sarna departs from the principles of traditional Jewish interpretation when he denies what the text is plainly saying. The Talmud says, "A verse cannot depart from its plain meaning."[10] Guides to the Talmud reiterate this point: "The text does not lose its literal meaning"[11]

One rabbinic authority, Rabbi Kahana, held that this rule applied only where Torah lays down laws and principles of behavior, but not to "proverbial or poetical passages." But another authority, Mar b. R. Huna, argued that the rule applied to the poetic passages also, and it was this view that prevailed.[12] The plain, the literal, the natural meaning of a text is what is meant. Therefore, whatever further interpretations the language may stimulate, there is good reason to insist on the literal meaning of Psalm 148: Creation is being called to praise God.

It seems that the early rabbis also interpreted Psalm 148 literally:

> As Scripture says, *The Lord hath made every thing to bear witness to His glory* (Prov. 16:4). He created the heavens to sing His praises, and so they sing them, as it is said *The heavens declare the glory of God, and the firmament showeth His handiwork* (Ps. 19:2). And even as the heavens and all that is in them sing praises of God, so also the earth and all that is in it sing His praises, as it is said *Praise the Lord from the earth*. . . .
>
> After God's praises are sung from the heavens, who ought to be the first on earth to sing His praises? He that is larger than his fellow creatures. And who are the largest? The sea-monsters, of whom it is said *And God created the great sea-monsters* (Gen. 1:21). Therefore, the first on earth to sing God's praises are the sea-monsters, to whom it is said *Ye sea-monsters, and all deeps* (Ps. 148:7).[13]

Here, the literal meaning presupposes that, to some degree, all of Creation is sentient, feeling, and able to respond to this encompassing cry of "Halleluyah. Praise the Lord!"

The Song of the Three Jews

Closely related to Psalm 148 is the Apocryphal addition to the Book of Daniel, the Song of the Three Jews. One of a number of popular Hebrew works in existence at the time that the text of the Bible was selected and dating probably from the second century B.C.E., this stirring prayer was recited by Hananiah, Mishael, and Azariah from the fiery furnace into which they had been thrown when they refused to betray God by bowing to the idols of Nebuchadnezzar (Dan. 1, 3). The prayer opens with proclamations of the blessedness of God and then enjoins all created things to bless the Lord:

> Then the three with one voice praised and glorified and blessed God in the furnace . . .

"Bless the Lord, all you works of the Lord;
   sing God's praise and exalt God for ever.
Bless the Lord, you heavens;
   sing God's praise and exalt God for ever . . .
Bless the Lord, sun and moon;
   sing God's praise and exalt God for ever." (Song of Three
   28–40)

The hymn continues with calls to stars, rain, fire, wind, snow, mountains, plants, springs, whales, cattle, birds, and finally, people. "Bless the Lord!" (*Barechu et Adonai*), the *Barechu*, the classic Hebrew call to prayer, introduces every verse except one. Hananiah, Mishael, and Azariah are calling upon all of nature and Creation to bless God with them, which suggests that animal, vegetable, and mineral alike are capable of responding to a call to worship.

Perek Shira, All Creation Salutes God

One final example of Jewish acceptance of panpsychism is *Perek Shira* (A Chapter of Song), a mystical hymn from sometime between the fifth and seventh centuries.[14] Commonly used as a preface to the morning service,[15] the prayer includes such biblical verses as the following:

The heavens say: "The heavens declare the glory of God; the sky
   proclaims his handiwork." (Ps. 19:1–2)
The desert says: "The arid desert shall be glad; the wilderness shall
   rejoice." (Isa. 35:1)
The rivers say: "Let the rivers clap their hands, let the mountains
   sing for joy together." (Ps. 98:8)

Cows, camels, serpents, snails, elephants, eagles, mice, starlings, spiders, frogs, fish, cranes, butterflies, and even trees and grasses offer praise to their Creator and fill the universe with their hymns.

Perek Shira is a refreshing antidote to the excessive human pride that can stem from the notion that we alone among God's creations offer praise to the Creator. In the introduction to the song itself, the following rabbinic tale is cited:

Our rabbis tell the following story: "At the time that King David completed the Book of Psalms, he became full of pride and said to the Holy One, blessed be He, 'Surely there is no creature which you have made that can sing songs and praises greater than mine.'"

"At that exact moment a frog appeared before him and said, 'David, do not be so proud, for I can sing praises and songs even greater than yours!'"[16]

The song is consistent in ascribing sentience to the entirety of Creation. Its inclusion in traditional Hebrew prayer books is testimony that it has found a place in Jewish tradition.

Thus, Jewish texts provide abundant evidence that all of nature reverberates with life in all its possibilities. The qualities of "mind" and "feeling," which once described only humans, are here attributed to nature: The ability to participate in covenant. To praise God. To respond to God's call. To sing. To speak. To be glad. To rejoice. To clap hands, awake, declare, and proclaim. Each of these terms implies sentience. In light of such textual evidence, Pedersen's claim may seem even more convincing:

> . . . the Israelite does not distinguish between a living and a life-
> less nature. A stone is not merely a lump of material substance.
> It is, like all living things, an organism with peculiar forces of
> a certain mysterious capacity, only known to him that is famil-
> iar with it. . . . The earth is a living thing.[17]

The earth is *alive*. Yet in a world that diminishes the value of the sacred, we have grown blind to this profound mystery.

Renewing Our Wonder

Where does this leave us? If we recognized the fact that the earth and all of Creation is alive, what would this mean? It will be helpful to begin by pointing briefly to what it does not mean. It does not mean, for example, that rocks and people are equal, since both are sentient. Here, our discussion takes a different tack from the deep ecologists, many of whom would argue that all of Creation is equal and has equal rights.

John B. Cobb, Jr., and David Griffin, eminent theologians at the Claremont Graduate Schools, address this issue of distinctions within sentient creation. They affirm that all existence "can enjoy some degree of experience" and hence should be treated with respect. At the same time, they do not fly in the face of common sense: "Our attitude toward a rock is properly very different from that toward a dog." Cobb and Griffin invoke a distinction between "mere aggregates with no unity of experience or enjoyment" and "higher-level actualities" whose complexity of organization permits a more intense kind of existence.[18] In other words, a rock, although composed of countless tiny units, apparently has no further organization that would permit intensification of experience. A dog, on the other hand, has a central nervous system that does yield more intense experiences than those available to a rock.

Such distinctions must be made, yet one must not be overzealous. John Ruskin, the influential nineteenth-century British writer and social critic, arrived at a balance. "Things are not either wholly alive, or wholly dead. They are more or less alive."[19] William Barrett, the invaluable interpreter of existentialist philosophy, was equally thoughtful: "Whoever thinks matter is mere inert stuff has not looked long at rocks. They do not lie inert; they thrust forward, or crouch back in quiet self-gathered power."[20]

Understood in this way, grass is no longer merely a green ground cover devoid of any possible sensation. And now it is not only imaginable but also thinkable that Rabbi Nachman's well-known meditation is more than a mere figure of speech:

> It is especially precious
> to go out into the fields at the beginning of spring,
> when nature awakens from her sleep,
> and to pour out a prayer there.
> For every fresh blade of grass, every new flower,
> all join themselves with the prayer,
> for they too yearn and long for God.[21]

In recent centuries, our latent sense of companionship with other species has been largely viewed with suspicion. But now that a sense of kinship has become intellectually respectable (through the emergence of the field of eco-philosophy), we are free to follow the invitation to explore possibilities that were previously unseen. The universe, still vast beyond imagining, can become a more companionable place. Once again, mind can join with heart in affirming the profound outcry of the modern Hebrew poet Micah Joseph Berdichevski:

> It is not you alone who pray, or we, or those others; all things pray, and all things pour forth their souls. The heavens pray, the earth prays, every creature and every living thing. In all life, there is longing. Creation is itself but a longing, a kind of prayer to the Almighty. What are the clouds, the rising and setting of the sun, the soft radiance of the moon and the gentleness of the night? What are the flashes of the human mind and the storms of the human heart? They are all prayers—the outpouring of boundless longing for God.[22]

Will a shift of perception also affect how we treat the environment? Although there is no absolute certainty, it is hard to imagine that a renewed sense of wonder will not encourage caring behavior toward *all* life. Choices will remain challenging, and dilemmas will not disappear. Yet slowly, over time, this sense of nature as holy but not Deity, alive but not necessarily animistic, might help reestablish our sense of respect toward the world around us. And wonder and respect are the primary qualities needed to inspire a community to consistently engage in environmental practices.

Few Jews can now call upon a family folklore to capture their ancestors' connections to the land in Eastern Europe. Charles Fenyvesi can. In this piece, he treats us to the story of a love for farming and the land, interwoven with kabbalistic motifs, as it was passed from generation to generation in his family. As a farmer of a 7.5-acre plot in Maryland, Fenyvesi carries on the family's tradition.

7

Practical Kabbalah: A Family History

CHARLES FENYVESI

The beginning is a story, a *meise*, as it usually is, and as it should be.

Once upon a time, more than two hundred years ago, in the tiny village of Derzs in the Hungarian part of the mighty Habsburg empire, there lived a young Jew with a smile that was as quick as his mind. His name was Daniel, and while others in his village were content to earn their living by following in their parents' footsteps, he kept thinking about new ideas. He had a favorite phrase: "It will work if we give it a try." One of his ideas was to raise sheep for wool and sell the fleece in the great markets beyond the borders of his native Szabolcs County. His parents and their friends and neighbors doubted that anything could come out of such a risky enterprise, but Daniel was stubborn.

He also had a plan for the profits he hoped to make, but it was so ambitious that he did not dare share it with his parents, who were farmers renting land from a nobleman, just as their parents had before them.

Daniel was thinking of buying land, which Jews could not legally do at that time. But whether legal or not, investing in land, which, unlike most possessions, could not be strapped on one's back in case the need arose, did not seem a sensible proposition to Jews, whose history consisted of expropriations and expulsions.

At age eighteen, Daniel borrowed his father's wagon and horse and set out for Buda, the capital, more than 150 miles to the west. Sacks of fleece from the first shearing of his sheep's fleece filled the wagon as tightly as seeds in the head of a sunflower. He spent the first night of the long journey in a spacious roadside structure with sturdy wooden pillars and a thatched roof. It offered safety and shelter for people, their wagons, and their animals.

But he could not sleep. He got up, and as he walked around, he discovered another Jew who could not find rest. His name was Isaac, and he had just completed his rabbinic studies in Poland, hundreds of miles to the north, and he was now walking to Kallo, then the capital of Szabolcs County, to apply for the job of rabbi.

The two young men quickly noted that they were the same age, and soon they traded confidences. Daniel acknowledged, for the first time, that he had doubts about the wisdom of his idea of raising sheep for wool. Isaac said he had doubts not only about his chances of getting the job of leading a large congregation, but also about serving as a rabbi. He liked to sing, he liked walking through fields, and he hated to be caged inside a room. Perhaps he was not meant to be a rabbi, a scholar expected to spend his life immersed in the Torah.

Daniel said that Jews in Szabolcs County loved songs and that members of his family also enjoyed walking through the fields.

Then he asked the question that troubled him all his life. Rabbi, he asked, is it acceptable for a Jew to want to own land and to work on it? His parents and their ancestors had been renting land for centuries, he explained, but now he thought they should finally buy land.

For the first time, Isaac was confronted as a rabbi with a *shaila*, a question, and he was surprised how easy it was to answer. He said that as their biblical ancestors owned land so they could tend animals and raise crops, there was no reason for a Jew in Hungary not to own land and raise sheep or wheat, if that is what Daniel's heart longed for. He said he had heard that unlike Empress Maria Theresa who hated Jews so much that she would speak to them only through a screen, Crown Prince Josef was an enlightened man who wanted Jews to help build his empire. The rabbi predicted that the law would soon allow Jews to own land.

Morning came, and Daniel insisted on delivering Isaac to Kallo, even though it was not on the way to Buda. Before they parted company, the rabbi put his hands on his new friend's shoulders and asked God's blessing for Daniel's enterprise and for his other enterprises that were sure to follow. Finally, the rabbi said, "May the Lord bless you and favor you and all your descendants who keep the laws of Moses and work on the land."

Loving the Land

Daniel's venture was more successful than he had ever imagined. He sold the fleece at a higher price than anyone in his village thought possible and received orders for more.

In the years to come, Daniel took good care of his flock of sheep, which increased and multiplied and brought good profit. He went on to become, in the first years of the nineteenth century, the first Jew in Szabolcs County to buy a plot of land even before it became legally permissible for a Jew to own land.

As for Isaac, in due course he was elected rabbi of the town of Kallo. By the first years of the nineteenth century, he had become Hungary's most beloved rabbi and was known as the Kallever Rebbe rather than by his name, Isaac Taub. Jews and Gentiles alike believed that he had miraculous powers, as his study of Kabbalah had opened his eyes to the secrets of souls and nature. He also composed songs in which the flowers and the animals of the visible world served as hints of the supernatural. One hauntingly sweet melody, as much a Hungarian folksong as a Hasidic *nigun*, about a rooster walking through woods and fields to announce the coming of the Messiah and the rebuilding of the Temple, is still sung in Hungarian and in Yiddish in the two worlds in which he lived—in Hungary and in Hasidic congregations across the globe.

The rabbi's blessing turned the secret longing Daniel had for land into his family's keystone of faith. In the years that followed the rabbi's words at that fateful meeting in the 1770s, first Daniel and then his descendants came to think of the land they bought as an extension of the Holy Land, *Eretz Yisrael*. Resisting the temptations of the cities as well as the professions and business, many of Daniel's descendants remained engaged in agriculture. From generation to generation, they quoted the Kallever Rebbe's explanation to Daniel that since our ancestors were banished from the Holy Land, land everywhere became holy, just as after the Romans' destruction of the Holy Temple in Jerusalem, wherever Jews built a temple, it became the surrogate Temple.

For a century and a half, Daniel's descendants in Hungary faithfully observed the talmudic laws concerning farming, even though those laws were supposed to be applied only in *Eretz Yisrael*, such as leaving the edges and the corners of their land to be harvested by the poor and burning the fruits of trees for the first three years after their planting. For five generations, they were successful, and the speed of their acquisition of wealth in a proverbially poor county was considered amazing. One twentieth-century descendant, Samuel Schwarcz, better known by the nickname of Shumi, explained it his way: "They loved the land, and the land returned their love."

Daniel was my grandfather's grandfather's grandfather. Having heard stories about him and his descendants all my life—ever since I remember remembering—and having delved into their sayings that have come down to contemporary generations, I think I understand the reasons for my ancestors' abiding love for land.

My Schwarcz ancestors were not content with looking at nature as the wonder of God's Creation, as described in the conclusion of Maimonides' *Guide to the Perplexed*, which they doubtless studied, or as the ultimate expression of beauty, as was the conviction among the Hungarian Gentiles, whose music and poetry they were so fond of. Unlike their fellow Jews in the city, who thought of words like seeds and roots, trees and harvest as mere figures of speech, my ancestors were deeply engaged in the realities behind those metaphors and knew full well what the metaphors were borrowed from. After all, the Hebrew word for metaphor, *hashala*, comes from the word "to borrow," implying that whatever is borrowed needs to be returned to its source. Under the influence of the Kallever Rebbe, who himself echoed some of the teachings of that other Hasidic master and lover of nature, the Baal Shem Tov, my ancestors came to believe that nature constitutes a critical link in the chain of divine manifestation and in that way is most like Torah.

They enjoyed a comforting certainty that they participated in carrying out the divine design. I have no doubt that somehow kabbalistic books reached their village and that they avidly studied the hidden wisdom, in addition, of course, to the Talmud. When, in the summer of 1993, I was reading *Shomrei Adamah*'s English translation of the *Peri 'Ez Hadar*,[1] a little-known kabbalistic classic that was first printed in 1728, I felt like shouting: This must have been a text my ancestors read and loved! Reading the abstruse language and trying to understand the classification system that ascribes metaphysical significance to natural phenomena—such as the differences between the wholly edible grape from the shell-bound walnut and the apricot with a pit inside—I could imagine the Kallever Rebbe exulting in such mysteries. He must have discussed them with my ancestors during long walks across orchards of apples and apricots, followed by a rest in the shade of a centuries-old walnut tree, his favorite tree. (According to *Peri 'Ez Hadar*, the walnut symbolizes Ezekiel's chariot.)

Just as the invisible writing of spies becomes legible when exposed to certain chemicals, the abstract principles of Kabbalah have gradually begun to appear to me as standing behind the practical, everyday decisions of my ancestors.

Restoring the Wholeness of Creation

One important aspect of the Hasidic-kabbalistic world-view is the belief in the existence of angels, mysterious creatures who span the vast distance between *HaShem* enthroned on top of the spiritual hierarchy of emanations and us earth-bound mortals rooted in the material world. In the family stories passed down to me, angels played key roles, and their appearances were unexpected and decisive. Each angel was in charge of carrying out one assignment, one specific part in the grand divine design. The angel's will was responsive to a human being who pleaded with a pure heart and a soul on fire, what Jewish mystics call *kavannah*. In my family tradition, we believe that an appeal to heaven has the best chance of winning when it echoes the needs of the land, land impatient for improvement and grateful for human persistence. And the angel's intervention opens the way to a positive outcome.

My grandfather Akiba used to say, "Behind every blade of grass is an angel who says, 'Grow, grass, grow.'" One fine sunny day in early spring, he decorated his carriage and his two best horses with long, brightly colored ribbons and took his wife, Rachel, and their children on a joyous carriage ride around all the lands he owned to inspect the fresh green growth of the wheat and potatoes. "This is the good life," he would cry out, hug and kiss his wife, and then chant the *Shehecheyanu*, his favorite blessing and the incantation of every optimist. He would conduct another ceremonial tour on another fine day during the summer, after the wheat fields had become a sea of golden waves and the potato plants shaded into a dark, dense green.

He and his brothers, all seven of them farmers, and their one sister, married to a farmer, loved to experiment with new plants, including hybrids. But they stayed away from those that mated cherry to apricots or tomatoes to potatoes. Their children remember how they were forbidden to eat the fruit of trees that were grafts from different species. The Talmud pronounces such trees impure, and Kabbalah posits that a mixed-fruit tree "confuses the angels assigned to the species in question." (A parallel is drawn to the prohibition in the Torah of mixing species, as mixing destroys the integrity of a species.) As *Peri 'Ez Hadar* explains, "Failing to keep the two domains separate in the natural world allows the forces of impurity to penetrate the side of holiness in the metaphysical domain."

My ancestors praised the bounty of God's Creation and exulted in their recitation of the appropriate blessings. Those who remember my grandfather's generation have always cited the fervor of their prayers and the joyous, self-confident nature of their faith. In the village, the caretaker of the Calvinist church, who was born in 1920, the year my grandfather died, told me, "Members of your family were famous for their smiles on their faces, and that was because they really believed that God was on their side." He explained to me how in his family—his father worked for my grandfather just as his grandfather worked for my great-grandfather—it was related to him that the Schwarczes thought of

God as someone they knew intimately, "the way one knows a grandfather though he died long ago."

One of my ancestors' fundamental beliefs was in the need to pursue *tikkun olam*, the duty of a Jew as defined in the sixteenth century by the incomparable kabbalist Rabbi Isaac Luria Ashkenazi, better known as the Holy Ari. According to him, improving or, as others translate it, restoring the world is the first kabbalistic commandment because *tikkun* means restoring the original wholeness that Creation itself shattered. In the Holy Ari's explanation, God's infinite power had to restrain itself to bring about the creation of a finite world. Thus in Creation, the omnipresent divine essence chose to focus on a tiny point in all the worlds: our earth. However, that self-imposed contraction of power, *tzimtzum* in the holy language, proved too powerful for the world it poured into. The world, or what Lurianic Kabbalah poetically calls "vessels" or *kelim*, broke into millions of small fragments, mere shards. Or to use another of the Holy Ari's metaphors: sparks of the divine light fell from the heavens into the lower realms, where they remain concealed in the material world of rocks, animals, and people. A subsequent catastrophe occurred when Adam disobeyed the divine command: the great fire of the human soul separated into sparks.

The programmatic part of the Holy Ari's cosmology is that to restore the world to its original condition of harmony and wholeness, Adam's descendants must search for and gather the fragments.

The Power of Practical Mysticism

My Schwarcz ancestors perceived land as the material substance that was closest to them and within their power to improve. The soil of their patch of the earth was windblown sand virtually empty of nutrients, about as fertile as the sand of a beach. So the *tikkun* my ancestors engaged in was to forever upgrade the soil of the land they worked. This must have seemed strange to their neighbors, who sowed and harvested year after year but added little to improve the soil.

My ancestors collected leaves, wheat stalks, kitchen scraps, and organic debris of all types to toss into the sort of heap that we moderns call a compost pile. They eventually carted the compost off to their fields and vegetable garden. My mother's first cousin Shmuel, who was born in 1899 in Szabolcs County and died in the 1970s in Beersheba, told me once how "religiously" our forebears insisted on saving everything from melon rinds to fireplace ashes. "Nothing should go to waste!" was their motto. He also recalled that even though their method was demonstrably successful, neighbors shook their heads at the Schwarczes' *meshugas*, their craziness.

Now I understand that Cousin Shmuel's use of the word "religious" in referring to our ancestors' zeal in gathering material for the compost pile was not a mere figure of speech. Their insistence on recycling what was customarily cast off reflected another kabbalistic principle, as defined by the Holy Ari: *klitat ha'nitzot*, or the collection of holy sparks that have fallen to a lowly status. *Peri 'Ez Hadar* uses other imagery: *klipot*, the skins or shells of a fruit, are *tuma'ah*, or impure; however, their descent into evil is not irreversible.

To the minds of our Schwarcz ancestors, the redemption of all sorts of *klipot* must have taken place in the heat of the pile, which, as every modern gardener knows, transforms disparate organic wastes into one heap of supernal soil. I have a hunch that in setting up the compost pile at least as early as the mid-nineteenth century, my ancestors might have been inspired by kabbalistic imagery. But regardless of their source of inspiration, they must have perceived that their compost piles reflected a mystical abstraction. As *Peri 'Ez Hadar* said it, "As things are below, so they are above. For there would be no shadow if there were none to cast it."

The most important of all the materials of lowly origin the Schwarczes put back into the soil was manure, considered in their days the lowliest of lowly substances. They systematically collected it in big piles and pits to mature. Every fall, they and their workers spread the manure on the fields, replenishing the soil, which then gave higher yields the following year. That meant that more wheat stalks and potato peels were given to the cattle, which in turn produced more manure, which was again plowed back into the soil. Such a productive loop—the opposite of a vicious circle—was the source of the Schwarcz wealth.

The Schwarczes were practical mystics. They insisted on applying in their everyday life the ethereal wisdom they studied on *Shabbos*. This was their way of approaching lofty principles. Tilling the land was their life, and to be a good steward—*balaboos* in Yiddish, *gazda* in Hungarian—was their highest objective. Their patient and persistent piecing together of shattered fragments was an effective realization, in the lower or material world, of a high kabbalistic abstraction: a *tikkun* leading to an *olam shalem*, a favorite phrase of theirs, a world that is whole.

My Uncle Shumi, to his eternal regret, auctioned off his portion of the inheritance in 1927 to pay off debts incurred by his father, who had kept buying large plots of land during the golden afternoon of peace and plenty before World War I, the last quarter of Emperor Franz Josef's reign. But, as Shumi was the first to acknowledge, he also lost the family talent for dealing with land. Nor did he believe. He could not believe, he told his father, who was greatly disappointed. And all his life Shumi felt guilty for not observing the laws of Moses and for not being able to carry on the enterprise blessed by the Kallever Rebbe.

For Shumi and his brothers and sisters, the loss of their land was the tragedy that foreshadowed the Holocaust. In 1927, Shumi led the sad procession of his family, his mother and his three brothers and three sisters, from their ancestral village. Many of Daniel's other descendants also went bankrupt around the same time. Those who held on to their land in other villages of Szabolcs County were marched off to Auschwitz in June 1944.

The departure from the ancestral land led by Uncle Shumi occurred ten years before I was born. I visited the village only once in my life, in 1989, to say Kaddish for Uncle Shumi, my grandfather Akiba (after whom I am named), and all my ancestors buried in our family cemetery over many centuries. A villager in his eighties who knew us as though we were still neighbors showed me the 30-acre plot Daniel had originally bought. This, he said, was still the best piece of land in the village. My eyes also rested on some of the hundreds of acres eventually acquired by Daniel's descendants, one of the most ambitious among them being Grandfather Akiba.

All Life Is Part of a Grand Design

The Schwarczes believed in reincarnation, *gilgul nefesh*, which is another kabbalistic principle that flows from the notion of *tikkun olam*. A long series of lives are needed to gather the sparks of Adam's shattered soul, an enterprise that includes retrieving sparks that fell to the nonhuman parts of Creation such as animals, plants, and even rocks. In the Schwarcz tradition, which is as self-centered as it is practical, there is a belief that sparks of the departed souls tend to stay within the same family. This process is encouraged by giving a newborn child the name of an ancestor who "died a happy person" and was known as "a wholesome spirit." The child's link is later reinforced by telling him or her tales about that ancestor. Unmistakably, the stories, such as the Kallever Rebbe's blessing, have the function of what the German philosopher Friedrich Schelling called "narrative philosophy." Our Hasidic masters understood that more than any rabbinic rule or scholarly exposition, a good story or even a good metaphor can charm our minds with its magic, and the enchantment can last more than one lifetime.

In my family, the children and grandchildren of Holocaust survivors are now settled in moshavim and kibbutzim in Israel. They are successful farmers, though emphatically secular. In 1984, I bought a small farm in Maryland, where I now live with my family. As I plant it and work with animals, it is self-evident that we tend the same earth wherever we invest our strength and our affection. What matters is good stewardship, which need not concern itself with maximizing a profit. I now think that the Kallever Rebbe detected the flammable essence of Daniel's soul and lit a fire. The rabbi's blessing—a transfer of vital energy—confirmed and justified, magnified and sanctified the irrepressible affinity Daniel had felt with land.

Each year, I weed and improve parts of a land that lay neglected. When planting walnut trees and blackberry brambles, hazelnut bushes and black-eyed Susans and ornamental grasses, I recite the blessing: be fruitful and multiply. Kabbalistic principles have come to make common sense to me. Nature is indeed comparable to the Torah as the unfolding of the divine will, and a blessing said over a fruit we grow helps the flow of divine energy sustaining the plant. The blessing completes the loop linking the Creator, the plant, and the steward of the land, whose responsibility is to restore harmony. Along with my ancestors, I believe that each plant has not only its own particular personality but also its own energy source—why not call it an angel?—which ensures its minute part in a vast design.

I am aware that I, too, am a spark from a particular fire that has been burning for generations. I know I take up a project begun long ago when in the spring I dig up the soil on which I spread manure the previous fall. In choice moments—for instance, when harvesting our first walnuts and inhaling the bitter scent of their husks or when sharing with friends the cheese we make from the milk of the goats that we raise—I have the heady feeling that I, too, am a beneficiary of that blessing conferred more than 200 years ago.

As I walk my plot of land, I hear a chorus of hoarse honking, and I look up. Across the sky flies a flock of wild geese. Our rooster responds by crowing lustily.

Our lives are completely intertwined with the natural world. Every day, we use products that are derived from nature: the food we eat, the air we breathe, the homes we build, the clothes we wear. There is nothing inherently wrong with using the natural world in these ways. The earth is good, and we are invited to partake of it. However, when we abuse this privilege, when we take more than we give back, when we consume excessively, we deplete and potentially ruin the system that provides for us. Since this is the situation today, it follows that our habits of consumption have become a prime environmental concern.

In this piece, Dr. Eliezer Diamond examines Jewish tenets that promote balance in the lives of individuals, communities, and the environment.

8

Jewish Perspectives on Limiting Consumption

ELIEZER DIAMOND

We have been taught all our lives that abundance is good. We take pride in the standard of living that our economic and political system makes available, at least in theory, to all Americans. At the same time, we feel significant dissatisfaction, either because we are not as affluent as we had hoped to be or ironically, having achieved our hoped-for affluence, we still feel empty.

Jewish tradition is aware of this ambivalence. On the one hand, the rabbis considered sensual and material impulses to be "very good." Without these impulses, a man would not build a house, marry a woman, or beget children.[1]

On the other hand, Ecclesiastes voices the reflection of a man who has spent all his life pursuing wealth, pleasure, and power without finding real fulfillment.

> I said to myself, "Let me experiment with pleasure and have a good time!" but this also turned out to be [unsubstantial as] a vapor. . . . For when I considered all the things that I had done and the energy I had expended in doing them, it was clear that the whole of it was futility and a grasping at the wind, and none of it was profitable [for a man's life] under the sun. (Eccles. 2:1, 11)

Ecclesiastes' tone of world-weariness and bitterness is familiar to many of us. We pursue our dreams of wealth and comfort only to discover that they are a chimera, and we are unable to find a viable vision to replace our shattered dreams. We feel like cogs in a machine, unable to change the course of our own lives, much less the complexion of society.

The Jewish view of consumption begins with the belief that the earth belongs to God. We are encouraged to partake of it and told that when we do, we receive a divine gift. That is why Jews are required, before partaking of any food, to recite a blessing that acknowledges God as its Creator. Not to do so, says the Talmud, is to be considered a thief.[2]

A particularly striking affirmation of this-worldly pleasure is found in Deuteronomy, which states that officials should make the following declaration to Israelites assembled for battle:

> "Is there anyone who has built a new house but has not dedicated it? Let him go back to his home, lest he die in battle and another dedicate it. Is there anyone who has planted a vineyard but has never harvested it? Let him go back to his home, lest he die in battle and another harvest it. Is there anyone who has paid the bride-price for a wife, but who has not yet married her? Let him go back to his home, lest he die in battle and another marry her." (Deut. 20:5–7)

The recurring phrase "lest he die in battle and another. . ." suggests that one should not face death without first tasting life.

Rabbinic literature, while exhibiting more ascetic tendencies than the Bible, is replete with positive assessments of physical pleasure. One illustration is a fascinating statement by Yaltah, the wife of Rabbi Nah-man, a late-third-century Babylonian rabbi, which begins with the proposition that "whatever the Torah has forbidden it has permitted something like it." She then offers several examples to make her case: The fat of the domesticated animal is forbidden, but the fat of the wild animal is permitted; pork is forbidden, but the brain of the mullet (which supposedly tastes like pork) is permitted; another man's wife is forbidden, but if he divorces her, she is permitted; and so on. Yaltah therefore asks her husband in what form the Torah permits eating meat together with milk, which is generally forbidden. He replies that one may eat the udder of the cow although it contains milk.[3] Yaltah's point seems to be that although certain behaviors are forbidden by the Torah, no form of experience or pleasure is totally denied.

Balance and *Halachah*

The positive view of material and sensual pleasure outlined above must be placed in the context of biblical and rabbinic theology, which is dedicated to achieving balance. Judaism ensures the proper balance between enjoying and exploiting the world by establishing a system of boundaries or laws called *halachah.*

Halachah requires that periods of work, of being actively involved with the world, alternate with periods of rest and retreat: the Sabbath. This can help restore balance in people's lives and in the world. Commenting on Gen. 2:15, "The Lord God took the man and placed him in the Garden of Eden, to work it and to tend [or keep] it," the sages state that "to work it" refers to the phrase "Six days you shall work" and "to keep it" refers to "Observe the Sabbath day."[4] "Work," a transformative process, consumes human and material resources, while "keeping" preserves resources. The biblical imperative requires finding a balance between transformation and preservation.

This six-and-one cycle applies to years as well as weeks. Every seventh year is a year of rest for the land. No cultivation of land takes place (Lev. 25:3–5), but whatever grows of its own accord may be eaten (Lev. 25:6–7). The year 1993–1994, or 5754 according to the Jewish calendar, was a Sabbatical year. At least 3,500 Israeli farmers refrained from working their land, and numerous others modified their farming practices.

The limitations placed on Jewish individuals and society through the laws of the Sabbath and the Sabbatical year, as well as the restrictions governing diet and sexual behavior, are intended to help people fathom life's hidden limits, so that rather than being seen as a curse, the limits are considered the starting point from which one constructs a meaningful life. "Who is wealthy?" ask the rabbis rhetorically. "One who is happy with one's lot."[5]

Halachah concerns itself not only with balance in the individual and collective life of the people; it also seeks balance and equity in the distribution and consumption of the fruits of labor. Thus, the biblical obligations of *peah*, leaving a corner of one's field for the poor at the time of harvest (Lev. 23:22), and *ma'aser*, giving one-tenth of one's harvest to the landless Levites (Deut. 14:27–29), are expanded by the rabbis into an obligation to give between ten and twenty percent of one's income to the poor.[6]

Moreover, *halachah* specifies that familial and religious celebrations, rather than being occasions for excessive consumption, should be restrained so they do not create pressure on others in the community who are less well off to spend beyond their means. These affairs should also include the poor. An attempt to achieve the first goal was the formulation of sumptuary laws that limited conspicuous consumption. A 1637 ruling of the national Jewish Council of Lithuania stated that since "people are spending too much money unnecessarily on festive meals, every Jewish community and settlement . . . is expected to assemble its officers and rabbi and to consider the number of guests which it is suitable for every individual, in view of his wealth and the occasion, to invite to a festive meal."[7]

The second objective, sharing with the poor in times of celebration, is described by Maimonides as he evaluated the relative merits of the three obligations of the Purim festival: to feast, to send gifts to one's friends and to give gifts to the poor. "Better for one to give many gifts to the poor than to have a sumptuous feast and send many gifts to one's acquaintances; for there is no greater or more elegant joy than to gladden the hearts of the poor, the orphan, the widow and the stranger in our midst."[8]

Given the emphasis Judaism places on restraint, it is particularly important for community leaders, who are role models for others, to modulate their consumption. Excessive consumption by community leaders can also lead to moral corruption and create financial burdens on the people. The Bible states: "[The king] shall not keep many horses or send people back to Egypt to add to his horses. . . . And he shall not have many wives, lest his heart go astray; nor shall he amass silver and gold to excess" (Deut. 17:16–17).

The Talmud relates a story in which the saintly Pinhas ben Yair was invited to dine at the official residence of Judah the Patriarch. "When he reached the gate, he saw several white mules, a rather rare and expensive breed, tethered there. Saying, 'Must my fellow Jews feed all these?' he turned on his heel and left."[9]

Judaism's concern for modesty also affects its attitudes and practices regarding consumption. A talmudic passage suggests that the 613 commandments can be summed up by the following verse in Micah: "He has told you, O man, what is good, and what the Lord requires of you: Only to do justice, to love goodness, and to walk modestly with your God. . ." (Mic. 6:8). Broadly defined by the rabbis, modesty applies to consumption that is excessive or overly conspicuous. The rabbinic tradition discourages one from eating in the marketplace, from eating and drinking to excess, and from wearing clothes of such fine materials that they are likely to draw too much attention.[10]

The Spiritual Effects of Consumption

Excessive consumption can wreak havoc in one's personal life and rob one of the life of the spirit. The attempt to satisfy every fleeting impulse, a common phenomenon in our world of ubiquitous advertising and malls, begins with our thoughts. The Torah recognizes this when it commands as the tenth commandment, "You shall not covet" (Exod. 20:14 and Deut. 5:18).

The Torah fosters inner balance and harmony and inhibits the addictive impulse by limiting indulgence in material and sensual pleasures. *Halachah* specifically restrains one from becoming a gastronomical or sexual gourmand. For example, Rabbi Johanan, a third-century Palestinian sage, said that if one starves his sexual desire, "it will be sated; if one sates it, it will remain hungry."[11]

Environmental Implications of Consumption

The Torah speaks even more directly to the environmental implications of consumption, specifically, to the issue of sustainability. Consider the verse:

> If, along the road, you chance upon a bird's nest, in any tree or on the ground, with fledglings or eggs and the mother sitting over the fledglings or on the eggs, do not take the mother together with her young. Let the mother go, and take only the young, in order that you may fare well and have a long life. (Deut. 22:6–7)

The Bible gives no reason for this prohibition, which has been the subject of much rabbinic debate. Nahmanides suggested "that Scripture does not allow the total destruction of a species, although it allows us to slaughter some of its kind."[12] More provocatively, Don Isaac Abravanel, a fifteenth-century Spaniard, wrote:

> The Torah's intention is to prevent the possibility of untimely destruction and rather to encourage Creation to exist as fully as possible. For God made the continued existence of animals possible by enabling them to produce fruit. . . . And God has commanded not to destroy that which generates progeny or produces fruit; rather, just as picking fruit is permitted while destroying the tree is forbidden—as Scripture states, "You shall eat from the tree but you shall not cut it down" (Deut. 20:19). . . . Instead, we should send away the mother so that we may partake of her offspring while the mother produces other progeny and thereby perpetuates God's creation.[13]

He concludes:

> And this is the meaning of . . . "in order that you may fare well and have a good life." This commandment is given not for the sake of the animal world but rather so that it shall be good for humankind when Creation is perpetuated so that one will be able to partake of it again in the future. This, too, is the meaning of "and [you will] have a lengthy life," namely, because you are destined to live for many years on this earth, you are

reliant upon Creation perpetuating itself so that you will always have sufficient food.[14]

This directive could be applied today to limit consumption to what is necessary for a sustainable economy. While this concept is notoriously difficult to define, in some branches of our economy—such as forestry and fishing—applying this principle would seem fairly straightforward, once foresters and fishermen and their clients realize that healthy future production depends on limiting the present harvesting of resources. Of course, once such environmental concerns as threats to endangered wildlife enter the picture, we are again plunged into murky waters.

Finally, some consider the following biblical verses to be the focal point of Judaism's environmental concerns:

> When in your war against a city you have to besiege it a long time in order to capture it, you must not destroy its trees, wielding the ax against them. You may eat of them, but you must not cut them down. Are the trees of the field human to withdraw before you into the besieged city? Only trees that you know do not yield food may be destroyed; you may cut them down for building siegeworks against the city that is waging war on you, until it has been reduced. (Deut. 20:19–20)

Verse 19 prohibits cutting down fruit-bearing trees in a time of war. Biblical scholars have suggested that the Bible is alluding to scorched-earth military tactics common in the ancient Near East. In this view, no direct advantage could be gained by felling the tree; the intent was punitive or a form of psychological warfare. But from the fact that the next verse permits cutting non-fruit-bearing trees only for some immediate positive use—namely, constructing siegeworks—it would appear that the prohibition of the previous verse includes cutting down fruit-bearing trees for a similar purpose. In short, then, fruit-bearing trees may not be cut down even for the purpose of using their wood because this would destroy forever their generative capabilities. This analysis is consistent with Abravanel's understanding of the requirement to send away the mother bird when taking her eggs or fledglings.

Rabbinic interpretation of these verses extends—and qualifies—the biblical law. Extensions include applying this prohibition, known as bal taschit, "you shall not destroy," to the entire material world. Thus, although it is Jewish practice to tear one's garment as a sign of mourning, anyone who tears one's garment "excessively" (the rabbis do not quantify the term) is said to violate this prohibition.[15] This ruling raises interesting questions about the amount of resources an individual or a society can expend for emotional catharsis or, as it is more popularly known, escapist entertainment. Moreover, inefficient use of resources is forbidden just as total destruction is. The Babylonian Talmud says that anyone who does not properly adjust the air flow of a lamp, thereby causing unnecessary fuel consumption, has violated the *bal taschit* prohibition.[16]

However, this efficiency criterion also leads the rabbis to qualifying *bal taschit*. According to one interpretation of a talmudic passage, if the transformative use of any raw materials, including fruit-bearing trees, will produce more profit than using it in its present form, its transformative use is permitted.[17] Thus, if a fruit-bearing tree will produce only $10 worth of fruit per year for the next ten years, but its wood can now be sold for $200, it may be cut down and its wood sold.

There are at least two problems with this interpretation. One, which is technical, arises when the long-term production of the tree far outstrips any immediate profits but felling the tree now will lead to larger short-term profits. Do the short-term profits justify felling the tree? Secondly, this analysis seems to reduce the status of even the fruit-bearing tree to raw material.[18] Does the tree's beauty and vitality count for nothing?

Rabbi Moses Sofer, an eighteenth-century Hungarian scholar, responded to this issue in a case in which he allowed cutting down fruit-bearing trees not only to use their wood, but also to use the land on which they grow. Nonetheless, says Sofer, there is a difference between these two instances. One who wishes to use the land is obligated to replant the trees elsewhere, if possible.[19] Sofer recognized that trees are alive and had to be protected against residential and commercial development. They are not simply obstacles to be removed.

It should be clear that halachic literature contains directives and concepts that can be used to construct sane, fair economic and environmental policy. If the earth is God's, does it not deserve the care and the concern of our tradition? We have sacrificed the natural for the commercial and found that trade-off wanting. Is it not time to strike a more fruitful balance within God's world?

The Jewish connection to nature can most often be found in psalms, poetry, and stories. It is here, I believe, that the feeling comes through with the greatest power. So, I was delighted when I happened across Robert Sand's story in *Story* magazine several years ago. When I asked Robert's permission to print it in this volume, he wanted to know something about my work, and I forwarded to him a copy of my teaching guide on Judaism and environment, *Let the Earth Teach You Torah*, and several issues of *Shomrei Adamah*'s newspaper, *Voice of the Trees*. He responded, "I want you to know how moving everything I've read has been to me. As someone whose agnostic father drove him to his Orthodox bar mitzvah in a 1958 Plymouth—'For God's sake, Dad, I can't ride to Congregation Sons of Israel! I have to walk.' 'Walk? Whddya talkin? Walk? It's over twenty blocks!'—it's shocking to find that my own Jewishness, which I thought was dead, was merely dormant."

9

New York Is a Girl

ROBERT SAND

It was 1950 and Poppy Weiss was dead, and my mother, in an attempt to win back her family, sent away for tickets for me and my sister to appear in the Peanut Gallery on "The Howdy Doody Show."

It had been my mother's dream to get my sister and me on that show, but Poppy had forbidden it. Poppy, who had one eye and a lifelong reputation as an impossible man, had come to live with us after Nanny

Weiss died three years before, and he immediately became the man of our house, forbidding us, essentially, to live our lives as we'd grown accustomed to living them. This included not watching television, much less sending away for tickets to one of its most popular regular shows.

My father, the only Jewish motorcycle cop in Jersey City and one of only two Jews on the entire force, was a very tough man everywhere in the world, except in the presence of Poppy Weiss, and he let Poppy make the rules even though Poppy was living in his apartment. This made my mother, who'd looked upon her marriage to my father as her salvation, deeply disappointed and, as she put it, "different towards him"; and it made my father, a dashing mustachioed figure with a profile like Barrymore's and the torso of a garage who had therefore prided himself on what he liked to refer to as his "remarkable inner fortitude," just as deeply disappointed in himself.

Poppy was killed by a ninety-six-pound marble gargoyle that fell four stories in a terrible storm from the facade of an apartment building at Hudson Boulevard and Tonnele Avenue. Poppy wouldn't have been killed—and would probably still be alive and making trouble today, at one hundred and eleven—if he hadn't had a passion for being outdoors when everyone else was inside. He was addicted to it, and his addiction got worse every year. The more horrifying the storm, the better he liked to be in it. "Just me and the elements," he used to say, "that's the way I like it."

Once, on a rainy November weekend when my parents had gone to Grossinger's with Ray Pfeffer, the other Jewish Jersey City cop and his wife, and my sister was sleeping over at Mindy Zavodnick's, Poppy took me out into the horror. "It's time," he said, as he dressed me in my winter coat and leggings, "that you learn what I know."

We walked through freezing rain from my building to Sip Avenue and then up toward Journal Square. It was 6:05 in the morning, the sun wasn't yet up, thin short blades of water were cutting into my face like berserk flying metal, and there wasn't another soul to be seen on the street except for the occasional rain-beveled silhouette of a stranger passing by in a car.

"Is this not marvelous?" Poppy asked me in his thick accent. "Is this not the most fabulous thing you ever done?" I told him that it was, and I believed that it was. "This is beauty," he said. "Beauty is right here, right now."

What was beautiful to him, essentially, was the smell of the air and the sound of the world. Rain slicing down from the heavens has its own language, and Poppy Weiss believed he understood it when it spoke. And he considered the smell to be God's, His aura, the scent you'd ingest if, for some reason, you had the opportunity to hug Him on a happy occasion. "You have no way of knowing this," he said, "but rain is God's aftershave."

After twenty minutes, we were drenched and shaking. Poppy hustled me into Greenspan's delicatessen, which had just opened, and lectured me over hot tea and apple cake on the merits of trying to see that which isn't always visible to the naked eye.

"Everything in life has a life," he said, "not just things with a soul and a brain."

I nodded, terribly relieved that hot tea and warm apple cake were beginning to reverse what felt to my frozen heart like imminent death, and I tried to look as taken by what he was saying as he was.

A few minutes later, he said, "The reflection of natural morning light on a wet street is a living thing that will never let you down," and a few minutes after that, as his wet cold hand squeezed my arm through my soaked overcoat, he said, "When I'm home, I gotta be with people. But out in the world, I needa be alone."

I knew then, even though I was only five, that the family line on Poppy was probably true: Nanny's death had driven him crazy. But the more he said insane, unrelated things, the more I loved hearing them, and the more I loved him.

"Come on," he said, slapping two dollars onto the table. "I want you to see the girl from the rooftops."

We walked back into the awfulness. It was now colder, and the shrapnel rain slashed into every exposed part of my body, even slipping through my open mouth to soak the apple cake I was still chewing. I was trying to figure out who the girl was when he asked me something particularly nuts.

"How old are you now?"

"Five."

"Do you remember anything from before your birth?"

"Huh?"

"From the womb. You know, Marion's belly. Come on, think back. Five years is nothing."

"I don't . . ."

"Try . . ."

"I did, but I don't."

"Shame," he said. "I certainly would like to hear that environment described."

The girl, as he called her, turned out to be New York City, the majesty of which made him sob softly to himself as we stood closer to the eye of the storm on the rooftop of another building, further east, just barely making out the still-lit skyscrapers at attention in the rain across the Hudson.

"Every city in the world has a gender," he said. "A personality, an identity, a definition. You know what I'm saying?"

I told him I didn't.

"New York is a girl," he said. "A big red-lipped girl, in her late twenties, who still looks damned good in clothes."

At this, he clapped his hands together and laughed like hell, his face pointed upward toward the starting point of the storm, and then he stopped laughing and looked across the river toward the city, his face suddenly pained, his good eye spilling more tears.

"She makes me cry, New York," he said. "I love her so goddamned much, she makes me goddamned cry."

When my parents returned from Grossinger's the next night, my fever was a hundred and three and climbing, and when Poppy told them where he and I had been the previous day, my mother hit the roof.

She screamed at him far beyond the point where her anger at his having exposed me to the elements should have been vented. Looking back, I realize that she was screaming about her life, about his dominance of it. She screamed for the better part of an hour, and when she was done, Poppy walked to his room and packed his bag. I got out of my sickbed and stood at his archway and watched him pack, and when he sensed my presence he looked up, smiled, and said, "You sorry we done it?"

"No," I said.

"Me neither," he said. "Now you know what I know."

Then he stuffed the last of his short-sleeved dress shirts into the bag, shut the lid, threw on his coat, and walked out into the now dissipating storm as my mother begged his forgiveness and my sister, who'd come back from Mindy Zavodnick's while my mother was still screaming, stood in her coat and cried. My father, who'd retreated to the kitchen much earlier, sat smoking Lucky Strikes by himself on the fire escape in the dark, his legs hanging out over the edge, his feet jiggling nervously as he watched Poppy, bag in hand on the sidewalk below, disappear into the darkness.

My mother was distraught. Although relieved that Poppy was gone, her guilt over having made him leave was monumental. She asked my father to find out where he was living, to go there, and to bring Poppy back to live with us.

It took my father three days to learn that Poppy had a room at the Concourse Hotel on Journal Square, a rat hole of a place where the Irish detectives on the force regularly made vice arrests. He promised my mother he would go there the next morning and bring Poppy home. But that night there was a terrible storm, through which Poppy was walking, just him and the elements, when the gargoyle on the Mayflower Arms apartments was blown loose and came down on his head. He died, said one of my father's colleagues on the force, instantly. "He never knew what hit him, Harry," said the cop, but I knew differently.

Poppy Weiss, you can be sure, knew what hit him. I believed with all my heart that Poppy, grief stricken and daughterless and lonely, had directed the gargoyle to fly down onto his head from its facade and put him out of his misery as a profound favor from one living thing to another.

After his death, Poppy became my obsession. His face was a picture hanging permanently on the wall inside my head, and I was his museum, exhibiting his view of the world everywhere I went. When Miss Berkle, my kindergarten teacher at P.S. 23, asked me why I was sitting off in a corner of the playground at recess when all my friends were playing dodgeball, I told her that when I'm home, I gotta be with people, but out in the world, I needa be alone. She called my mother that night and expressed her concern for my mental health.

Within thirty-six hours, I was nodding at Dr. Herman Topnik, a North Bergen child psychologist recommended to my mother by the

B'nai B'rith Women, as he asked me things like "Do you understand that your grandpa was your grandpa and that you are you?" He also made me draw individual pictures of my mother, my father, my sister, my grandfather, and myself and then one of all of us in a group. Afterward, while he talked to my mother in his office, I sat in his outer "playroom" by myself and built the New York City skyline with his erector set. The next day, my mother mailed her request for "Howdy Doody" tickets to NBC at Rockefeller Center.

We waited five months for the tickets, time during which my father became, seemingly from out of the blue, my buddy. He and I, who had never done anything together (he'd always spent his weekends asleep on the couch in his undershirt and boxers, a copy of *Detective* magazine covering his eyes), were suddenly playing softball at Lincoln Park, and going to the Stanley and the Loews and the State theaters for matinees, and taking the tube train into Manhattan, and visiting the library, while over on the female side of the family, my mother and sister were finally telling each other about what it was like to be a girl and what it was like to be a woman. As our family renewed its vows, Poppy's memory began to recede, but for me it never faded.

On "The Howdy Doody Show," Buffalo Bill Smith stuck a microphone in my face as I sat next to my sister in the Peanut Gallery and asked me, on national television, what I would do to make Mister Bluster less "ornery."

I said I would stand with him on a Jersey City rooftop in a big storm, very early in the morning, and look out across the river toward New York, which was a big red-lipped girl in her late twenties who still looks damned good in clothes.

The muscles in Buffalo Bob Smith's heavily pancaked face twitched involuntarily, and his eyes fluttered up into his head as though he'd been hit by a fist, but he recovered and said, "My, my, my! Would you look at the imagination on this little fella!"

When my son turned twenty last fall, I took him back across the country with me to Jersey City, and he and I walked in the rain. It wasn't a terrible storm, but it was real New Jersey rain, and he didn't want to be out walking in it in his California tank top and Bermudas.

"Why are you doing this to me?" he asked.

"Because," I said, "it's time you learned what I know."

Sacred Time

Cycles of the Jewish Year

In the 1950s, Abraham Joshua Heschel wrote that sustaining our "technical civilization" requires sacrificing "an essential ingredient of existence, namely time."[1] In many ways, time is our most precious natural resource over which, to some extent, we have control. Yet many of us unwittingly exploit it for the sake of personal and professional advancement or to help us gain power and things. When we *use* time to acquire things, we start to measure our lives by what we have rather than who we are. This sort of gauge for the kind of people we are is exactly where our spiritual and environmental problems begin. The more things we want, the more we need to work to make the money to buy the things, the more we need to exploit the earth to provide the resources to make the things, the less time we have to enjoy our lives.

In Judaism, there is another side to time. In his book *Time's Arrow, Time's Cycle*, Steven Jay Gould describes two dimensions of time that coexist in the Bible: linear time and cyclical time.[2] We in the West are more familiar with the linear dimension. This is the forward-moving aspect of time or history: God created the earth, brought on the Flood, took the Israelites out of Egypt, revealed himself to the people at Mount Sinai. Most of us live within this "time frame." Cyclical time, on the other hand, is the undercurrent of the Bible: the never-changing constant round of the seasons and the months, which Judaism marks by its cycle of holidays. This dimension of time does not move forward; it is timeless and eternal.

Cyclical time can be just the right antidote for a society obsessed with linear time. In Judaism, Shabbat and the various holidays scattered throughout the year afford opportunities to step out of the rat race into a different time dimension. They give us time to reconnect with family, friends, community, the seasons, and the rhythm of life; time to taste the timeless, the eternal; time to remember who we are and what really matters. Keeping time by the Jewish calendar may provide just the orientation we need to live environmentally aware and balanced lives.

D.H. Lawrence, writing in the first half of this century, lamented the fact that our civilization has grown so disconnected from nature:

> Oh, what a catastrophe, what a maiming of love when it was made a personal, merely personal feeling, taken away from the rising and setting of the sun, and cut off from the magic connection of the solstice and the equinox! This is what is the matter with us, we are bleeding at the roots, because we are cut off from the earth and the sun and stars, and love is a grinning mockery, because poor blossom, we plucked it from its stem on the tree of life, and expected it to keep on blooming in our civilized vase on the table.[3]

During early Jewish history, time, nature, and community were bound together inextricably through the calendar. In this piece, Debra J. Robbins traces the historical development of the Jewish calendar and offers it as a way for Jews to find a connection to nature today.

10

The Sun, the Moon, and the Seasons: Ecological Implications of the Hebrew Calendar

DEBRA J. ROBBINS

God said, "Let there be lights in the expanse of the sky to separate day from night; they shall serve as signs for the set times—the days and the years. . . . " —Gen. 1:14

The sun and the moon mark the basic units of time in the Hebrew calendar. They determine our days, months, and years. The sun prescribes our agricultural seasons and yearly cycle, while the moon dictates the rhythm of the months. Together, they provide a framework for our holidays.

Jewish tradition has long recognized that we need the basic cycles of nature in our lives. By heralding the first barley crops on Passover, celebrating the earth's bounty on Shavuot, and praying for rain at Sukkot, our calendar aligns us with nature's way. If we embrace it, the Jewish calendar can define the pattern of our lives. In cultivating a relationship with nature, we cultivate a relationship with the One who provides for us.

Today, an inquiry into the Hebrew calendar can teach us about the ecological sensitivities of our ancestors and guide us on a path that integrates their "natural" wisdom with our modern lives.

The Origins of the Jewish Calendar

The Israelites lived in Egypt until the time of the Exodus and did not have their own system for measuring time. Like the rest of Egyptian society, they reckoned seasons and months by the agricultural seasons and by solar and civil calculations.

In its earliest stages, the ancient Egyptian calendar was based on three seasons. The year began in midsummer with *Akhet* or "Inundation," when the Nile rose and overflowed the fields. During *Peroyet* or "Coming Forth," the fall, the waters receded and arable land again emerged. This was the time of seeding, tilling, growing, and harvesting. After the harvest, the year concluded with *Shomu* or "Deficiency," when the Nile was at its low point.

Originally the calendar was solely based on events of the agricultural cycle, but over time, the Egyptians integrated astronomical factors into the agricultural cycles.

From the moment the Israelites left Egypt, they lived by their *own* calendar, which evolved out of their experience in Egypt *and* their life as a free people in the desert. With the emergence of this calendar came the expression of a new Israelite identity.[1] The Bible gives us repeated evidence of the significance of the calendar in the life of the Israelites: "This month shall mark for you the beginning of the months" (Exod. 12:2). "You go free on this day, in the month of *Aviv*" (Exod. 13:4). "You shall observe the Feast of Unleavened bread . . . at the set time in the month of *Aviv*, for in it you went forth from Egypt . . . "(Exod. 23:15).

Aviv in modern Hebrew means "springtime." In the Bible, *Aviv* refers specifically to the period when the grain is beginning to ripen after the stalks have hardened.[2] These biblical passages testify to a new orientation for keeping track of time in which the celebration of liberation must coincide with the spring harvest. The need to observe Passover at the time of the ripening grain will eventually be the dominant factor in determining the Israelite calendar.

The general season of the Hebrew festivals was set by the cycle of the sun, while the specific dates were determined by the cycle of the moon. The significance of the moon in determining the calendar is apparent in the Hebrew language itself. In Hebrew, the word for "moon" is *yerach*, which also means "month." *Yerach* is related to the verb that means "to travel" and refers to the journey the moon makes across the night sky. The new month begins when the moon is first seen as a sliver in the evening sky and continues until the moon is seen at the same stage again, about twenty-nine days later.

Similarly, the Hebrew word *chodesh* refers to both moon and month. In different eras, it has referred to the new moon, to the festival of the new-moon day, and to the whole month.[3] *Yom Hachodesh*, "Day of the New Moon," and *Rosh Chodesh*, the first day of the month, indicated for the Israelites the significance of the moon and the first day of the month.

The Exodus passages cited earlier command the Israelites to celebrate liberation in *Aviv*. For Passover to be celebrated in the proper month of the spring season at the time of the ripening grain, both cycles—lunar and solar—must be used. If they are not, if only the lunar cycle is used, Passover would wander backward each year, like Ramadan, the major Islamic festival (the Muslim calendar is lunar based). The necessity of celebrating Passover in a particular season—defined by the cycle of the sun—on a particular date—defined by the cycle of the moon—separated Israel from her neighbors and required that the Israelites develop a lunisolar calendar. Through the Israelite calendar, faith, nature, and history were inextricably linked.

The Canaanite Influence

After the Exodus from Egypt and forty years of wandering in the wilderness, the Israelites settled in Canaan, and their calendar went through several stages (1275–1000 B.C.E.). Unlike the Israelites, who used both the moon and the sun to determine their calendar, the Canaanites measured time by the sun alone. The names of several Canaanite months, known to us from the Bible, reveal the significance of the solar cycle and its corresponding agricultural events: *Ethanim* (1 Kings 8:2), "the month of steady flowing," when only perennial streams contain water; *Bul* (1 Kings 6:38), the rain month; *Aviv*, the time the grain ripens; and *Ziv* (1Kings 6:1, 37), the month of splendor, of blooming flowers.

Canaan's diverse climatic zones—hills, valleys, mountains, and desert—affected the Israelite farming and holiday cycle. Grains growing where it was colder—in the north and in the mountains—ripened later than those growing where it was warmer—in the south and the valleys. Accordingly, the Israelites found themselves celebrating their holidays at different times, depending on the climate.

Throughout this period, the Israelites struggled to maintain the connection between time and agriculture. Evidence of an integrated system is found in the Gezer Calendar, discovered by the archaeologist R.A.S. McAlister in 1908 at Gezer, northwest of Jerusalem.[4] Dating from around the tenth century B.C.E., the calendar is one of the oldest written documents of agricultural life during the biblical period. The archaeologist W.F. Albright translates the text as follows:

> His two months are [olive] harvest,
> His two months are planting [grain],
> His two months are late planting;
> His month is hoeing up of flax,
> His month is harvest of barley,
> His month is harvest and feasting;
> His two months are vine-tending
> His month is summer fruit.[5]

Albright asserts that the Gezer Calendar is a mnemonic device. By remembering the events pertaining to three double months, three single, then a double, and then a single, the agricultural seasons could easily be remembered. He explains that, to a child, this mnemonic would be "just as useful as our familiar 'thirty days hath September'. . . ."[6]

This may well have been a childhood rhyme originally and was probably well known in Israelite society. If Albright correctly analyzes the Gezer Calendar, the Israelites followed a calendar that was defined by the agricultural events of everyday life. They based their units of time, seasons, and months not on abstract numbers and calculations, but on the reality of the environment in which they lived.

The Calendar of the Monarchies

By approximately 1000 B.C.E., the Israelites had established a monarchy. During Solomon's reign, power was centralized in Jerusalem. The calendar became a political tool of the monarchs and the natural extension of consolidation during this period. For the purpose of unification, it was critical for all people to celebrate festivals and pay taxes at the same time. But because of the climatic differences in the northern and southern regions, the festivals of the Israelites did not necessarily correspond to the farming cycle. The kingdom of Ephraim in the north was forced to celebrate the harvest holidays of Passover, Shavuot, and Sukkot before their harvests were ready.

When the Israelite kingdom was divided, Jeroboam took control in the north. He moved the date of Sukkot from the seventh to the eighth month to ensure that the northern Ephraim would again celebrate its agricultural festivals at the time of its harvest (1 Kings 12:32–33). The people's easy acceptance of this change indicated their connection with the natural cycles—and that they wanted a calendar that made sense to them.

Until the fall of the northern kingdom, the north and the south had independent calendars. When Hezekiah came to power after the fall of the northern kingdom in 722 B.C.E., he tried to unite the remnant of Ephraim with Judah and to synchronize the two calendars, but the northern Ephraimites refused to take on the southern calendar of Judah (2 Chron. 30). To assuage the Ephraimites, Hezekiah was forced to establish the festivals for all of Israel according to the Ephraimite calendar.

When Josiah came to power a century later, the power shifted from north to south and with it, so did the calendar; Josiah finally imposed the southern Judean calendar on the remnant of the Ephraimite people (2 Kings 23:22–23; 2 Chron. 35:17–19).

In the midst of political changes and calendar manipulation by the monarchy, one idea clearly emerges. To control the calendar was to dictate the political, religious, social, and economic lives of the people. It was imperative for the Israelites, an agriculturally based people, to have a calendar that reflected the events of nature taking place in their fields. Despite all of the political changes made by the various monarchs, agricultural and natural cycles continued to play a dominant role in determining the Hebrew calendar.

Babylonian Influence

During the period of exile, the Jews in Babylonia drew upon the developing ideas of their host country to help them concretize their own lunisolar calendar and astronomical methods. To make sure that the lunar months would fall during the appropriate season, the Babylonian astronomers inserted a leap month, *Adar*, into the calendar. In a nineteen-year cycle, they added the month of *Adar* seven times.[7]

When the Jews returned to *Eretz Yisrael* after the exile, they brought with them a new sophistication in the calendar arts. In addition to the nineteen-year cycle and the insertion of *Adar*, they had new month names. As the Israelites became unified around their own religious beliefs and observances, they sought to divorce themselves from the Canaanite time-keeping system, which was closely linked to pagan religious practices. They replaced the Canaanite month names with ordinal numbers to create a system of reckoning that was more consistent with the new monotheistic views of the Israelites. These numeric names were subsequently replaced by Babylonian-influenced names.

By the end of the monarchy period, the Jews had become a people with their own calendar, festivals, and culture and hence their own distinctive Jewish identity. These elements still set the pattern for the religious life of Jews today.

Witnessing the Moon:
The Democratization of the Calendar

The early rabbis refined ways of determining the new moon and corre-
lating it with the holidays. Authority for determining the calendar rested with the Sanhedrin, the rabbinic court, which was charged with
inserting months into the calendar as necessary and with sanctifying
the new-moon day. In this way, the Sanhedrin maintained unity in the
vast community.

Although the Sanhedrin made the final decisions concerning the
calendar, the entire Jewish community participated in the process of
calendar determination. It was important for the leaders to create a balance of power in order to keep the people involved in a process that so
significantly affected their lives. While the rabbis were capable of calculating the calendar, Jews from all over *Eretz Yisrael* still regularly observed
the heavens, awaiting the appearance of the new crescent moon. Many of
those who saw it came to testify before the Sanhedrin. If the evidence
was good, a new month was proclaimed.

It was both an honor and a mitzvah to witness the new moon, and
the court enthusiastically encouraged people to participate:

> There was a large courtyard in Jerusalem. . . and there all the
> witnesses used to assemble, and there the court examined
> them. And they prepared big meals for them, so that they
> should acquire the habit of coming.[8]

The court was so intent on urging people to fulfill this mitzvah
that all witnesses could testify before the court. The rabbis ruled that
Shabbat could even be violated to fulfill this mitzvah:

> If one sees the new moon and is not able to walk, they bring
> him on an ass or even on a litter. . . . If the journey be a long
> one, they may carry food in their hands, because for a journey
> lasting a night and a day they may profane the Sabbath and go
> forth to give evidence about the new moon. . . .[9]

To be an acceptable witness, one had to be upright, honest in daily
and ritual life, and familiar with nature and have full knowledge of the
moon's twenty-nine-and-a-half–day cycle.[10]

When it was determined that the new moon had been sighted at its proper time and expected place, the court declared the beginning of the new month: "The chief of the court says, 'It is hallowed!' and all the people answer after him, 'It is hallowed! It is hallowed!'"[11] Because the new month was not official until the whole community joined in the ceremonial announcement, the public pronouncement was essential.

To signal the new month to the neighboring communities, the people would set bonfires atop the tallest hill:

> They used to bring long poles of cedar-wood, and rushes and pine-wood, and tow-flax; and a man tied these together with twine. He went up to the top of the hill and set them on fire, and waved them to and fro and moved them up and down until he saw his fellow doing likewise on the top of the next hill. . . .[12]

Over time, problems arose with direct community participation in calendar assessment. The fire signals used to proclaim the new month were often sabotaged by enemies. When messengers replaced the fire signals, there were still problems with communicating the new month in a timely fashion.

Fortunately, while direct observation of the moon laid the foundation for the development of the calendar in early Jewish history, by the first and second centuries, rabbis also began to hone their astronomical and mathematical abilities. Mathematical calculations enabled the rabbis to determine the calendar without directly observing the moon's phases and without being in Jerusalem. Over time, mathematical calculations took precedence.

Control of the calendar was as powerful a tool in rabbinic times as it had been under the monarchy. A Babylonian rabbi, Mar Samuel, for instance was nicknamed *Yarhina'ah* (from the word for "moon" or "month") to refer to his ability as a lunar expert.[13] But Mar Samuel's confidence about calendar calculation brought him into conflict with the Sanhedrin in Jerusalem. The friction between Palestine and Babylonia resulted in concrete consequences. Because the calendar was determined in Palestine and word of the new month and festival celebrations had to be sent by messenger to the Jews in Babylonia, the Babylonian Jews very often had to observe two days of festivals to ensure that they celebrated on the correct day. Mar Samuel argued that the Babylonian Jewish community could accurately determine the calendar on its own, without relying on Palestinian authority.[14]

Between the years of 200–500 C.E., *Eretz Yisrael* underwent radical upheaval. Roman authority was unstable. The power of Christianity increased. Jewish communities suffered from increases in taxation and persecution, and many Jews moved to other countries.

In the face of this social and political upheaval, Hillel II aspired to preserve the integrity of Jewish institutions. Fearing that central Jewish authority would become dispersed and the institution of the calendar would be lost, he made public the formula for calculating the calendar in *Sod ha-Ibbur*, "The Secret of Intercalation" and *Kevi'uta de-Yarha*, "The Fixing of the New Month."[15] By declassifying these methods, Hillel II essentially authorized the whole community to participate in determining the calendar. The rabbinic court no longer needed to sanctify the new month; the proper time was widely known and accessible to anyone who wished to master the calculations.

Control of the calendar and determination of the dates of the festivals was, and still is, vital to the unification of all Jewish communities. Jews are connected despite distance because we all celebrate "Pesach in *Aviv.*" In the biblical period, the calendar reflected the life of a people bound to their land and served as a nexus for the interaction between nature, humanity, and the Divine. In the early rabbinic period, calendar determination involved the collective witnessing of the moon, which helped the people maintain an intimate relationship with the natural world.

Today, although the calendar is calculated mathematically, we can still follow our ancestors' practices to bring the richness the Jewish calendar offers into our lives: we can familiarize ourselves with the cycles of the sun and moon and the wheat and the barley. In these ways, we can celebrate our sacred relationship with nature and with the Creator.

Since Judaism emphasizes *historical* redemption, it has often been credited with introducing linear time to civilization. Jewish historians and theologians have further identified Judaism with linear time and dismissed Judaism's reliance on cyclical time to distinguish it from paganism, which emphasizes sacred time and the cycles of renewal. Yet by diminishing the value of cyclical time, Jews have lost a vital link to the sacred and to creation. In this piece, Rabbi Lawrence Troster attempts to counteract the tendency to view only the historical face of Judaism by drawing out the Creation theology inherent in the liturgical cycles of the day, week, month and year.

11

"In Your Goodness, You Renew Creation": The Creation Cycles of the Jewish Liturgy

LAWRENCE TROSTER

Jewish prayer reflects two perspectives; one is historical, the other is Creation centered. Although the two themes have been harmonized over many hundreds of years, it is still possible to separate them and examine the distinct views of the world each expresses. In the historical cycle, the central focus is the story of the people and their God; the story begins when God brings the people out of the land of Egypt. The Jewish liturgical year is structured around this fundamental experience. Passover celebrates the Exodus itself, Shavuot celebrates the giving of the Torah at Mount Sinai; and Sukkot celebrates the wandering in the desert. This is the historical cycle, the one with which most Jews are familiar. But another cycle, the Creation cycle, exists alongside the historical cycle and needs to be recognized.[1]

The Creation cycle transcends historical or secular time; it returns to mythic time and to the original Creation. Anthropologist Mircea Eliade has pointed out that the notion of "eternal return"—a return to the origin of life, to Creation, to unity with God—is central to most indigenous traditions. Religion, then, devises escapes from real time so we can return to mythic time. Across cultures, people engage in rituals to revisit or reenact the moment of the Creation of the world. This is an attempt to overcome the chaos and contamination that comes with historical time. In such traditions, historical progression does not arise, for it would be invalid, no more than a departure from the primal act of creation.

It has long been assumed that Israelite religion rejected the necessity of "eternal return" and instead introduced linear time with "an emphasis on unique historical events that were supposed to have taken place at particular points in time."[2] Crucial events like the Exodus occurred at a particular time and place in history. History, then, had meaning in its own right. It would have been absurd to talk about God's purposes in history if history were nullified by endless cycles of creation. For the Israelites, history was an authentic arena in which to encounter the Divine. It has been argued that the view of history that prevails today arose from the innovative religion of the ancient Israelites.[3]

While it is difficult to determine if this is so, it is undeniable that linear time played a significant role in Christianity also. Jesus was born, crucified, and resurrected at specific moments in history. The idea of an "eternal return" and repetition of these events was rejected by the developing church.

It is simplistic, however, to see only historical time portrayed in the Bible. In fact, the Bible traces a "grand cycle" from the time of Creation to the time of the Messiah in which both creation and historical cycles are incorporated.[4] This idea of recurrence is implicit in the Jewish liturgical cycles of the day, week, month, and year. In addition, Jewish mysticism has based an entire series of Creation cycles on the biblical idea of the Jubilee year.[5]

The Creation theology of ancient Judaism owes much to the priests, especially those associated with the Temple in Jerusalem. The Temple service amplified the Creation motif. The Temple was a conduit for divine energy, and the function of the various rituals was to maintain the sacred center of Creation, to control chaos, and to bring God's blessings into the world.

When the First Temple was destroyed in 586 B.C.E., the synagogue became its metaphoric substitute, and the various sacrificial services of the Temple were transformed over time into synagogue liturgy. This liturgy was further developed and codified in the centuries after the Second Temple was destroyed in 70 C.E. The historical relationship of God and the people of Israel, especially through the recitation of the Exodus story, was a prominent feature in the evolving liturgy. The Passover Seder, for example, is devoted almost entirely to recapturing the Exodus experience. Nonetheless, the Creation theology of the priestly tradition remained a major theme in the structure and content of Jewish prayer. In the transformation from Temple to synagogue and from sacrifice to liturgy, the balance of sacred time/space/person shifted more toward sacred time than ever before. Thus, Shabbat became a more prominent feature of every Jew's religious life, and new Shabbat home rituals, such as lighting candles as a sacred act, began to develop. Sacred space survived metaphorically not only in the synagogue, through its architecture and liturgy, but also through home rituals. Sacred personage survived in the veneration of the sages.[6]

Jewish Liturgy: Creation and History Merged

Jewish liturgy includes four creation cycles—the daily, weekly, monthly, and yearly—and each Jewish service builds on the theme of two central prayers, the *Sh'ma* and the *Amidah*. In each service, the strand of Creation, represented by references to Creation, eternity, and the Temple, is juxtaposed with the historical strand, represented by the Exodus, covenant, and Torah.

The morning service begins with two prayers that introduce the *Sh'ma*, the central prayer of Jewish tradition. One reflects Creation, the other reflects history. In the first prayer, the Creation theme is addressed: God is the One "Who forms light and creates darkness, makes peace and creates everything." This is followed by a series of prayers praising

God as the creator and the renewer of the world. In the second blessing, the historical element is introduced. Here, God is giver of Torah and partner in the covenant with the Jewish people.

Next comes the *Sh'ma* itself, consisting of three paragraphs from Deuteronomy (6:4–9, 11:13–21) and Numbers (15:37–41). In recalling the original covenant experience, the *Sh'ma* represents the historical cycle in the liturgy. The *Sh'ma* is not a prayer in the conventional sense, but rather an act of centering in which worshipers accept the yoke of God.

The other major prayer, the *Amidah*, is the silent prayer. The *Amidah* recalls the Temple as the community comes together to stand before the Throne of God. The image of the Temple returns us to mythic time, to the sacred center, and to Creation. The *Amidah* asks God to transform the world we know back into Paradise. In effect, we ask God to annul history in favor of the Eden that will be restored at the "end of days." Taken together, the *Sh'ma* and the *Amidah* synthesize the historical and Creation cycles and unify God the Creator with God the historical lawgiver.

The *Sh'ma* and *Amidah* represent a journey in which we first accept the covenant and then are admitted—with praise and thanksgiving—into the metaphorical Temple, the microcosm of Creation. We start with history and move to eternity. We experience a return to the original or renewed order of Creation. The liturgy directs the worshiper to a sense of oneness, purity, and connection.

The weekly cycle most clearly illuminates the Creation elements of the Jewish liturgy. The week is the most enigmatic of our markers of time. Unlike the day, the month, and the year, it is totally unrelated to any external events or natural phenomena. This demarcation of time may appear arbitrary, but it is not. The seven-day week is rooted in the Creation narrative of the Bible. Each day of the week from Sunday to Friday corresponds to a day of Creation depicted in Genesis 1, with Shabbat being the completion and culmination of Creation. The first chapter of Genesis was probably recited day by day while the Temple stood to mirror the Creation of the universe. In Hebrew, the weekdays are known by their number alone. Only Shabbat, the day designated for Creation and eternity, has a distinct name and identity. Since antiquity, the Jewish people have measured time in weeks in order to celebrate each Shabbat as holy, as a day of rest.

The monthly cycle is the least well-known of all the temporal cycles and in modern times has lost its significance. *Rosh Chodesh*, the celebration of the new moon, was a significant event in ancient Israel,[7] but today we are left with remnants of this festival such as the proclamation of the new month, the special blessing for the moon based on the Talmud (*Sanhedrin* 42a), a special grace after meals, and *Yom Kippur Katan*, the "minor Yom Kippur," a monthly fast day for the moon. There are also legends of the moon being restored to its true size and being made equal to the sun in the days of the Messiah. In all these sources, the renewal of the moon is tied to the notion of the renewal of Creation.

The yearly holiday cycle can be understood from both historical and Creation perspectives. The three pilgrimage festivals—Passover, Shavuot, and Sukkot—are historical, since they celebrate events in the early days of the Jewish people: the Exodus, the giving of the Torah on Mount Sinai, and the wandering in the desert. This national/historical cycle replaced an earlier Creation/agricultural cycle. Passover marks the spring planting season; Shavuot, the grain harvest; and Sukkot, the vegetable harvest. While Passover is probably the most historically connected festival, it originated as an agricultural/Creation pilgrimage festival of spring purification and renewal.

Sukkot is particularly rich in Creation character. In the time when the Temple stood, Sukkot was the autumn Creation festival. Yom Kippur, the "day of purging," cleansed the nation of sin and returned the world to a pristine state in preparation for the ritual of re-Creation at Sukkot.[8] Today, the sukkah, or booth, is reminiscent of the symbol of Creation: the Temple. And, of course, the sukkah, decorated with the fruits of the harvest, and the waving of the *lulav* and *etrog* reflect the agricultural roots of the Jews.

The third of the pilgrimage festivals, Shavuot, was originally called "the festival of *Katsir*" or "reaping of the barley harvest." It celebrated the first harvest of the year, which occurred in late spring.

While little of the Creation character of these festivals survives in the holiday liturgy, there is ample "theological room" for reclaiming this aspect of the tradition.[9] The liturgical year provides significant spiritual resources for a Jewish Creation theology. With its Creationist character reemphasized, the liturgy yields opportunities for a heightened appreciation of and relationship with the natural world.

Many environmentalists claim that the consumer cult of America is the greatest obstacle to creating a healthy world. To counter this consumer habit, some people advocate taking one day off per week—one day of complete rest. On that day, we wouldn't drive or use electricity; we wouldn't buy anything or do anything that intervened with nature. Rather, we would just "be." We would appreciate all the gifts of life: nature, family, friends, and community that we have been given.

The one-day-a-week would serve as a weekly reminder that what really matters cannot be bought and that all of our actions have consequences in the natural world. The one-day-a-week promises to orient us toward an attitude of stewardship and greater sensitivity towards life on the other six days. In Judaism, such a day already exists; it has been there since before the world was created. That day is Shabbat. In this essay, Rabbi Dan Fink proposes that Shabbat provides an antidote to our contemporary lifestyles, which are largely devoid of environmental awareness and practice.

12

Shabbat and the Sabbatical Year

DAN FINK

The Sabbath is a day of harmony and peace, peace between man and man, peace within man, and peace with all things. On the seventh day man has no right to tamper with God's world, to change the state of physical things. It is a day of rest for man and animal alike. —ABRAHAM JOSHUA HESCHEL, *The Sabbath*

Most measures of time reflect nature's cycles. Each year, the earth makes another revolution around the sun; each year brings a full cycle of seasons. The month is roughly based on the twenty-nine-and-a-half–day cycle of the moon as it goes from new to full and back to new again—a connection that is even more apparent in the lunar-based Jewish calendar. Finally, a day represents the interval it takes for earth to complete one rotation on its own axis, turning us from sunlight to darkness to light renewed.

There is, however, one measure delineated by our calendars that seems completely arbitrary: the week. It is totally unrelated to any external events or natural phenomena. Why do we group together periods of seven days? Wouldn't a five-day or a ten-day week make as much sense as the current arrangement?

In fact, the week is not arbitrary at all. The contemporary seven-day week is rooted in the Creation narrative of the Hebrew Scriptures. Since antiquity, the Jewish people have measured time in weeks so they can celebrate each Shabbat as holy, as a day of rest. God gave us Shabbat, and our seven-day week came into being on its account.

Ironically, it is precisely this time period, which is unrelated to events in nature, that may constitute one of our best hopes for preserving the natural world. The Jewish understanding of Shabbat places strict limits on our dominion over nature. While the year, the month, and the day celebrate one particular aspect each of the Creation, Shabbat celebrates its entirety. It is, as the words of the song *Lechah Dodi* fittingly declare, "the last in Creation but first in intention."

As we turn to the environmental implications of Shabbat, we should note that its significance is not limited to the Jewish people. Although Shabbat is characterized by a host of many uniquely Jewish observances, it still retains a level of universal importance. The rabbis remind us that Shabbat is given to Israel and to all the other nations of the world. Unlike other Jewish holidays, Shabbat precedes the existence of the Jewish people. It is part of the very fabric of Creation. In our broken world, diverse faiths and peoples observe it differently. But we continue to work and pray for the speedy arrival of that day when we might speak of a world repaired and whole, sharing one Shabbat together.

Eternity Utters a Day

Shabbat is mentioned frequently in the Torah, beginning with the tale of its origins in the second chapter of Genesis: "And God blessed the seventh day and declared it holy, because on it God ceased from all the work of Creation that God had done"(Gen. 2:3). This passage is narrative. It is not law. It does not explicitly command humanity to do any particular action. Yet, it establishes the theological basis for abstaining from work on Shabbat. Our moral duty as human beings created in the divine image is to act as "godly" as possible. If our ethics are guided by this principle of *imitatio dei*, then the Creation story offers us a case of God teaching by example: God rested on the seventh day of Creation and sanctified it, so we, too, should hallow the Sabbath day by not working on it.

Later passages in the Torah make this demand more explicit. In the version of the Ten Commandments recounted in Exod. 20: 8–11, Shabbat observance is extended to the entire community, including servants, resident aliens, and even the animals:

> Remember the sabbath day and keep it holy. Six days you shall labor and do all your work, but the seventh day is a sabbath of the Eternal your God: you shall not do any work—you, your son or daughter, your male or female servant, or your cattle, or the stranger who is within your settlements. For in six days the Lord made heaven and earth and sea, and all that is in them, and God rested on the seventh day; therefore the Eternal blessed the sabbath day and hallowed it.

This, the fourth commandment, recognizes that not only human beings need a weekly day of rest. Shabbat provides all nature with a much-needed respite and an opportunity to recover from the heavy strain imposed by humanity's labors.

People were undoubtedly tempted to break this law from its onset. It is costly to halt production for a full day each week. Perhaps this is why in Exod. 34:21, God insists that farmers abstain from working on Shabbat even at prime plowing and harvest times. The Creation is worth more than any monetary considerations. Only one thing can override Shabbat observance: the obligation to save a life.

A Day of Rest and Joy

Though the Torah commands us to refrain from working on Shabbat, neither the fourth commandment nor any of the Torah's subsequent references to Shabbat observance offer much insight into what, exactly, constitutes "work."

This task fell to the rabbis of the Mishnah and the Talmud, who transformed the somewhat vague biblical ordinances pertaining to Shabbat into a vast and detailed body of legislation. Significantly for those concerned with Shabbat as a day of environmental peace and responsibility, they based their concept of "work" on the tasks required to build the Tabernacle that the Israelites carried through the desert.

Rabbi Hannina b. Hannina explains this connection between the Tabernacle and Shabbat as follows:

> They [the categories of "work" prohibited on Shabbat] correspond to the forms of labor in the Tabernacle. They [the builders of the Tabernacle] sowed, hence you must not sow (on Shabbat); they reaped, hence you must not reap; they lifted up boards from the ground to the wagon, hence you must not carry from a public to a private domain.[1]

The building plan for the Tabernacle and the details of its subsequent construction occupy much of the latter portion of the Book of Exodus. In the midst of this lengthy discussion, there are two repetitions of the commandment to observe the Sabbath by abstaining from work (Exod. 31:13–17 and 35:1–3). For the rabbis, everything in the biblical text has a purpose; nothing in Scripture is arbitrary. Therefore, they determined that this repetition of the commandment regarding Shabbat observance, within the context of the building of the Tabernacle, teaches us that "work" officially constitutes any of thirty-nine major tasks involved in creating that structure.

Why is this definition of work significant to an environmental understanding of Shabbat? There are numerous parallels between the biblical accounts of the building of the Tabernacle and the creation of the world. The same key words and phrases appear in the two narratives. Just as God created heaven and earth, Moses and the people built the Tabernacle. In other words, the construction of the tabernacle is a paradigm of human creation, just as the Genesis story is a paradigm of divine creation.

If this is the case, then the commandment to abstain from "work" on Shabbat really prohibits all forms of productive or creative work—namely, any type of activity that changes the natural order of things. During the week, we are free to use natural resources responsibly for the betterment of human society. However, on Shabbat we refrain from any work that uses nature for human ends. The following passage from Mordecai Kaplan, the founder of Reconstructionism, illustrates the power of Shabbat to counterbalance humanity's tendency to abuse our power over the rest of the Creation.

> As a result of the mechanization and over-industrialization of present day life, the human being has come to stand in greater need of the Sabbath than before. . . . The function of the Sabbath is to prohibit man from engaging in work which in any way alters the environment, so that he should not delude himself into the belief that he is complete master of his destiny.

Shabbat and the Environment Today

Mordecai Kaplan and Abraham Joshua Heschel, writing in the mid-1900s, sound prophetic today, for the environmental crisis has worsened as the new century begins. Both men surely would have recognized that the current state of the earth—acid rain, global warming, holes in the ozone, filthy air and water, the destruction of the rain forests and overflowing landfills—makes the need for Shabbat even more urgent than it was when their books were first published. Shabbat, a day that sets realistic limits on our consumption, has never been more vital than it is now. We need its commanding voice, which reminds us to walk lightly upon our planet. By revitalizing Shabbat, the Jewish people can help lead the way for all people toward increased ecological awareness. We can set an example by avoiding environmentally harmful types of work traditionally prohibited on Shabbat (such as driving and the unrestricted use of electricity) and creating new Shabbat observances (such as eating vegetarian meals, conserving water, and reducing waste).

Another way to celebrate Shabbat is to spend time in nature. After all, it is not enough to simply refrain from work; Shabbat also calls for study, prayer, and *oneg*—joy. God commands us to make the day a delight. By enjoying a walk in the woods, we fulfill this aspect of Shabbat and refresh ourselves for the coming week.

There is good Jewish precedent for this practice. The Talmud tells of Rabbi Hannina, who would wrap himself in a robe on the eve of each Shabbat and say, "Come, let us go out and greet the Sabbath Queen!"[2] Later, in the sixteenth century, the Kabbalists of Safed would follow his example, gathering outside just before sunset every Friday evening to welcome Shabbat. They taught: "Shabbat is received in the field. You must stand facing west, presumably in a high place, and there must be an open space behind you."[3]

The rabbis and the mystics recognized that we can learn to love Creation by spending time in nature. Shabbat is the perfect time for this.

A Shabbat for the Land

Shabbat is not just for people. Nature gets a rest each week as well. Comparable with the cycle of seven days, there is a cycle of seven years. And on the seventh year, the Torah provides a special Shabbat for the land. The basic requirements of this Sabbatical year are found in Lev. 25:2–7:

> When you enter the land that I assign to you, the land shall observe a sabbath of the Lord. Six years you may sow your fields and six years you may prune your vineyard and gather in the yield. But in the seventh year the land shall have a sabbath of complete rest, a sabbath of the Lord: you shall not sow your field or prune your vineyard. You shall not reap the aftergrowth of your harvest or gather the grapes of your untrimmed vines; it shall be a year of complete rest for the land. But you may eat whatever the land during its sabbath will produce—you, your male and female servants, the hired and bound laborers who live with you, and your cattle and the beasts in your land may eat all its yield.

The Sabbatical year pertains only to Jews living in the Land of Israel. Even there, few currently keep this mitzvah. Yet, despite the relatively low level of its observance, the Sabbatical year is, in principle, extremely important. It represents the first recorded agricultural policy to provide for the replenishment of the soil. In this sense, the Sabbatical year, which reminds the farmer that the earth is not inexhaustible, is an example of sound land management.

Furthermore, during each Sabbatical year, people were forced to live frugally, forsake luxury, and focus on basic sustenance. While some farmers must have found it difficult to comply with these rules, others undoubtedly found the experience liberating. Freed from the burden of long hours in the fields, the sabbatical gave them the opportunity to be with their families, study Torah, and enjoy the beauty of Creation. Perhaps they returned to their work the following year as wiser women and men, imbued with a truer sense of themselves and the limits of their land.

The basic idea still makes sense: take a sabbatical every seven years, and use the time to explore what life is like outside the "rat race." Genuine sabbaticals provide a precious opportunity for relaxation and renewal. They can also ease the burden on the earth. If every industry shut down for one year out of seven, imagine how pollution levels would decrease. While this scenario may appear extreme and utopian, the principle is sound. One more aspect of the Sabbatical year underscores its relevance for today's environmentally conscious Jew: its concern for the poor and underprivileged. Exod. 23:10–11 addresses the sabbatical year:

> Six years you shall sow your land and gather in its yield; but in the seventh you shall let it rest and lie fallow. Let the needy among your people eat of it, and what they leave let the wild beasts eat. You shall do the same with your vineyards and your olive groves.

This text adds the element of social justice to the Sabbatical year, drawing a connection between caring for the earth and concern for the needs of humanity. It is not sufficient to let the land rest while you consume all of its "wild" produce. You must offer the fruits of the Sabbatical year to the needy.

This is vital. Too often, environmental issues are presented as the domain of the white, upper-middle class. Critics argue that the poor cannot afford to worry about the state of the earth when they have all they can do just to put food in their mouths. The Sabbatical year's concern for both social justice and the environment demonstrates why this critique is ill founded. Most often, abuse of the earth and human poverty go hand in hand. Nuclear and chemical waste dumps are not located in Palm Beach and Beverly Hills. It is the destitute who are most vulnerable. The underclass disproportionately suffers the effects of Love Canal, Chernobyl, and Bhopal.

Jubilee Year: The Earth Is the Lord's

The Sabbatical year demands that we attend to the state of the entire earth, not just to parts of it occupied by the privileged. It is binding on rich and poor. It teaches us that the health of the planet is everybody's business and that ecology cannot be separated from other issues of social justice. These lessons are reinforced by the Jubilee year, a sabbatical of sabbaticals—seven times seven years, every fifty years.

The Jubilee's uncompromising credo is that "the earth is the Eternal's." The most complete description of this Jubilee is in Lev. 25: 8–12, 23:

> You shall count off seven weeks of years—seven times seven years—so that the period of seven weeks of years gives you a total of forty-nine years. Then you shall sound the horn loud; in the seventh month on the tenth day of the month—the Day of Atonement—you shall have the horn sounded throughout your land and you shall hallow the fiftieth year. You shall proclaim release throughout the land for all its inhabitants. It shall be a Jubilee for you: each of you shall return to his holding and each of you shall return to his family. That fiftieth year shall be a Jubilee for you: you shall not sow, neither shall you reap the aftergrowth or harvest the untrimmed vines, for it is a Jubilee. It shall be holy to you: you may eat only the growth direct from the field. . . . The land shall not be sold in perpetuity, for the land is Mine; you are but strangers resident with me.

The Talmud indicates that the Jubilee year had already ceased to function by the time of the Second Temple. This is not surprising, as its provisions for the regular redistribution of land are radical even by today's standards.

As with the Sabbatical year, however, the concept of the Jubilee retains great significance for a Jewish understanding of environmental issues. Its fundamental premise is that human beings can never really own land. The earth belongs to God; we are only tenants dwelling upon it. We tend to forget this and too often exploit what is not ours. Therefore, by commanding that the land be redistributed every fifty years, the Torah powerfully reminds us of our proper place in the scheme of things. The Jubilee year helps ensure that people will fulfill their role as stewards of the Creation rather than succumb to the tendency to exploit nature. Because it legislates against permanent, large-scale land acquisition, the Jubilee year might also serve as a manifesto for the small, self-sufficient family farm in its struggle against the growing power of agribusiness. It would discourage those who view the land purely in terms of profit and protect the men and women whose devotion to working the soil is rooted in love.

Hope for the Future

The Sabbath day, Sabbatical year, and Jubilee all offer enormous hope and promise: the vision of a world in which we live in harmony with each other and our environment. At times, that world seems impossibly distant from our own.

Our sages recognized this discrepancy. They knew that these sabbaths were more a messianic dream than current reality. Indeed, they declared Shabbat to be a foretaste of the world to come, a harbinger of a day that would be "all Shabbat." But they also believed that together with God, we could hasten the arrival of that time. They observed that "if all Israel were to keep one Shabbat, the Messiah would come."[4] Environmentally speaking, their words still ring true. It is in our power to renew the earth. If we work—and rest—together, we can bring about the day when the air will be clean, the rivers run clear, and the land break forth in blossom. Then we will experience the deepest and truest Shabbat imaginable.

For a while, when I was in my twenties, I ran white-water river trips for a living. What was so wonderful was not just the adventure of navigating the waters, the surrender to nature, or the pleasure of a community in the wild, but the sense that time was expanding. The minute we got our feet in the water and began loading up the rafts, we were on "river time," and there we remained until the journey's end five days later. Once on "river time," our experience of time completely changed. We had no watches, no obligations to meet, no calendars to schedule. Everything happened organically according to the natural rhythm of the day. It was on "river time" where I found the most profound relaxation.

When I "found" Judaism, I discovered that my tradition—to my surprise—integrated "river time" into its weekly calendar. The Jews I knew fondly referred to this special time, this sense of timelessness, as Shabbat time. In the following essay, Rabbi Marc Sirinsky explores the relation between the two.

13

The Land of Your Soul

MARC SIRINSKY

Getting into the woods or onto the river is not usually the easiest journey to begin. There is so much to do: finding the right maps, inspecting equipment, packing the car. While putting a trip together, there are moments when I wonder if it's really worth the effort. Why not just stay home and relax? These thoughts quickly disappear when I finally arrive

at my destination and the second part of the journey begins. The grand
and awesome splendor of place, be it river or wilderness path, elicits a
profound change "in the land of my soul."

This internal change finds its closest parallel in Shabbat. Six days
prior to Shabbat, I organize, create, coordinate, and move about in the
world. I work to earn a living for myself and my family. I try to do my
part to make the world a better place in which to live. Mindful of Shabbat rapidly approaching each week, I also become aware of all that needs
to be done so I can be ready for Shabbat's arrival. I must work to prepare to stop; it is not always easy. Yet without fail, when I greet Shabbat,
all the preparation melts away into memory, and I experience one of
the most delightful feelings in the world. A change takes place in the
"land of my soul."

What is this change? Words of Rabbi Shlomo Carlebach, z"l, hint at
an answer:

> Return again, return again,
> return to the land of your soul.
> Return to what you are, return to who you are,
> return to where you are, born and reborn again.

What is it about Shabbat and about being in wilderness that lets me
return to what I am, to who I am? Perhaps an answer to this question lies
in one of the most wondrous of Jewish concepts, the *neshamah yeterah*,
the additional soul. The first references to *neshamah yeterah* are in the
Babylonian Talmud. We read that "Simeon ben Lakish said, 'On Sabbath
eve the Holy One, blessed be the One, gives a person an extra soul (a
neshamah yeterah).' At the conclusion of the Sabbath, this extra soul
(*neshamah yeterah*) is taken away. . . ."[1]

What is the nature of this additional soul? Put simply, it lets us
forget our worries and problems so that we may focus on the joy and
happiness of Shabbat. Traditional Jewish mystical writings teach "with
the Sabbath-soul all sadness and anger are forgotten. Joy reigns on high
and below."[2] The *neshamah yeterah* emotionally renews us. Rashi, the
great eleventh-century biblical commentator, says, "When Shabbat
comes, rest comes."[3] He means not only physical rest, but also the rest
that restores wholeness.

The *neshamah yeterah* can enter us at other times. According to some, we have access to this additional, enlarged soul on holidays.[4] Other writings speak of a sage who, on behalf of the common folk of his community, carries and maintains his *neshamah yeterah* all week, never losing access to it.[5] Thus, access to the additional soul is not limited to Shabbat and holidays. A journey into some of the regions of our planet that are the least touched and altered by human hands may also be a way to gain access to this special divine part of our soul. The sense of wholeness that we find in wilderness, the place where God's handiwork is perhaps most palpable, is akin to the experience we have with each Shabbat.

Just as Shabbat can restore wholeness like no other *time*, wilderness can restore wholeness like no other *place*. This may be why we often feel sad when we part from either Shabbat or wilderness. It is not only the place or time that we wish to enjoy a moment longer; it is our access to our additional soul that we wish to prolong. The *Havdalah* service, the service that separates Shabbat from the rest of the week, helps us with this natural sadness. Moses Maimonides, the preeminent twelfth-century Jewish thinker, asks in his *Mishneh Torah*, "Why is a blessing recited over fragrant spices at the conclusion of Shabbat?" He responds, "It is to cheer the soul which is saddened at the departure of . . . [Shabbat]"[6] and the departure of our *neshamah yeterah*. The *Havdalah* ceremony, in which we enliven and use all our senses, helps carry the sweetness of Shabbat into the six days of the week. Perhaps we must learn to leave time at the end of a wilderness experience for a ritual that, like *Havdalah*, would help prolong and reinforce the teachings and awareness that we gain from being in close proximity to our enlarged soul while in nature.

In comparing Shabbat and wilderness, we should remember that Shabbat arrives regularly as a gift from God; it arrives wherever we are. Shabbat comes whether we are ready or not. Every seventh day since Creation, Shabbat has graced the world. Wilderness, too, is a gift from God. Like Shabbat, it needs to be protected. Yet for most of us, wilderness does not enter our lives regularly. We need to choose to make time for it.

It is clear from classic Jewish mystical teachings that the additional soul, the *neshamah yeterah*, can change a person spiritually, psychologically, emotionally, even physically. We should not underestimate the transformative powers of Shabbat or of wilderness. Each blessing of Shabbat, each journey into the wild, and each moment in nature can give us an opportunity to participate more fully in the mysteries of the divine world and, in so doing, to live more fully in the "land of our soul."

The Holidays

All I knew of the Jewish holidays growing up was Rosh Hashanah, Yom Kippur, Chanukah, and Passover. In my family, the holidays were simply occasions for new formal clothes and large meals. The dressier the clothes, the more somber the holiday. Yom Kippur was most somber and seemed the most important. Passover was the most fun, for the sheer joy of having all the cousins around. I remember feeling very proud about having these honored guests in our house. But there it ended. The holidays didn't have any real meaning to me. I had no reason to continue to celebrate them as an adult.

It wasn't until I was about twenty-five—when I had begun to seriously explore Judaism—that I started to discover that the Jewish holidays are not isolated moments that commemorate some seemingly foreign historical event, but are connected to each other and to the seasons of the year. Holidays are markers for the seasons, and they had been, long before they commemorated historical events.

I began to recognize the underlying "natural" dimensions of Passover: the *karpas*, the greens, symbolize the renewal of spring; the egg represents fertility and rebirth; the shankbone illustrates the season of lambing. Over time, I learned how all the holidays reflect the moods of the year. Fall, when nature reaches the peak of its maturity and is sloughing its outer self, is the right time for us to turn inward, reflect on the past, and clarify our life's direction for the next year. Sukkot, which follows closely after Yom Kippur, provides the necessary release and celebration after a period of intense self-examination. Purim, which marks the end of the our hibernation through the long winter darkness, is, like Mardi Gras, a time for letting loose and revelry.

I also understood that it is, in part, this holiday system that has kept Judaism alive for these thousands of years, since each holiday affords an opportunity to teach particular values, to organize a community, and to pass on a tradition.

Exploring the holidays became like a quest for buried treasure. My greatest find was Tu B'Sh'vat—all the more so because it is so obscure: the New Year of the Trees, the Jewish Arbor Day, the Jewish National Fund's tree planting holiday.

The essays and vignettes in this section take the reader on a "natural" journey throughout the Jewish year. As you will see, the holidays that are the most substantive from a naturalist's perspective are not necessarily the holidays with which most assimilated modern Jews are familiar. But they are the holidays that celebrated our ancestors' lives as they lived on the Land of Israel.

14

Rain and the Calendar

ELLEN COHN

I must have been eight years old. It was the year when my brother's friends were each having their bar mitzvah, and it was the year when I first noticed the *prayer*. Since I had studied the basic Jewish prayers in religious school and our family regularly attended the Reform temple, I enthusiastically joined the congregation in words that I knew even though much of the service at this Conservative synagogue was different from our own.

One prayer was prominent in our temple, the *Sh'ma*. I had learned, "*Sh'ma Yisrael* . . . The Lord is One." But I noticed that the Conservative prayer, unlike ours, continued with these words: "And if you diligently obey my statutes, which I teach you this day, to love the Lord your God . . . then I will cause the rain to fall in your land in its proper time, the early rain and the latter rain. You will harvest your grain and your wine and your oil. I will give grass in your fields to your animals and you will eat and be satisfied. . . . "

I turned to my parents, questioning: Why was this Judaism different from the one I knew? "This prayer is about *rain*," my mother answered. "The paragraph in the Conservative prayer book says that God gives rain and takes away rain." Then she muttered scornfully, "As modern Jews, we are not superstitious. Only science can explain the rain. Religion has nothing to do with it!"

Growing up in the 1950s—the era of progress and industrialized science—I watched the landscape change before me. New highways let us drive ever faster across the Atlantic seaboard. "Megalopolis!" my brother would exult, as though the "Future City" of roads and mass communication joining our home in the Washington suburbs with Boston and New York were a dream come true. On weekend drives, we discovered expanding suburbs, enlarged apartment complexes, higher sky-scrapers. "Everything's being built up!" my family exclaimed. "Every-thing's falling apart," I retorted, fearing we were irreversibly swallowing up nature.

My family's "progressive" Judaism reflected the pure worship of unre-strained science. We did not have to worry about old-fashioned "supersti-tious" laws or other "antiquated" customs because "we had science." In this vein, we studiously avoided the second paragraph of the Sh'ma.

Yet, I began to find that the entire Sh'ma prayer reflected my own deepest values. Its second paragraph was not an incantation to bring the rains and grain. Rather, it suggested a deeper mystery in which our actions bind us to God and nature. God created the world, taught us to care for it, and demanded that we comply. We would be rewarded with bounty or famine depending on how we lived, how we treated each other, and how we treated nature. This was a basis for living in harmo-ny with the earth. Dump pollutants into the waters, and the river would die. Strip hillsides of trees, and the soil would erode. Long before the environmental movement became popular, I was finding in Judaism a program for an environmentally sound lifestyle.

Judaism loved the world in a way that 1950s science and progress could not. I committed myself to the task of learning more about this Judaism and the spiritual texts that expressed and enriched it. That jour-ney took me deeper into the tradition; it took me to Israel.

Rain: A Gift from God

I arrived in late August and was greeted by hot, dry breezes and Jerusalem's brown, dusty hills. Yet soon after the High Holy Days, the days were marked by cold persistent rains; summer turned to winter almost overnight. I had learned quickly that Israel has just two seasons: wet and dry. My neighbors told me that if I could persevere until Passover, I would reap the fruits of the rainy season. By the late winter, the Jerusalem hills were green with flowers poking out of the rock crevices. On Tu B'Sh'vat, the Jewish Arbor Day, I noticed new buds on the trees and the branches leafing out, and I joined with the Israeli children to plant my own tree—a Tu B'Sh'vat custom. I had come to Israel to learn

Hebrew and Jewish texts, never thinking that the Jewish prayers—particularly the Sh'ma—that had captivated me as a youth might, indeed, be grounded in a physical reality. But in Israel, I could actually observe the centrality of rain and the seasons in the cycle of Jewish life.

The Jewish relationship with rain was from the first precarious, uncertain, and connected to our relationship with God. Before we entered the Land, God promised a "good land" flowing with milk and honey, an abundant land rich in the "seven species": wheat, barley, grapes, figs, pomegranates, olives, and dates (Deut. 8:8). And what made these seven species flourish was the right amount of water at precisely the right time, just as the Sh'ma taught: "I will cause the rain to fall in your land in its proper time: the early rain and the latter rain."

The Land of Israel would not be like the parched land of Egypt, dependent on the Nile's flooding for water for crops.[1] Instead, rain would bring the needed water as a gift from God. "For the land that you are about to enter into is not like the land of Egypt from which you have come. There the grain you sowed had to be watered by your own labors, like a vegetable garden; but the land you are about to cross into, a land of hills and valleys, soaks up its water from the rains of heaven" (Deut. 11:10–12).

The rain in Israel follows a predictable yearly cycle. Rain brought crops, which inspired celebrations, hence, the Jewish holiday system was originally determined by agriculture. Now, living in Israel, I could actually witness the rain and see how its cycle is the foundation upon which the Jewish calendar and, indeed, Jewish life is built.

At the end of the summer dry season, the Jewish New Year begins with Rosh Hashanah. On Rosh Hashanah, we reexamine our lives, change our ways, and begin again. Our change can impact on the rains and our collective livelihood:

> Sometimes the Israelites have been complete sinners, so on Rosh Hashanah, when God determines our fate for the year, it is decided that Israel will receive only a small rainfall for the coming year. But then they change their actions, and God decrees that the rainfall will be increased.[2]

The sense is that, both individually and communally, we are capable of change, of leaving behind our negativity, of shaking the very foundations of our existence. Rosh Hashanah is just the beginning of a ten-day purification period that culminates on Yom Kippur. Four days after Yom Kippur—once we've emerged from the days of awe and reflection—comes Sukkot, the harvest holiday and the most joyful time of the Jewish year, since it is then that the fruit and vegetable crops are gathered in.

Sukkot marks the end of the dry season and the beginning of the rains. During the time of the Temple, the priests held an elaborate water ceremony in which they danced, juggled, and played music as they drew water below the Temple Mount from the pools of Shiloah and brought it in gold-clad buckets up to the Temple. Our ancestors celebrated water to invite in the rain.

During the week of Sukkot, people circle the sanctuary in synagogue, waving their *lulav* and *etrog*, and chanting poems of praise. On the seventh day, they circle the sanctuary seven times and then shake the willows in a dramatic finale called *Hoshana Rabah*. The custom is a cathartic transition as we leave the withered summer behind us and enter the new year afresh, with a prayer for water to nourish our crops and souls.

During the time of the Temple, willows for the *lulav* were gathered from a place called Motza, just outside Jerusalem. I discovered Motza quite by accident one summer day while riding a horse I had rented from the stable near the Jerusalem Forest. Following my young Israeli guide into the Judean hills, he quickly pulled up, and I signaled my own mount to stop. "This is Motza," he announced, although we were a bit higher and just east of the Motza I knew. "This is where they take the water willows for the Temple for *Hoshanot*," he proclaimed with that authority many Israeli tour guides easily command. I doubted him until I looked over and saw that the trees were full of the type of willow we put into our *lulav* and banged for *Hoshana*—straighter and less droopy than the more common weeping willow. Willows need abundant water to survive, and finding one generally indicates that a stream is present. But here there was no water. Then I noticed that the trees' roots rested in the wadi we were riding through. I suddenly realized that in the winter after Sukkot, these dried creek beds have water coursing through them. I was reminded that the willows I bought for my *lulav* always tended to dry out quickly.

Not just the individual willows need water, but also the entire country—the land itself and even the economy. That day, as I rode my horse through the wadi, I understood why *Hoshana Rabah* ended the period of repentance and personal change. If I could—if we all could—put aside our personal ambitions, greed, and problems and shift our focus to the larger needs of the world, then we would truly change, and the year could begin on the proper note.

On the eighth day of Sukkot, Shemini Atzeret, we publicly proclaim the change from dry season to rainy season in the synagogue. For the next six months, we utter these words in our daily silent prayer: *"M'sheve ha-ruach u'm'rid ha-geshem,"* "Who causes the winds to blow and the rain to fall."

If the rains don't fall, the Talmud details an organized system of prayers and fasting. Even today, with technology, irrigation, and the proliferation of non–agriculturally based industry, Israel is still dependent on the rain in its proper season. Middle Eastern leaders and political scientists often cite water as their most precious resource and the one over which political disputes are most likely to arise. So every year, after Sukkot, economists and statesmen join with the religious as they anticipate the winter rains. As the talmudic rabbis believed that God's favor was shown with rain in these crucial weeks (God's disapproval was shown with drought), so the modern political state takes an accounting of its resources and calculates its economic fate in this same period. In Israel today, the price of groceries and the financial yield from exports are in part determined by the size and quality of the harvests, which depend on the same early and late rain that the rabbis mapped out in the Talmud.

By midwinter, at Tu B'Sh'vat, the New Year of the Trees, the majority of rains have fallen, the water begins its climb in the trees as sap, and the almond trees start to bud. In his commentary on the Talmud, Rashi explains how the New Year for Trees came to be in the month of Sh'vat: "Already the majority of rainy days have passed—this is the time to be fruitful, the sap rises in the trees and we find the fruits beginning to form from now on."[3]

Passover heralds the beginning of spring and, with it, the end of the rains. Passover falls in the Hebrew month of Nissan and marks the Omer period—the time between Passover and Shavuot when we wait appre-hensively for the spring grains to grow. Wheat, in particular, is very ten-der. Just as the lack of rain in winter would cause a shortage of the earli-er winter crops, so too much rain in springtime will damage the wheat and the economy that depends on it. Rain in the *proper* season promises wheat flour and bread for the coming year and hope for the future. Those who have spent a year or more in Israel know that it seldom rains after Passover. In fact, a second month of Adar is added on a regular basis so that Passover will come in spring after the rains.

And so the year is complete. The cycle of rain maps the Jewish year, determining our crops and our holidays and defining our lives. By pur-suing the "rain" that had spoken to me as a child, I was launched on a spiritual journey. Rain was my way to God and my Jewish agricultural heritage. It linked me to the meaning of my tradition.

15

Sukkot: Holiday of Joy

ELLEN BERNSTEIN

One day while working on my computer and looking for another word for *home*, I clicked on my word finder. To my delight, the first synonym given for *home* was *earth*, then *world, globe, planet, country, land, homeland,* and *soil.* I was delighted that my Macintosh has an ecological vision! The root of ecology—*ecos*—means "house" in Greek. Ecology understands the earth as home; it is the study of the web of relationships that contribute to the earth's hospitality. This finding was all the more timely given that the Jewish harvest holiday of Sukkot was just around the corner. Sukkot is undeniably the earth's holiday and the time to remember that the true meaning of *home* is "earth."

Sukkot—as harvest holiday—first teaches that life is intimately tied to the cycle of nature. The holiday assumes that we are ecologists, that we know the species and habitat of our home, and that we participate in the life of our ecosystem. An authentic celebration of Sukkot presupposes that we have been tending our crops all season; now is the time to reap what we have sown. It is also time to gather the four species and build a sukkah.

Sukkot, also known as the Festival of Joy, provides another teaching: that pleasure is essential to our livelihood.

"Rejoice for Seven Days"

The sukkah, the simple open-air hut we build to remember our holiday, had its origin in the temporary structures the Israelites built to shelter their harvest. Living far from the fields, they constructed sheds to protect freshly harvested fruits and vegetables until they were able to transport the crops home.

The Torah obligates us to build a sukkah from materials of nature; we are directed to make it beautiful with choice fruits and herbs and to eat and sleep there for seven days. We are also told to invite guests and to share all the bounty and joy with friends and neighbors and those less fortunate.

Today, the symbol of the sukkah might serve as the logo for an environmental organization. During this week-long camp-out, we cannot help but learn that the earth is home and the only true shelter is under God's wing. The pleasures of life come from the things we most often take for granted: good food, straight from the earth; good friends; and fresh air. This is a lesson we must learn time and again. No home can protect us the way the sukkah does; no money can buy the joy that comes from this humble holiday. What Sukkot teaches—that earth is home—is much easier said than done.

Besides the mitzvah of dwelling in a sukkah, we are commanded to gather four species. The Torah says: "You shall take the fruit of the goodly tree, palm branches, foliage of leafy trees, and willows of the brook, and you shall rejoice before your God for seven days" (Lev. 23:40). This practice is reminiscent of old harvest festivals, like the Maypole, during which every member of the community comes bearing a bunch of greens in token of nature's rebirth. Our bunch consists of "the fruit of the goodly tree," the *etrog* (also referred to as the citron); palm branches; leafy myrtle; and the willow that grows by the brook. Why these four? Our ancestors took the most pleasant fruit of the land, the *etrog*; the branches with the sweetest scent, the myrtle; the branches with the most prominent leaves, the palm; and the most prized herb, the willow. (Salicylic acid, the primary component in aspirin, comes from willow bark, which many cultures use as a healing herb.)

There is really no mystery about why we select these three greens. In Palestine, they were plentiful; everyone could pick them. They are aesthetically pleasing and, unlike pomegranates, say, or peaches, they will stay fresh and green for Sukkot's seven days.

"The Fruit of the Goodly Tree"

The *etrog* has long been something of a mystery. It is a member of the citrus family and looks very much like a lemon. The *etrog* is never referred to by name in the Torah; rather, Leviticus tells us only to gather "the fruit of the goodly tree." The talmudic rabbis advanced many arguments in support of the *etrog* as the fruit to which the Torah refers. They maintained that both the tree and the fruit had to be "goodly"; in other words, both the wood and the fruit must taste good. Only the *etrog* met these specifications. Further, many rabbis claimed that the *etrog* tree was the original Tree of Knowledge of Good and Evil, thus adding to its significance.[1]

The *etrog* has been the prescribed fruit of Sukkot since the fifth century B.C.E. The tree was native to East Africa and southern Arabia. Active trade routes between these areas and Mesopotamia introduced the *etrog* to Israel. By the first century C.E., it had become so important in Jewish religious observance that it traveled with Jews to foreign lands wherever the climate permitted its growth. In this way, the *etrog* spread through North Africa, Asia Minor, the Aegean Peninsula, Greece, and Italy. Indeed, it has been claimed that thanks to Jewish cultivation of the *etrog*, the peoples of these lands became exposed to and interested in all the citrus fruits—lemons, oranges, and grapefruits—and the Mediterranean became established as a center for citrus farming.[2]

The *etrog* story becomes particularly dramatic in the seventeenth century, when Jews began settling in northern climates where the *etrog* could not grow, and they had to rely on imported *etrogim* from commercial growers. But the Jews were not confident that non-Jewish farmers would cultivate the *etrog* in a way acceptable to *halachah*, or Jewish law. Many commercial growers began grafting *etrogim* onto lemon trees to produce an inexpensive *etrog*-like fruit. Production of this ersatz *etrog* became a popular business among non-Jews and, many suspected, among Jews as well. The rabbis forbade the use of grafted *etrogim*, but unless you see the tree from which the *etrog* is harvested, there is no way to tell an *etrog* from its look-alike grafted variety. This resulted in widespread trade in illegitimate *etrogim*, the Sukkot scandal of the century. Concern about the purity of *etrogim* has continued to the present day in some Jewish communities.[3]

The Festival of Joy

Besides its intimate link to the natural world, Sukkot is the Jewish holiday most linked with joy. In ancient days, it was called *HaChag*, The Holiday. The Torah does not mention joy at all with reference to Passover, and there is only one mention of it at Shavuot (Deut. 16:11), while at Sukkot the Torah tells us: "And you shall *rejoice* before the Lord your God (Lev. 23:40). . . . And you shall *rejoice* in your festival (Deut. 16:14). . . . And you shall be only *joyous* (Deut. 16:15)." Three times the Torah orders us to be joyful, as if joy is something to strive after *on this particular day.*

Most of us don't pay enough attention to creating joy in our lives. We concern ourselves with material survival, intellectual achievement, career development—all worthy goals, of course, but not more honorable than cultivating joy.

I am always struck by the fact that although Sukkot is historically a major festival, it has a minimal following today. It falls soon after Yom Kippur, the Day of Atonement, the one day a year when Jews flock from out of the woodwork to be counted. Why are we more committed to examining our failings and our limitations than we are to creating joy?

Similarly, many of us act out of a sense of guilt and obligation in our efforts to be environmental citizens. We feel oppressed by recycling, carpooling, and paying attention to all of the details of living a healthy life. We do it, but if we do it out of a sense of duty only, it will be difficult to keep us engaged in the long run.

Joy, on the other hand, is a great motivator, because it comes from inner desire and conviction rather than an outside authority or morality. It is more rewarding to do things because we enjoy them than because someone tells us that we should. If we choose to be Jewish, if we respond to the challenge to steward the earth, we need to find the joy that will sustain us on the quest. We can act out of appreciation of our home and our culture rather than out of burdensome guilt; however, it will take a reorientation of our lives and values. For most of us, it will require serious intention and work; this is what a spiritual path is about. Sukkot is the marker on the path that reminds us to follow our joy.

16

Sukkot: Gathering the Boughs

DAN FINK

*One generation goes and another generation comes, but the earth
abides forever. . . . What has been is that which will be, what has
been done is that which will be done again, and there is nothing
new under the sun.* —ECCLES. 1:4, 9

After two weighty weeks of penitential prayer and atonement—from
Rosh Hashanah through Yom Kippur—I am glad to be back in the
autumn woods, bathed in brilliant sunshine. I delight in the signs of
the season: my breath clouding in the crisp air, hints of red spreading
through the sumac and sweetgums, the raptors overhead returning to
their winter nesting grounds. Then I shift my gaze downward toward
the underbrush in search of coniferous boughs snapped off by late summer storms. I have come, again, to gather *s'chach*—the branches that
will cover the roof of my sukkah.

Every fall, I make this pilgrimage to the forest, a day or two before
Sukkot. Over the years, I have traveled to the deciduous uplands of
northern Kentucky, to the last stands of virgin hemlock in the Shenan-
doah Valley, and to the riparian belt of cottonwood and willow that lines
the steep banks of the Missouri River outside Omaha. Now, I live in
Idaho and collect my *s'chach* from the ponderosa pine forest that covers
the northern Rockies like a great green mantle.

Yet wherever my journeys have taken me, I have never felt far from
the small suburban woodlot just behind my childhood home. Every
forest I have entered since I was a boy still carries me back to that place,
where my friends and I built tree houses, caught crawfish, and played in
the remnants of bunkers dug by Union soldiers during the Civil War.

Late on Shabbat afternoons, my father would hike with my brother, my sister, and me in those woods, telling his stories, listening to ours, and teaching us the names of trees and wildflowers. During my sophomore year of high school, I took my girlfriend there and carved "D.F. + S.V." into the shining silver bark of a beech tree. She looked on admiringly, then gave me my first kiss. A decade later, when my parents told me of their plans to get divorced and sell the house where I grew up, the three of us walked and talked together in that forest, the one place I knew we could always speak from the heart. No one I know lives near those woods any more, but it still occupies a central place in the geography of my life.

This morning, the s'chach is abundant. I load the greenery into my trunk and head toward town. I'll be back by lunchtime, grab a bite, then start building my sukkah. Now, as I wind down the mountain roads, I daydream of the ushpizin—the mystical guests whom we invite to dine with us throughout the festival. Abraham, Isaac, and Jacob, Sarah, Rebecca, Rachel, and Leah will all be in my sukkah, reminding me of my Jewish roots. And as the wind blows through the fragrant branches, others will be there, too: my parents, my brother and sister, my friends, walking together in a forest behind my childhood home. In every forest. In every home.

17

A History of Tu B'Sh'vat

ELLEN BERNSTEIN

Tu B'Sh'vat, the Jewish New Year of the Trees, falls on the full moon of Sh'vat, which is the fifteenth—in Hebrew, *tu*—day of that month. Legend has it that the trees specifically asked the Creator for this unlikely mid-winter date for their new year because they realized that only after the winter rains had fallen could they flower and sprout new growth.

Tu B'Sh'vat is not mentioned in the Torah or the prayer book. It first appears in the Talmud, in the section dealing with Rosh Hashanah:

> There are four new year days: the first of Nisan is the new year for reckoning the reigns of kings and the feasts; the first of Elul is the new year for the tithe of the cattle; the first of Tishrei is the new year for reckoning of the years and taking stock of human lives; the first of Sh'vat is the new year for the fruit trees. That is according to the school of Shammai; the school of Hillel says, on the 15th of Sh'vat.[1]

Tu B'Sh'vat's beginnings, then, are strictly secular. It was originally a bookkeeping day, a day to pay taxes on fruit trees. This date—when the almond trees were starting to bloom—was an obvious marker to calculate the trees' new year. To pay taxes on the fruit trees, it was necessary to know to which year the fruits belonged. In Israel, fruit trees lie dormant during the cold rainy season from December to mid-February, when cold prevents the trees from using available moisture and nutrients. The trees' new year began when the trees awakened from their winter dormancy and started to use the water in the ground. Fruits that began to form before that date were considered to be using the rainwater from the previous season and were taxed along with the produce from that year.

How did the fifteenth of Sh'vat become a day of joyous celebration, a condition rarely associated with tax collecting? One of the oldest references to Tu B'Sh'vat as a festive day is in a poem by Rabbi Yehuda ben Hillel Ha-Levi, who lived in Israel in the tenth century. The poem praises and blesses trees and is evocative of the Israelite landscape; it introduces the concept of Tu B'Sh'vat as a day of judgment, a Rosh Hashanah for trees.

A Return to Fruitfulness

In the tenth century, Rabbenu Gershom, the leading rabbinic authority, prohibited public fasts on Tu B'Sh'vat, since it was a time of celebration, not deprivation. One of the first festive traditions to be associated with Tu B'Sh'vat was a ritual meal of fruits. In Ashkenazic communities, fifteen kinds of fruit grown in Israel were eaten, representing the fifteenth of the month, *Tu*. The ritual recalled the days when the Israelites were living on their own land and could carry out the talmudic instructions for tithing their fruit trees.

Although there were no special prayers, early traditions included reciting the Psalm 104, which celebrates the central role of water in nature: "Who waters the mountains from the upper chambers . . . God's trees have had their fill, the cedars of Lebanon which he planted" (Ps. 104:13–16). In the eleventh century, a set of psalms was composed especially for the Tu B'Sh'vat *Amidah*, the silent prayer.

Tu B'Sh'vat was a relatively minor holiday until the 1600s, when the Kabbalists who lived in Safed developed an interest in it. They created a *tikkun*—a fixing of the world—for this day, based in form on the Passover Seder. The Tu B'Sh'vat Seder included four cups of wine, three categories of fruit, and readings about nature.

With the distribution of the text for the Tu B'Sh'vat Seder, communities around the world began to develop customs for celebrating the New Year of the Trees. In Bucharia and Kurdistan, the holiday was known as the "day of eating the seven species" (see Deut. 8:8), and a dinner of thirty kinds of fruit was prepared. In India, fifty varieties of fruits were readied for the feast. In rural Morocco, the rich invited the whole town to their homes and filled the guests' hats with fruit. In Persia, it was customary to climb onto neighbors' roofs and lower an empty basket down the chimney. The basket would be returned laden with fruit. In Turkey, each member of the family had a special relationship to one species of fruit. In Persia and Afghanistan, Jews purchased new fabrics on Tu B'Sh'vat, from which clothing for Pesach was sewn. A Greek legend claimed that on Tu B'Sh'vat an angel tapped the head of every plant, commanding it, "Grow!" Another Greek legend related that the trees embraced on this day and everyone who witnessed this miraculous event would have a wish fulfilled.

There was a widespread custom of eating jelly made from the *etrog* of the previous Sukkot on Tu B'Sh'vat and praying for *etrogim* of fine quality for the next Sukkot. Some barren Jewish women planted raisins and candy near trees on Tu B'Sh'vat night and prayed for fertility. Young girls eligible for marriage were brought to trees, where an imitation marriage was enacted. If buds were soon found on the trees where they were "married," they knew their turn would come soon.

In some areas, Tu B'Sh'vat celebrations were held by families who had lost a loved one during the past year. As a holiday of rebirth, Tu B'Sh'vat is a symbol for mourners of the possibility of resurrection.

Only in this century, with the Jewish National Fund's efforts to restore Israel to its former "fruitfulness," has Tu B'Sh'vat become associated with tree planting. Tu B'Sh'vat provided an opportunity to ritualize the act of planting and to involve masses of people in it. However, when this custom was inaugurated, the agricultural realities in Israel were not fully understood. The optimal planting season is earlier in the fall with the accompanying rains. Nevertheless, the custom of planting trees was established on Tu B'Sh'vat, and today, tree-planting ceremonies take place throughout Israel on the fifteenth of Sh'vat. Jews from around the world participate by contributing money to purchase trees.

Meanwhile in North America, the Tu B'Sh'vat Seder has enjoyed unprecedented popularity over the last two decades. Because there is no specified liturgy for the holiday, Tu B'Sh'vat readily lends itself to creative interpretation. Celebrate it! You and your families and communities can enjoy this festive holiday, creating your own Seder using the material that follows.

18

The Tu B'Sh'vat Seder

ELLEN BERNSTEIN

May it be Your will O Lord our God and God of our ancestors, that through the sacred power of our eating fruit, which we are now eating and blessing, while reflecting on the secret of their supernal roots upon which they depend, that shefa, *favor, blessing, and bounty be bestowed upon them. May their angels be filled by the powerful* shefa *of their glory; may it return and cause them to grow a second time, from the beginning of the year and until its end, for bounty and blessing, for good life and peace . . . [M]ay all the holy sparks which were dispersed by us or by our ancestors and [also] through the sin that Adam committed with the fruit of the tree, now return to be included in the splendid power of The Tree of Life.*

—PRELIMINARY BLESSING, *Peri 'Ez Hadar*[1]

For most of us, when we hear the word *seder*, Passover immediately comes to mind. However, *seder* means "order," and a Seder can be used to structure a ritual for any holiday. The beauty of a Seder is that it speaks through all of our senses to the soul, and the "order" provides opportunities for everyone, no matter what their abilities, to participate. The Kabbalists of Safed used a Seder to design a ritual for Tu B'Sh'vat.

We don't know exactly who wrote the text for the Tu B'Sh'vat Seder, the *Peri 'Ez Hadar*, or Fruit of the Goodly Tree, or when it was written. It was first published as part of an anthology of kabbalistic customs called the *Hemdat Yamim*, and it was printed as a separate volume in 1728 in Venice.

Until recently, Tu B'Sh'vat Seders were popular only among the Sephardic communities, where the *Peri 'Ez Hadar* has enjoyed continuous printing and distribution for almost three centuries. On the other hand, no mention of the *Peri 'Ez Hadar* or its customs is found in the Ashkenazic literature, undoubtedly because Ashkenazic community derided Sephardic customs as antiquated and magical and condemned the entire *Hemdat Yamim* as heretical.

The Tu B'Sh'vat Seder is structured around an introduction, a preliminary blessing, a prescribed order of the eating of the ritual fruits, and a series of nature-related readings from the Bible, early rabbinic texts, and the Zohar. For anyone unschooled in Kabbalah, the *Peri 'Ez Hadar* is almost impossible to understand because it is built upon layers of symbols. To begin to unravel it, readers must grasp the kabbalistic orientation toward the world.

The Kabbalists believed that humanity holds the power to move the universe. Before Adam and Eve ate the apple in the Garden of Eden, there was one unified, collective soul. Creation was bound to Creator. When Adam and Eve ate the apple, they broke God's law and ruptured the soul.

Just as humanity holds the power to destroy, it also has the power to heal. The Kabbalists believed Adam and Eve's first act of defiance toward God separated nature from its divine source. It would be the charge of successive generations to help to heal this relationship; we do this by performing mitzvot, good deeds.

The mitzvah that Kabbalists emphasized on Tu B'Sh'vat is the one of blessing. Blessings can heal wounds when we recite them with sincere intention. The whole purpose of eating so many fruits on Tu B'Sh'vat is that it offers us the opportunities to make more blessings. The Seder is a "wondrous *tikkun*," the Kabbalists wrote, that we can do to "fix" the broken universe.

According to the Kabbalists, when people eat the fruit of a plant, they are eating of the plant's divine energy. It is the job of the plant's guardian angel to restore the "energy" so the plant can produce more fruit. The angel seeks the energy from the persons who originally ate the fruit. When they recite a blessing, they offer up divine energy that the angel can direct back toward the fruit. If the persons who eat do not recite a blessing, or if the fruit goes to waste on the tree, it is as if a robber stole the divine energy from the plant. The angel cannot replenish the energy, and the plant will not bear fruit again.[2]

This is the reason for so many blessings on Tu B'Sh'vat. Blessings are the power that can fix the world. Since each kind of fruit requires its own blessing, we taste many kinds of fruit—in some Seders, forty-five—and recite blessings upon blessings that we send to the Creator to help repair all that is broken.

The Order of the Tu B'Sh'vat Seder

Said Rabbi Simeon: "Mark this well. Fire, air, earth and water are the sources and roots of all things above and below, and all things above, below, are grounded in them. And in each of the four winds these elements are found—fire in the North, water in the South, earth in the West; and the 4 elements are united with the 4 winds—and all are one. Fire, water, air and earth: gold, silver, copper and iron: North, South, East and West—altogether these make 12, yet they are all one."[3]

The order for the Tu B'Sh'vat Seder is embedded in the kabbalistic concept of "the four worlds." The Kabbalists defined four levels of meaning in all experience, and they termed those levels "worlds." According to the Kabbalists, God dwells in a perfect realm called *Atzilut*, the world of spirit. The world in which we, humans, live is called *Assiyah*, which means "making" or "doing." This is the physical world, the only one we can perceive with our senses. Between these are two other worlds: *Briyah*, the world of the mind, and *Yetzirah*, the world of the emotions.

Even though we live in the lowest world, *Assiyah*, we still have access to the "higher" ones. All four have the same underlying structure: "As above, so below." If we pay close attention to the world of *Assiyah*, we can begin to learn about the "upper" worlds. By meditating on the habits of animals, the patterns of trees, the workings of the human body, we can begin to realize God's essence.

The Kabbalists represented the four worlds with different types of fruits for the Tu B'Sh'vat Seder. The edible part of each fruit—the fleshy part—symbolizes holiness, while the inedible portion—the shell, skin, or pit—represents protection.

The following chart indicates the quality, season, and fruit that correspond to the four worlds in the kabbalistic framework. I added the category "element" to give the Seder a distinct environmental *kavannah*, or intention.

WORLD	QUALITY	SEASON	FRUIT	ELEMENT
Assiyah	Action	Winter	Hard outer, soft inner	Earth
Yetzirah	Emotion	Spring	Soft outer, hard inner	Water
Briyah	Thought	Summer	Soft throughout	Air
Atzilut	Spirit	Fall	Essence	Fire

Assiyah, the world of physical action, the world of the earth, is symbolized by fruits and nuts that are hard on the outside and soft within, such as walnuts, pineapples, bananas, and coconuts. The hard outer covering corresponds to the protection we need to live in the world. It symbolizes our defenses. Like the spiny cactus and the armadillo, we need to protect ourselves from the invasive forces of life. The pulpy inner refers to the sweet interior that marks our essence.

Yetzirah, the world of feeling and forming, the world of water, is symbolized by fruits that are hard on the inside and have a soft outer coat. Among these are apricots, cherries, and olives. This world is one step higher than the world of *Assiyah*, one step less defended. The hard inner pit symbolizes inner strength and a character that needs less protection.

Briyah, the world of thinking and analysis, the world of air, is symbolized by fruits that are soft all the way through, such as strawberries, grapes, and raisins. In this world, which approaches pure spirit, we can drop all our defenses, all our hardness, and we can begin to relax into joy.

Atzilut, the world of spirit, the world of fire, transcends form in the physical world. It is not represented by any fruit in the traditional Kabbalist Seder. I have used incense or maple syrup to symbolize the essence of this world, the spirit that transcends everything.

According to the Kabbalists, there are also four cups of wine (or grape juice) to symbolize the four seasons: white wine for the winter slumber; red wine for the vital life force; and combinations to indicate the seasons in between. First, we drink a cup of white wine as a reminder of winter—*Assiyah;* then a cup of white wine with a dash of red for spring—*Yetzirah;* red with a dash of white for summer—*Briyah;* and pure red for autumn—*Atzilut.*

This Seder can best be understood as a four-course meal or a four-part play. We begin with the world of *Assiyah.* We recite readings about earth and our actions; we bless and eat fruits that symbolize the earth. Each section/world repeats this pattern.

- Introduction to the world: What does it mean to you?
- Readings: Choose approximately ten. For the "world" of earth, choose ten *short* readings about land, plants, soil, agriculture, toxic dumps, and action. For the world of water, choose ten readings about rivers, rain, oceans, water pollution, and emotions. For air, choose readings about air and the power of thought. For fire, choose readings about the sun, nuclear power, and the spirit.
- Blessings, eating fruits, and drinking wine.

Note: Since there are no halachic requirements for a Tu B'Sh'vat Seder, feel free to add music, dancing, meditation, storytelling, and discussions as desired.

A Tu B'Sh'vat Seder can be held indoors or out, with any number of people of all ages. *Seder* means "order," and when a beautiful orderly space is created, the entire Seder can be a powerful ritual. Any space with a peaceful atmosphere and that is evocative of nature will do. Candles, flowers, tablecloths, artwork, and branches will enhance the aesthetic experience. The Seder is a vehicle for people to participate and express their appreciation for nature in whatever way they know best. Local musicians, artists, or dancers may want to compose pieces specifically for the event.

Food Preparation

Cut up five to ten types of fruit for each "world." Flowers, incense, spices, or a burning candle may represent *Atzilut,* however, it can be left completely without symbolism. You will also need adequate supplies of red and white wine (or grape juice) so each person can have four glasses to symbolize the four seasons.

At the end of the Seder, you may want to have a meal using foods from the biblical verse that is quoted in the *Peri 'Ez Hadar,* "a land of wheat, and barley, and vines, and fig trees, and pomegranates; a land of olive oil, and honey; a land in which thou shalt eat bread without scarceness" (Deut. 8:8–9). Some suggestions are hallah, mushroom-barley soup, cheeses, and honeycake.

Study

Like the original Kabbalistic Seder, much of this Seder is devoted to reading aloud texts from traditional Jewish sources. I prepare ten readings per "world" and use the categories of earth for *Assiyah,* water for *Yetzirah,* air for *Briyah,* and fire for *Atzilut* to direct those present toward nature and environmental concerns. I like to juxtapose biblical and Jewish nature readings with contemporary nature, science, or environmental readings. One source for Jewish readings is *A Garden of Choice Fruit* (David Stein, ed.; Philadelphia: Shomrei Adamah, 1992), and sources for the nature readings include nature writers, newspapers, environmental books, and nature centers.

Blessings and Eating

Blessings, followed by contemplative eating—either in silence or with soft music or focused conversation—culminate each section of the Seder. You may want to offer one of these readings as a *kavannah*—intention before eating.

> Just as one can contemplate a flower or a melody, one can contemplate the act of eating. One opens one's mind completely to the experience of chewing the food and fills the awareness with the taste and texture of the food. One then eats very slowly, aware of every nuance of taste. (Aryeh Kaplan)

> R. Hezkla R. Cohen said in the name of Rav, "In the future a person will have to account for everything that he saw and did not eat." (Talmud)

. . . Would that I merited hearing the sound of the songs and praises of the grasses, how every blade of grass sings to the Holy One of Blessing, whole-heartedly with no reservations and without anticipation of reward. How wonderful it is when one hears their song and how very good to be amongst them serving our Creator in awe. (Rabbi Nachman of Breslov)

BLESSINGS FOR ASSIYAH. For *Assiyah,* we eat nuts and fruits with a tough skin to remind us of the protection the earth gives us, and we acknowledge that we need protection, both physical and emotional. We bless our defense systems, which help us to survive.

Recite the *berachah* over fruit:

Ba-ruch Atah A-do-nai El-o-heiy-nu Mel-ech ha-olam bo-rei p'ri ha-etz.

Praised are You, Eternal, Our God, who creates the fruit of the tree.

Eat the fruits with the hard outer shell.

Our first cup of wine is white, since in winter, when nature is asleep, the earth is barren and sometimes covered with snow.

Recite the *berachah* over wine:

Ba-ruch Atah A-do-nai El-o-heiy-nu Mel-ech ha-olam bo-rei p'ri ha-gafen.

Blessed art Thou, O Lord our God, Ruler of the universe, who creates the fruit of the vine.

Drink the first cup.

BLESSINGS FOR YETZIRAH. For *Yetzirah,* we eat fruits with a tough inner core and a soft outer. Through this act, we acknowledge the need to fortify our hearts. With a strong heart and a pure vision, we can retract the protective outer shell and let our lives grow richer and deeper as we experience the miracle of nature that surrounds us.

Recite the *berachah* over fruit:

Ba-ruch Atah A-do-nai El-o-heiy-nu Mel-ech ha-olam bo-rei p'ri ha-etz.

Praised are You, Eternal, Our God, who creates the fruit of the tree.

Eat the fruits that are soft on the outside and have hard pits on the inside.

As spring approaches, the sun's rays begin to thaw the frozen earth. Gradually, the land's color changes from white to red as the first flowers appear on the hillsides. So, our second cup will be a bit darker. We pour a little red wine into the white.

Recite the *berachah* over wine:

Ba-ruch Atah A-do-nai El-o-heiy-nu Mel-ech ha-olam bo-rei p'ri ha-gafen.

Blessed art Thou, O Lord our God, Ruler of the universe, who creates the fruit of the vine.

Drink the second cup.

BLESSINGS FOR BRIYAH. For *Briyah*, we taste fruits that are completely edible. In this world, where God's protection is close at hand, we can let go of all barriers and taste freedom. Together with God, we create the world. And like God's, each of our thoughts becomes action.

Recite the *berachah* over fruit:

Ba-ruch Atah A-do-nai El-o-heiy-nu Mel-ech ha-olam bo-rei p'ri ha-etz.

Praised are You, Eternal, Our God, who creates the fruit of the tree.

Eat the fruits that are soft throughout.

In summer, when vegetable and fruits are abundant, we are reminded of the richness of life. We drink red wine with a dash of white.

Recite the *berachah* over wine:

*Ba-ruch Atah A-do-nai El-o-heiy-nu Mel-ech ha-olam bo-rei p'ri
    ha-gafen.*
**Blessed art Thou, O Lord our God, Ruler of the universe,
    who creates the fruit of the vine.**

Drink the third cup.

BLESSINGS FOR ATZILUT. As summer turns to fall, plants are preparing seed for the next cycle of nature. We, too, must nourish the world for the coming generation. Just as the natural world goes through changes to achieve its full potential, we also need to change: we need to get rid of anger, envy, and greed so that we can be free to grow. When we do this, we will become very strong, like healthy trees with solid roots in the ground and our limbs open to the love that is all around us.

The fourth cup of wine is full-strength red.

Recite the *berachah* over wine:

*Ba-ruch Atah A-do-nai El-o-heiy-nu Mel-ech ha-olam bo-rei p'ri
    ha-gafen.*
**Blessed art Thou, O Lord our God, Ruler of the universe,
    who creates the fruit of the vine.**

Drink the fourth cup.

19

Purim Rivers and Revels

DAN FINK

And the month was changed from sorrow to joy.   —ESTHER 9:22

During my college years, I was not much of a Jew. Perhaps, having grown up in the synagogue as a rabbi's kid, I simply needed some time away from it. Or maybe it was fate. I certainly took it as a sign when my Irish-Catholic suite mate, Charlie Murphy, and I attended the Hillel House kickoff brunch for first-year students—and he was invited back, without me. At any rate, my Jewish observance at the University of Virginia consisted of a token High Holy Day service, an abbreviated Seder, and diligently avoiding dining hall pork chops.

Yet, I never forgot how I had been raised. I remained proud of my Jewish identity, and my spiritual life flourished, nurtured by the natural world. I spent many hours in the nearby Blue Ridge mountains, hiking and studying. Living outside a major metropolis for the first time, I felt the rhythm of the seasons, the passage from equinox to solstice and back, the play of shadows and light. I experienced the eternal cycle of generation, decay, and rebirth that underlies Judaism's sense of sacred time: autumn's twinning of bounty and loss, the creative darkness of winter, spring's restorative hope, and summer's release. I bought a cheap tent, a battered aluminum canoe, and a good topographic map of the George Washington National Forest. I used them often, and I used them well.

By early March, however, I inevitably developed a powerful case of cabin fever. This was the toughest season, no longer winter but still not spring. Classes grew tedious, and the bleak gray drizzle did not cease. I longed for release, for the decadent exuberance of Purim, when we celebrate our surviving the dark times of winter with laughter and excess.

Perhaps that explains why the first decent day of the month found me out on the river with three old friends—even though the water was flowing dangerously high and cold. We knew that experts hesitated before running the Rapanahanock at such flood stages. We also knew that we were not experts. Scott and I had some canoeing experience, but the Cadenas brothers—TT and Pedro—had never paddled before. Still, we were young and desperately ready for spring, so we loaded our boats with gear and beer, put in at Ely's Ford, and hoped to make the twenty-four miles to Mott's Run by nightfall.

At first, we fared unexpectedly well. Scott and I negotiated the rapids, choosing the shoots with a combination of skill and luck. TT and Pedro followed our path, whooping as they went. Then, we reached the massive rock gardens at the confluence with the Rapidan. My canoe made it through, but when we turned around to see how the Cadenas brothers were doing, we beheld a scene I will never forget: their boat ramming head on into a boulder, throwing both TT and Pedro (who weighed a hefty 275 pounds) a good eight feet into the air and then down the river.

TT soon surfaced and made it to the shore, but Pedro disappeared. For the next hour we searched for him. TT ran along the banks, calling his name, while Scott and I paddled downstream, hoping to catch him. No luck. The three of us sat silently at a makeshift campsite, praying for a miracle. TT began to sob, "He's dead. My brother's dead."

Then we heard a rustling in the bushes followed by Pedro's enormous laughter. He emerged looking like the creature from the black lagoon, with a six-pack in each hand. "I went to save the beer," he chuckled, "and I was not going to leave that river until I found it."

We wanted to kill him and hug him at the same time. Instead, we breathed a collective sigh of relief and pulled some dry clothes out of a sealed plastic garbage bag. We changed, collected wood, and lit a fire. Then, like Hasidim at a Purim *shpiel*, we spent the rest of the evening toasting our survival, celebrating with raucous laughter and ice-cold Budweiser fresh from the river.

20

The Parsley versus the Potato:
A Passover Reminiscence

EVERETT GENDLER

Potato versus parsley? Surely a misprint, the reader might think, familiar with that old American standby, parslied potatoes. Yet, however harmonious their culinary relations, their ritual rivalry was quite another matter in the days of my childhood.

From as early as I can remember, each year our Passover plate had on it *charoset*, horseradish, an egg, a shankbone, a potato, and a bowl of salt water. Thus was the mandate from Sinai, rabbinically interpreted, played out at the Gendlers' table in Chariton, Iowa, the farming town of 5,000 where I spent my first eleven years. The familiarity of that plate was reassuring, and the potato dipped in salt water, eaten so soon after the sweet Kiddush wine, was just the carbohydrate fix that a small child needed to sit through those seemingly endless pages of prayers.

All was coherent, even the blessing, *Baruch Atah Adonai Eloheinu Melech ha-olam, bo-rei p'ri ha-a-da-mah*, Blessed are You God, Ruler of the universe, who creates the fruit of the ground. For the potato, like all vegetables, was not only appropriately designated fruit of the earth; it could even lay claim to a special connection with the soil. For most vegetables, after all, grow above the ground, while the potato tuber, the edible part, develops totally within earth's protective soil. If ever there were a proper candidate for the blessing "fruit of the ground," the potato had a strong claim to the honor. And so, from one Passover to the next, the potato occupied the place of honor as the first item eaten from the seder plate.

Now let it be admitted that even amid this wholeness and harmony, there was one discordant note. When I finally could read and flipped through the *Maxwell House Haggadah* myself, something seemed to be amiss. The instructions made mention of lettuce or parsley, not potatoes. Lettuce or parsley? What on earth could they be talking about? Concerned inquiries to my parents yielded no answer but merely the assertion that, whatever the *goyishe* book might think, *of course* the potato was the proper vegetable for the Seder plate. So it had been with their ancestors in the Ukraine, and so it was to be here in Iowa as well. There the matter rested—until we moved to Des Moines. There in the big city, our traditional country ways were once more seriously challenged. There too, the Haggadah seemed to favor parsley, lettuce, or even celery! Worse yet, from informal discussions with my Hebrew school classmates, it became obvious that ours was a backward home, out of step with the sophisticated Jewish world of those whose Seder plates were graced with delicate, lacy greens, not lumpen boiled potatoes.

Throughout my adolescence, the issue erupted anew as the time to prepare the Seder plate approached. Eventually, parsley also occupied the Seder plate, but boiled potatoes remained. The parsley was dipped first, followed immediately by potatoes. And even I, the advocate of the big-city assimilationist intrusions on our traditional Seder plate, even I had to admit to myself (though never to my parents) that the potato was, indeed, more tasty and more filling than the parsley newcomer.

Looking back, the reason for this variation on custom is obvious: it was a climatic variation determined by environmental conditions. Long ago in the Ukraine, where winter lingered late, where fresh greens from California or Florida were totally unknown, what else could serve for the blessing over fruits of the ground but some remainder of a root crop from the previous growing season?

Today on our family Seder plate, parsley and potato peacefully coexist, another sign of the marvelous adaptability of Jewish ritual tradition. In these days of increasing environmental awareness, they also remind us of the wondrous variety of climates and circumstances in which the Jewish people have lived through the ages. May both the awareness and the variety long continue!

21

Leaving Egypt

DAN FINK

Arise my beloved, my fair one, come away! For now the winter is past, the rains are over and gone. The blossoms have appeared in the land, the time of singing has come, the song of the turtledove is heard in our land. The green figs form on the fig tree, the vines in blossom give off fragrance. Arise, my beloved, my fair one, come away! —SONG OF SONGS 2:10–13

My wife and I did not fall in love at first sight. Indeed, during our initial year and a half together as classmates in rabbinical school, we barely even spoke. On those rare occasions when we did exchange a few words, it was usually with disparagement or disdain.

Upon looking back at the coolness of our early encounters, I must admit that the burden of responsibility for the lack of cordiality lies squarely with me. Over the course of my studies at the seminary in Cincinnati, I had swallowed a lot of anger. I became increasingly rigid, and while I learned a great deal about Bible, Midrash, codes, and commentaries, I did not laugh very much. I was not spending the time outdoors that I had treasured in the past and dearly needed now. Too many hours in classrooms and libraries under bad fluorescent light had restricted my horizons. I was in a state of *mitzrayim*—the Hebrew word for Egypt, meaning "a narrow place, an uptight world, exile." And so when Laura joined my class—a free-spirited feminist with spiked orange hair, fresh from a year off in Los Angeles—it was no great wonder that in my insecurity I greeted her with undisguised scorn.

The surprise came nearly two years later when, in the spring of 1987, our relationship began to thaw. One morning, when I was feeling

155

more generous in spirit than usual, I offered her a well-earned but unexpected compliment on a sermon she had just delivered. A few weeks later, she invited me and a mutual friend to join her and her roommate at their home for dinner. Shortly thereafter, the same friend accompanied me on the first backpacking trip I had taken in several years. While we hiked through the great stone arches of Red River Gorge, Kentucky, he told me that I should ask Laura for a date. I thought about this the rest of the day. At nightfall, as the crescent moon rose over the redbud trees and we made camp, I admitted that this sounded like a good idea.

The following Saturday night, I took Laura to see a modern dance troupe perform an incomprehensible routine in an aging, dimly lit hall. Things went well enough to ensure a second date. This time, we planned a picnic supper in Mount Storm park.

I was so excited I spent nearly a full day preparing the meal: white wine, salads, croissant sandwiches, pastries, and a mango. I picked up Laura, and we drove to the park. When we arrived, it was a magnificent spring evening, the warm air redolent with the smell of flowers and fresh-cut grass. We walked together, then spread out a blanket under an enormous oak and ate. By the time we got to the mango, the weather was turning a bit chilly, but we ate it slowly nonetheless, savoring its sweetness. We finished it, paused awkwardly, then shared a kiss that tasted like spring and mango, and I knew that my long and wintry world of exile was beginning to end.

22

Grow Your Own—Barley, That Is!

EILEEN ABRAMS

Last year at this time, the barley growing in a corner of my small front yard was higher than my knees. The Sukkot before, my friend Rivkah Walton had asked if she could plant barley in my sunny yard. She was building an Omer counter and wanted some barley to incorporate into the design. (Barley was brought to the Temple on the second day of Passover as an offering of the first of the new grain harvest; an Omer counter is a device for counting off the days from the second night of Pesach until Shavuot.)

"A barley crop in the front yard of my Philadelphia row house?" I mused. And then I thought, "Why not?" During the months between planting and harvest, I went from being a detached land lender to a passionate barley steward. Tending the crop between Sukkot and Shavuot deepened my involvement with Jewish living and my connection to the natural world in ways I never would have expected.

The seed for the barley came from Chuck Miller, a member of the local *havurah* community who had a working farm about a two hours' drive from Philadelphia. One chilly October afternoon toward the end of Sukkot, Rivkah came over and dug up a bed for the seed in a corner of my yard. The barley plot was small, about nine inches by nine feet. (The yard itself is a mere five feet by nine feet.) The plot was bounded by a hip-high wrought-iron fence on two sides, an azalea bush on the third side, and grass on the remaining side. In a few weeks, the seed sprouted vigorously. It was a wonder to contemplate thick green shoots pushing their way out of the earth toward the sun in the middle of November.

By Chanukah, in mid-December, the barley was about four inches high and looked like a patch of sturdy, dense, bright green grass—quite in contrast to the lawn grass in the yard, which had died back and yellowed with the onset of autumn. In December, I began taking snapshots of the plot, chronicling the barley's growth through the end of May. One of my favorite shots is of the hardy barley under a dusting of snow, a testament to the sheer vitality of this winter-growing grain.

Around Purim, the barley had a growth spurt. The blades lengthened and thickened, and I began looking for the barest beginnings of the heads of grain. Early one morning as I was inspecting the crop, as I now did routinely, I spied tiny protrusions in a few blades of grain still wet with dew. Heads of grain had begun to form. I drew a deep breath, and before I knew it was saying the *Shehecheyanu* (the blessing for seeing or doing something for the first time or for the first time in a long time).

As the grain was ripening between Purim and Passover, I felt what I imagined Eve and Adam must have felt in the first garden, startled and amazed by growth. I had never seen barley grow before. "It's so beautiful! What's going to happen next? How tall will it get? How big will the heads get, and what shape will they be? And how do you know when it's ripe and ready for harvest?" These questions had a practical significance because Rivkah had asked me to harvest and dry stalks of the barley in seven stages of its growth so she could incorporate them into the design of the Omer counter she was building. I harvested weekly between Purim and Shavuot, collecting samples that represented the stages of the barley's growth. That spring for the first time, I counted the Omer myself, although not as is traditionally done, in the evening. Every day between Passover and Shavuot, I visited the plot, usually in the morning, and every day there was new growth in the crop. It was impossible to watch the barley growing each day and not be aware of the "Omer countdown" at the deep inner level at which we are in touch with the natural world and, through it, with God.

That spring, also for the first time, I participated in a *tikkun leyl Shavuot* (an all-night study session) traditionally held on Shavuot, where the barley played a special, unexpected role. The *tikkun* was held in the home of a *havurah* member, and Rivkah brought a sheaf of ripe barley we had harvested the week before to decorate the living room in which we sat, studied, snacked, and (in some cases) snoozed through the night. At daybreak, about fifteen of us gathered for the service in which we would read the Ten Commandments from the Torah.

The service was about to begin, and nobody could find a *yad* (pointer used for reading the Torah). Then someone reached for the barley sheaf and removed a stalk. The stalk became the *yad*. I will remember for a long time watching the barley I had grown move across the page as the Commandments were being read. The moment unified for me the words from Sinai with the bread from the earth, and I recalled the lines from *Pirke Avot* (Ethics of the Fathers): "Where there is no bread, there is no Torah; where there is no Torah, there is no bread."

A week later, I made the final barley harvest. It was the full moon of the month of Sivan, which fell at the end of May. It felt right, somehow, to complete the harvest on the full moon. My barley now rests in a large white vase on a stand in my dining room. On Shabbat and holidays, it decorates my table.

23

Mountain Paths

DAN FINK

Do not urge me to leave you, to turn back and not follow you. For wherever you go, I will go; wherever you lodge, I will lodge; your people shall be my people, and your God my God. Where you die, I will die, and there I will be buried. —RUTH 1:16–17

Shavuot celebrates mountaintops and relationships. The covenant between God and the Jewish people may have commenced with Abraham and Sarah by the green banks of the Euphrates, but the relationship was not sealed until the first Shavuot, when the Israelites received the Torah from the summit of Mount Sinai.

It was fitting, then, that just after Shavuot, in June of 1989, Laura dropped me off at the base of Springer Mountain, Georgia, the southern terminus of the 2,100-mile-long Appalachian Trail. During the past year, we had been ordained, bought a house, gotten married, moved, and settled into our first jobs as the rabbis of Harrisonburg and Staunton, two towns in Virginia. All these major life changes concentrated in such a short time span had been difficult to handle. Like most newlyweds, we squabbled constantly, but these quarrels were exacerbated by our rocketing stress levels.

It was, therefore, with a mixed sense of sadness, anxiety, and relief that we uttered our tearful farewells at the trailhead. As Laura got into the car and pulled away, I hoisted my pack and set out. My plans were to hike from Springer to Damascus, Virginia, a small trail town just north of the Tennessee border. This meant walking nearly 500 miles, almost none of them flat. I gave myself forty days, the same amount of time that Elijah had journeyed on a single meal and Moses had tarried on the mountaintop. I hoped that, like those prophets, I would return home from my travels stronger and better.

Throughout my first week on the Appalachian Trail, I hiked alone. I rarely encountered other backpackers as I shuffled up and down the red clay hills of northern Georgia. However, upon crossing into the broader vistas of North Carolina, I met two companions who walked with me the rest of the summer: an aspiring opera singer from Pittsburgh and a Kentucky auto mechanic. Together, we trudged over the steep, eroded slopes of the Stekoahs, enduring fierce hail storms and rampant stinging nettles. We strolled through the Great Smoky Mountains National Park, where we reveled in lovely weather, spectacular scenery, abundant wildflowers, and easy paths cushioned by a thick mat of pine needles. We shopped for supplies in tiny valley villages and shared aspirin and Dr. Scholl's pads for aches and blisters. Despite our divergent backgrounds, we became friends.

Still, it was a challenge for us to stay together. Straggling over tough trails on sweltering summer days, we got ornery. We walked at different paces and argued over when to take breaks and how long they should last. After a while, we learned to travel alone, each of us at our own speed, meeting up at prearranged spots to eat lunch and make camp. This compromise enabled us to enjoy the luxuries of solitude during the day and the pleasures of companionship at night around the bonfire. These friendships sustained me. By the end of my forty days, I was sick with giardiasis—dehydrated, cramped, and exhausted—but with the help of my hiking companions, I made it to Damascus. We partook of one last meal together, toasting our accomplishment with Gatorade. Then they moved on, while I found a place to sleep until Laura arrived to drive me home and nurse me back to health.

My odyssey was not over. The following summer, I again went out on the trail, putting another 500 miles behind me. I still have 1,000 miles to go before I reach my dream of standing atop Mount Katahdin, the northern end of the Appalachian Trail. But after my first forty days, things changed—in the woods and at home. There were still plenty of obstacles to overcome, but I no longer felt the old sense of frenzied urgency. Upon my return, I knew that given time, things would work out right. I stopped worrying about whether I could climb the mountains and just laced up my boots, threw on my pack, and went to work.

24

In Search of the Omer

ELLEN COHN

It is said, "On the strength of counting the Omer, Abraham, our father, inherited the Land of Israel."

—MIDRASH RABBAH, PARSHAT EMOR 28:6

As I learned more about the agricultural dimensions of Judaism, I became curious about the 50-day period of the Omer between Passover and Shavuot, when traditional Jews count down for the spring grain to ripen. I had never even heard of the Omer until I was an adult, and yet this seemed like an important time in the Jewish calendar. I was curious about the Omer—generally translated as "sheaf." What was this mysterious countdown? Were we counting days? Were we watching the grain ripen? Which grain? Why? There were more questions. I didn't understand why *barley* was offered at the Temple on the second night of Passover and throughout the Omer, but *wheat* was offered on Shavuot at the end of the Omer. I also knew from the Talmud that Shavuot was the judgment day for the "fruit of the tree." Was there a connection between this *fruit* and the *wheat* offered on Shavuot? I hoped that by exploring the meaning of the Omer, I could answer these questions and better understand the relationship between my ancestors and their plants. I was eager to find another link back to the Land.

The conventional understanding of the Omer is both historical and spiritual: The Omer corresponds to the period when the Israelites left Egypt, wandered in the desert, and finally received the Torah. The journey began with the Jews enslaved in a foreign land and ended with their arrival in their *own* land, tilling their own soil. Journeying across the wilderness exposed the Israelites to relentless wind, heat, and sand, which tested their souls and prepared them for Torah. The Omer period, then, was a kind of spiritual countdown.

I wanted to learn more about the relation between the spiritual story of the Omer and the agricultural one. My curiosity piqued, I ventured out in the Judean hills in search of wheat fields. All across the hills, I found wild grasses shaped like wheat. I collected many grasses I thought were wheat, but all too often they turned out to be weeds or derivatives of other wild grains.

Although my outings among the grasses were enjoyable, my best information came from the agricultural and naturalist societies, which informed me that wheat needed special conditions to grow and that in Israel a brief wheat harvest followed the barley harvest. Wheat needed to be cultivated carefully. This was my clue to understanding the place of these grains in the tradition.

Given my somewhat questionable skills as a natural historian, I now turned my attention to Jewish texts.

Barley versus Wheat

I knew that Shavuot is called the "wheat harvest" (Exod. 34:22). Further, Maimonides confirmed what I had discovered from the agricultural center, "It is well known," he wrote, "that barley ripens before the wheat crop."[1]

Both crops were planted around Sukkot. They grew throughout the fall and winter with the rains and our prayers. But barley would ripen as early as Passover, while wheat would take an additional six weeks to mature. That's why barley, not wheat, could be used for the offering all throughout the Omer.

It surprised me that the early commentators focused so much on the differences between barley and wheat. The *Sefer HaChinuch*, a medieval Jewish commentary, suggests there is a qualitative difference between bringing *sheaves of barley* to the Temple at Passover and during the Omer and bringing *wheat as bread* on Shavuot. "The essence of life for all creatures is in grain," the commentator wrote, "Barley is used for the Omer because it is a more common (and weaker) grain than wheat...." Barley is a food for *all creatures*, but "wheat is the food for *people*." No wonder, then, that barley is brought as an offering in its raw state and wheat is brought as bread. "It is fitting that it [wheat] is prepared in precisely the way a person enjoys and actually eats it."[2]

Many of the early rabbis equated wheat with human knowledge, while barley was considered animal feed. In deriding a fool who calls out that the barley harvest is blossoming well, the rabbis answered, "Go and proclaim your good news about the barley harvest to the horses and donkeys."[3]

My textual research found support from an unlikely source, a young luncheon companion from Iran who was eating a vegetarian dish made of barley. He laughed, proclaiming he was a donkey, since he was eating donkey food. Remembering the rabbis' low regard for barley, I pressed him further. He responded that in his culture, barley is considered comparable to animal feed. Though I do not disdain donkeys or donkey food, I was glad for this bit of contemporary folk wisdom.

Now that I had some insight into the differences between barley and wheat, I could begin to understand why we made the offerings in the first place. The Talmud explained that on Passover, we offer the Omer at the Temple so "that the grain produced in the field will be blessed." On Shavuot, we bring "two loaves of bread so that the fruit of the tree will be blessed." And on Sukkot, "God says, draw water before me on Sukkot so that the rains of the year will be blessed on your behalf."[4]

At each season, our ancestors brought a *special* gift to God. This practice was the traditional way of asking for what we wanted in return. At Passover, we offered barley because we wanted God to provide barley for us throughout the period of the Omer. At Shavuot, we offered wheat bread in the hope of receiving healthy wheat crops. At Sukkot we offered water, trusting God to grant rain all winter long.

The Fruit of the Tree

The other puzzle these passages began to solve is the meaning of the "fruit of the tree." The "fruit of the tree" appears to be the wheat berry. While Shavuot is the holiday for bringing new fruits in general, wheat is considered the premier fruit.

I had no trouble thinking of wheat as a fruit because, in the 1970s, I used to grind my own wheat berries to make bread. And I knew that wheat was a special food because my friends drank wheat grass juice to cure their winter malaise. But was wheat the fruit "of the tree"? Rashi had declared that it was and supported his argument by quoting Rabbi Yehuda, who stated that the "Tree of Knowledge" that stood in the Garden of Eden and tempted Adam and Eve was not an apple tree, but wheat.[5] This interpretation of wheat clarified why the rabbis placed so much value on wheat as opposed to other grains. Wheat was a Jewish symbol of intellectual development.

I had come to a new appreciation of the Omer. The period between Passover and Shavuot molded the wandering Jews—weary and defeated by their own slave mentality—into a free people capable of standing together at Mount Sinai. The Omer period in the spring symbolizes the fruition of wheat and the fruition of the Jewish people.

For years, I tried to integrate the spring cycle of ripening wheat into my life. I joined an Omer support group to help me align myself with that season of freedom and commitment. I was careful to be conscious of the grain I ate during the Omer period. After Passover, I refrained from wheat products, wanting to ready myself for the wheat/knowledge of Shavuot. I was hungry for the essence of wheat.

Western society refers to wheat as "the staff of life." I can testify that it is almost impossible to avoid wheat. Most foods have wheat in them. For me, avoiding wheat took a tremendous effort.

In the weeks after Passover, I made wheat-free barley bread. As other grains became ready to harvest, I used them in my loaves: first rye, oats, then spelt (the rediscovery and popularization of which is only a few years old). An amateur baker, I cannot make barley bread rise. Barley is a weak grain with a sweet taste and gray color—a good addition to baking, but hardly capable of standing on its own. The other grains become increasingly more substantial, easier to knead, rise, and bake.

The first time I use wheat products during the Omer is just before Shavuot, about the time the stalks are beginning to stand straight. When I finally begin baking with wheat, I use the weaker wheat derivatives, such as semolina, prevalent in the Sephardic/Mediterranean culture—more bland, more mushy, and coarser than regular flour. Kneading my new fresh whole-wheat flour for my Shavuot loaves, the dough turns into real bread. It has consistency and malleability and is full of a "meaty" flavor.

And now, my understanding of the Omer is complete. At Passover, when the sickle hits the first standing grain, the barley harvest begins.

Then we count down seven weeks of the Omer to Shavuot and the wheat harvest, when the two loaves of wheat bread are offered. When we first left Egypt, we were like donkeys because we did not have the Commandments to inspire a conscious life; we were fit only for barley, the coarse food of animals. After seven weeks of preparation, we are ready for the food of human beings—wheat for the body and Torah for the soul.[6]

25

Of Dust, Ashes, Comets, and a Three-Year-Old

DAN FINK

Alas! How desolate sits the city once great with people! . . .
Take us back, Eternal One, to Yourself, and let us come back.
Renew our days as of old! —LAMENTATIONS 1:1, 5:21

On the evening of Tisha B'Av, in the Jewish year 5754, my daughter Tanya and I walk up the tree-lined path to the Neale Woods Nature Center Observatory. In cities and towns throughout the world, traditional Jews are gathering to fast and mourn the destruction of Jerusalem nearly 2,000 years ago. They will sit in their synagogues, on low stools or on the floor, reading from Lamentations and chanting dirges. For many, this is the saddest day of the Jewish calendar.

But Tanya and I are not at shul. Instead, we are standing in line, with hundreds of others, to witness a catastrophic event millions of miles away. Tonight the first fragments of Comet Shoemaker-Levy 9 are smashing into Jupiter, throttling its enormous surface and throwing off huge, flaming plumes. Tanya waits with remarkable patience for someone who is not yet three years old but shows little interest when we finally make it to the telescope. She peers into the eyepiece for an instant, then steps down.

Now it is my turn. I locate two of Jupiter's bright white moons, then focus on the great planet itself. At first I see nothing, but with some concentration I spot the tiny dark blotches caused by the collision. The telescope operator tells me they are, in fact, much larger than most nations here on earth.

Suddenly, I sense my own almost infinitesimal smallness. Peering across the immense blackness of space, I tremble and remember other times I have felt this way: alone among the redwoods, hiking in deep canyons, watching electrical storms. I think of the Midrash that teaches how God created and destroyed many worlds before this one, and I know that it is true. All around us worlds are being created and destroyed, every day. We are dust and ashes.

Then, my musing ends. Tanya pulls at my sleeve. "Hey, Daddy, it's time to go. I want to play!" Together, we turn away from the telescope and head out into the sticky summer night. The comet continues to level its blows upon Jupiter, but my daughter and I stroll toward the car, hand in hand, through a forest lit by fireflies.

Sacred Community

Anyone who cares about the environment is concerned about how the earth will *sustain* itself over time. The earth has been so ravaged by chemicals and so depleted by agricultural methods that take more nutrients from the soil than they return that there are serious doubts that sufficient food and timber can be produced for future generations. Is there a way we can live that will both sustain ourselves *and* sustain the earth?

Many Jewish teachings are implicitly linked to *sustainability*. This is evident by the fact that Judaism has been able to sustain itself for more than 3,000 years. While other cultures were building pyramids and conquering territories, the Jewish people—in particular, the rabbis of the first centuries of the Common Era—were concerned with creating a self-sustaining community. Having lost the Temple around which Jewish life had revolved, the rabbis realized they needed to develop a way of life that would ensure the survival of their faith and their people. They became adept at the art of community building and developed such techniques as a detailed body of law, an ethical system of right livelihood (mitzvot), and a mode of communal study that was both a source of pleasure and a path to God. Over time these became so seamlessly integrated into the fabric of Jewish life that they have almost imperceptibly *sustained* the community. Without them, there would be no community, no faith, and no survival.

In fashioning a community-oriented way of life, the rabbis, knowing the potential for human destruction as well as for human creativity, had to try to devise ways to minimize human arrogance. It is exactly this sort of arrogance that desensitizes us to the life all around us and tempts us to exploit the earth. So it is useful to understand how Judaism manages arrogance in order to create community, since only through community can we develop a vision and sustain a way of life that ensures a future for our planet and for all people.

"A sense of place" in the environmental lexicon refers to the relationship between an individual and the place in which he or she lives. The term captures the power and meaning that a place and everything about it—topography, weather, soil, plants, animals—can have on one's life. Environmentalists often argue that the great rush of our society has caused us to lose sight of the value of place. The disappearance of forests, marshes, and grasslands, as well as the breakdown of community life, is the unfortunate consequence of our culture's obliviousness to place.

It should be no surprise that the Bible's understanding of sense of place is religious. It begins by establishing an ordered world in which every living being has a particular place and purpose, and its first stories reveal the damage that can occur when individuals and nations deny and transgress their God-given place.

The Bible suggests that the struggle to recognize the limits of one's place is a core human tension that has challenged humanity since the beginning of time. Transgressing limits leads to a whole spectrum of societal ills from criminal behavior to "abuse" to global destruction. From an environmental perspective, knowing one's place and the boundaries of place is elementary to stewarding the earth. Knowing one's place is also elementary in the building of community.

In the following piece, Rabbi Neil Gillman explores the early stories of Genesis to uncover the Bible's perspective on a sense of place.

26

Cosmos and Chaos: Biblical Views of Creation

NEIL GILLMAN

The noted anthropologist Clifford Geertz contends that the central function of religion is to *order* our experience of the world. Religion seeks to present a world that manifests order rather than anarchy and meaning rather than absurdity, or, to use the terms that will become central to this discussion, cosmos rather than chaos.

Geertz maintains that the need for *order* is deeply rooted in the human personality. Geertz quotes philosopher Susanne Langer: "[Man] can adapt himself somehow to anything his imagination can cope with; but he cannot deal with Chaos. . . .Therefore our most important assets are always the symbols of our general *orientation* in nature, on the earth, in society, and in what we are doing."[1]

To speak of an "orientation" in nature, on earth, or in society is to assume that nature, earth, and society all manifest a fundamental order. A compass permits us to orient ourselves in the world because we structure the world so that it has a north, south, west, and east and because we know that the compass always points to the north. Once we know where north is, we know where the other points of the compass are, and then we know where we are located in that broad general structure. Without this order, we would be lost.

On an infinitely broader scale, then, the task of religion is to create the ultimate structure that underlies all things and to provide the orientation within that structure that permits individuals to "locate" themselves in the world, to provide a sense of "place." Without this, they would be irretrievably "lost."

Creation 1: Developing a Sense of Place

It is a generally accepted conclusion of modern biblical scholarship that Genesis preserves two distinct Creation stories. The first, which scholars call Creation 1, is recorded in Genesis 1–2:4a; and the second, called Creation 2, is in Genesis 2:4b–3:24.[2]

The major theme of Creation 1 is that Creation brings order out of chaos, out of the unformed and the void (*tohu va-vohu*), out of the darkness and the deep and the waters that cover the earth. For the phrase *tohu va-vohu*, the eleventh-century French scholar Rashi, preeminent among Jewish medieval biblical commentators, used the French term *etourdir*, which is the infinitive verb form for "dizzy" or "swirling about"—in other words, anarchy.

Out of this preexisting anarchy, God creates structures. Throughout the text, various forms of the Hebrew root B-D-L, "to separate," are used. Each day God creates by setting off an aspect of the original stuff of Creation. God does not create from nothing. Each element of Creation is assigned its special place and its own day. There is light and there is darkness, heaven and earth, waters above and waters below, a light for the day and a light for the night, vegetation and living creatures. At each stage, God sees that what God has created is good. Once all of Creation is in place, God creates the human beings in God's image and blesses them. The order of the cosmos is then complete. The literary framework of this first Creation narrative underlines its intention to establish order: each day of Creation begins with "God said . . ." and ends with "There was evening and there was morning, a first (second, third, etc.) day."

This theme of *order* in Creation 1 may be understood as an attempt to develop a sense of place. Every aspect of Creation has its *place* in the broad order of things. And since the world is pervaded with this sense of order, human beings also have their place. This distinctly ordered approach to Creation may be called "cosmic" to contrast it to what we will call the "anthropological" or human-centered approach of Creation 2.

Creation 2: Chaos in the World

Creation 2 gives none of the details of Creation 1. We are told nothing about the creation of heaven and earth, of land and seas, or of sun, moon and stars. Significantly, however, this story claims to tell of the creation of "earth and heaven" (Gen. 2:4b), not of "heaven and earth," as in Creation 1. The change is not accidental. In this story, we are not concerned with the order of the cosmos; we are interested in what transpires on earth. More to the point, we are interested in Adam, who is created first in the process, not last, as in Creation 1.

Creation 2, like Creation 1, begins with certain preexisting conditions: there was earth and a flow welling up from the ground that watered the whole surface of the earth (Gen. 2:5–6). God then forms the man from the dust of the earth and blows into his nostrils the breath of life so he becomes a living being. Once the living being is created, God proceeds to plant a garden. Twice we are told (Gen. 2:8 and 2:15) that the man is given a "place" in the garden. The second time, he is also given a role: "to till it and tend it." God then causes trees to grow in the garden and gives the man the right to eat of all the trees, except for the Tree of Knowledge of Good and Bad, ". . . for as soon as you eat of it, you shall die"(Gen. 2:17).

Only after the man and the garden have been created does God form the wild beasts and the winged creatures (Gen. 2:19). Then the man is asked to name them. There follows the creation of the woman, and the familiar drama with the serpent, which leads to God's expulsion of the man and the woman from Eden (Gen. 2:23).[3]

The ordering or structuring thrust of Creation 2 is not as evident as it is in Creation 1. But it is surely *implicit* in God's creation of the Garden of Eden, within which the man is placed and which effectively becomes the center of the world, an anticipation of the role Jerusalem and the Temple will play in the later tradition.[4] It is also evident in the man's naming of the creatures of the world. To name, of course, is to distinguish, to assign a distinctive character. It is, in this case, a way to structure Creation.

But the more interesting issue is the relation of Creation 2 to Creation 1. These are not simply two alternative versions of Creation that the editor(s) had to include because they were both sacred texts that could not be ignored. Rather, they supplement each other, and Creation 2 extends Creation 1.

If, in fact, Creation 1 describes how God brought cosmos out of the primordial chaos, Creation 2 provides one version of how chaos was reintroduced into the world through the primordial sin of Adam and Eve. In this story, the serpent warned Adam and Eve that God forbade eating the fruit of the Tree of Knowledge of good and bad: "as soon as you eat of it, your eyes will be opened and you will be like God" (Gen. 3:5). Unsatisfied with their own place and hungry to be like God, they ate of the fruit and crossed a boundary. It was through this act of transgression that Adam and Eve introduced chaos into their own lives and into the ordered world of the garden. As a result, they were exiled.

To have a place is to be secure. To be in exile is to be "lost," displaced, and vulnerable.[5] If cosmos is characterized by occupying an assigned "place," then chaos is signified by "displacement."

The transgression of boundaries and the resulting chaos is a theme that is established in Creation 2 and recurs in subsequent chapters of the Bible. In the next story, Cain violates a boundary in his attempt to displace his brother, Abel, to receive God's favor (Gen. 4:4–5). Cain, too, is exiled—"You shall become a ceaseless wanderer on earth" (Gen. 4:12)—and with Cain, the full implications of exile become explicit: "anyone who meets me may kill me" (Gen. 4:14).

In each of these two paradigmatic narratives, displacement (exile) is the punishment for trespass. But, it is a displacement of a different kind. If displacement indicates chaos, then chaos begets more chaos. Displacement is the source of chaos; it is also its consequence. We can now understand the "anthropological" dimension of Creation 2 in terms of humanity's reintroduction of chaos into the world.[6]

Tension between Order and Chaos

Creation 2, then, effectively introduces what we might call "the age of history," that eon between the cosmos that was and the cosmos that will be in the "days to come."[7] The age of history is marked by unremitting tension between cosmos and chaos. A good deal of that original cosmos still persists in, for example, the cycles of day and night and of the seasons. Yet chaos also persists, both in nature and in human affairs.[8] Indeed the first eleven chapters of Genesis can be viewed as a panorama in which moments of order or cosmos—*knowing* one's place—alternate with moments of chaos—*losing* one's place.

The first story of Creation begins with cosmos emerging out of chaos and concludes with the symbol of ultimate order, Shabbat, the seventh day, when God completed his work and rested (Gen. 2:1–3). This sense of cosmos is upset by three primordial sins, each of which transgresses boundaries: the story of Adam and Eve in Eden, the story of Cain, and somewhat more ambiguously, the story of the *Nephilim*, the offspring of the divine beings and human women (Gen. 6:1–4). The common theme of the punishments for each of these sins is displacement (exile) and death or at least the threat of death (Gen. 3:19; 4:12–13; 6:13).

By the end of chapter 6, chaos is rampant on earth. "The Lord saw how great was man's wickedness on earth, and how every plan devised by his mind was nothing but evil all the time" (Gen. 6:5). The individualized sins of Adam, Eve, Cain, and the *Nephilim* have now become a generalized human condition. God mourns the chaos that has emerged following Creation, regrets having made human beings, and resolves to blot out all living things. God will punish the humanly caused chaos by provoking another kind of chaos: the flood. The flood is explicitly portrayed as an uprooting of the order established in Creation 1. "All the foundations of the great deep burst apart, and the floodgates of the sky broke open" (Gen. 7:11). The boundaries established through the seven days of Creation are destroyed, and the world is reduced to the dizzy, chaotic state of *tohu va vohu.*

Toward the end of the story, there is a note of the consolation to come: "But Noah found favor with the Lord" (Gen. 6:8). There is also the ark, a safe "place" for human beings and creatures. Finally, God remembers Noah and the creatures in the ark. The waters disappear, and God promises never again to destroy the earth, "since the devisings of man's mind are evil from his youth" (Gen. 8:21). God seems resigned to the inevitably of a persistent tension between cosmos and chaos on earth.

The Noah story ends with the familiar organizing structures of Creation 1: "Seedtime and harvest, cold and heat, summer and winter, day and night shall not cease" (Gen. 8:23). God, once again—the echoes of Creation 1 are unmistakable—blesses Noah and his sons (Gen. 9:1) and establishes a covenant with them and with all creatures, never again to destroy all flesh. The symbol of that covenant is the rainbow (Gen. 9:9–17).

But again, chaos raises its head. Noah's drunkenness and his incestuous mating with his daughters (Gen. 9:20–27) are an act of transgression and clearly a sin of displacement, punished with exile. Next comes the Tower of Babel. Finally, these early narratives conclude with the birth of Abram, and we are launched (Gen. 12:1) into the reconstitution of cosmos culminating with God's covenant with Abram, later with Isaac and Jacob, and eventually with their posterity at Sinai. Torah and, by implication, the Jewish religion as a whole become the source of cosmos for this community.

Interspersed through these narratives (Gen. 4:16–5:32, 10:1–32, 11:10–32) are three genealogical tables. The placement of these genealogies may be obscure, but their import is clear: they represent an ordering device, a way of structuring human history during this early primordial age.[9]

The broad pattern, then, can be viewed as reflecting the ongoing tension between order and chaos. God creates a cosmic order out of primordial chaos, but that cosmos is constantly threatened by the chaos that human beings introduce into the world. God punishes the chaos of human transgressions with exile and then with more chaos, consistently returning the world to a state of order, only to see it upset once again. The final emergence of Abram and the later history of biblical religion should be seen within this context as God's further attempt to provide this community with the resources to maintain a sense of an ordered world.

Finally, it must be noted that from an anthropological perspective, this entire process reflects Geertz's and Langer's conviction that what the Genesis stories are portraying is a deeply felt, perpetual, and intuitive human need for an ordered world, a world in which human beings can orient themselves and thereby find their "place," along with an attempt at explaining the chaos that clearly persists in the human experience.

An Eternal Shabbat

Limiting ourselves to these Genesis narratives, two facets of this overview should be noted. First, God is the source of cosmos. Second, humanity is the source of chaos. In this view, God is engaged in a wrestling match with human beings, who perpetually and in various ways threaten the God-imposed cosmic order.[10]

Today, with cosmos and chaos still very much in tension, our task is to pray for—and to actively work for—the ultimate redemption to come.

A powerful symbol of the restoration of order and the knowledge of our place in it is the Sabbath, which is both a "memorial to the work of Creation" (as alluded to in Exod. 20:8–11 and 31:13–14) and a "foretaste of the age to come."[11] In another context, the age to come is referred to as "a day that is entirely Sabbath and rest for eternal life."[12] In this reading, every Sabbath reflects beginning and end and recalls the cosmos upon its creation and the cosmos that will be at the end.

The Sabbath, then, represents an age that is *already* quasi-realized: it is present in the here and now, however momentarily. Jews are also given other realized moments, such as the Day of Atonement and the climax of the Jewish marriage liturgy. But more broadly, Torah, *halachah*, and the very structuring of the Temple itself represent islands of realized cosmos within our chaotic world.

From this perspective, Torah, mitzvot, and the Temple cult are the resources God has given us to structure and discipline the chaotic impulses within us and teach us our proper place. The ultimate purpose of this system—which is nothing else than Jewish religion as a whole—is redemptive. It is nothing less than to bring about the eternal Sabbath, the age where cosmos will rule for all time.

For centuries people have read the Jacob and Esau story in the Bible and have identified Jacob as the hero and Esau as the villain. Esau's reputation has stuck, and his name has been associated with everything evil and everything "other": the Romans, the Crusades, the Nazis. In this essay, Shamu Fenyvesi revisits the brothers and questions our condemnation of Esau. What have we lost, as individuals, as communities, and as a culture, by banishing Esau and distancing ourselves forever from that which is unfamiliar?

27

Restoring a Blessing

SHAMU FENYVESI

Esau emerged from the womb first, covered with hair and silent. Jacob came out squalling, with one hand wrapped firmly around his twin brother's heel, like the many-fingered roots of a caper bush clinging to a limestone cliff.[1]

Esau fell in love with the mountains of Edom, the pyramid peaks, the steep canyons, and the long sandy plains stretching to the valley floor. Esau was a hunter and a wanderer. Jacob preferred the cool shadows of the tent; he was a thinker.

During the new moon, Esau would wait for the blanket of darkness atop a crumbling hill, embedded with tiny imprints of life from a time before Abraham and Sarah, before Adam and Lilith. He would kneel before a stone, the color of a camel's back, which had been planted in the ground and surrounded by a half-circle of rocks in the shape of a pre-festival moon. The assemblage was no Stonehenge. The hare had to crouch to conceal herself behind the rocks, and years later an angry foot would scatter them like so many seeds of a desert grass in the wind of a winter storm.

Esau awaited the mountain goats' descent to their favorite cluster of acacias. Their black tongues eagerly sucked in the green meat of the tiny leaves. Acacias are shaped like inverted pyramids with foliage so sparse that Esau often watched the moon through their branches and missed none of the orb's subtle features. As the fire of the dawn tipped the mountains, Esau would greet the sun with loud praises and lay on the altar the choicest meat of the goat he had speared.

Esau fathered a tribe of hunters and shepherds who worshipped sun and moon, leopard, and ostrich. They planted small altars of stone in the desert and knelt in front of them before the hunt. They danced in the winter rains and spoke with the many spirits of the plants.

Jacob, with a blessing stolen from their father, led a nation of shepherds and farmers who prayed to a God that they believed no stones could contain. They praised their one all-embracing God in as many ways as the wind blows and the rain falls. The earth was a sister to them, not a mother, and they would not speak with rocks or pray to figures of animals scratched into the soft sandstone cliffs. Jacob's people would eventually scatter the small stone circles and defeat the priests of Esau's nation in miracle contests. Centuries later, Jacob's wise men would speak of the absurdity of worshipping the sun and moon and turn their people's heads to the book and away from the mountains.

A few months ago, wandering in the abandoned mountains of my ancestors' desert home south of the Dead Sea, I stumbled upon a half-circle of rocks like a pre-festival moon, gathered obediently around a diminutive altar. The rocks, set against the dry slopes, all the color of a camel's back, drew in my eyes. Like Esau, I cover more hills and cross more brooks than I turn pages. I have chosen to read the red canyons and the advancing storm. Now, as I find myself walking through the words of Jacob's books, I ask that the blessing stolen by Jacob be restored to Esau.

Sun God, One God

Have we forgotten the reconciliation of the two brothers on the plains above the Jabbok River? Do we remember their long embrace?

A middle-aged Jacob, his obstinate righteousness tempered by tempestuous dreams that left him with a limp, crossed the river to make peace with his brother. In the deep rift valley, midway between the desolate salt lands of the Dead Sea and the verdant pine-covered hills of the Sea of Galilee, Jacob shed three tears for his brother. One tear fell from his right eye, one from his left, and one hung suspended from his eyelash.[2]

Esau approached without faltering. He was sure only of his readiness to forgive. Jacob was as conscious of his wrongdoing as a child is of his innocence. Thirty years after the deception, Esau accepted his brother's silent apology with the patience of a desert perennial enduring a long drought. They embraced with the love and fear and anger only bloodlines share.

In the months that followed, Esau would shake his brother from the comfortable confines of his thoughts to stalk wild asses in the resplendent light of the festival moon or to collect capers from the mustard-colored canyon walls. Jacob's limbs, soft from days in his tent, became dry and wiry, like branches of desert shrubs in the oven heat of the blinding summer.

As they walked across plateaus of sharp flint, black as a goat's tongue, Jacob, always at his brother's heel, would engage the silent Esau in questions of justice and morality. Esau, who moved with the loping speed of a young hyena, was schooled in the stern responsibilities of life on God's earth.

The brothers cultivated a small field of barley together in the sandy valley bottom. Jacob argued for a settled life. Like Abel and Abraham, Esau chose to wander the hills. Esau did not want to transform the open desert flats into a grid of grain, nor did he want to be tamed by the demands of cultivation. However, out of love for his brother, Esau agreed to farm a small field of barley. Esau's one condition was that they always leave the edges of the field for the poor and for the wild beasts; without such an offering, Esau insisted, the soil would cry out for justice, and thorns and thistles would flourish in place of grain.[3]

In their wanderings among the steep red canyons and the small oases, Jacob learned from Esau to tell history from the rocks, to foretell weather in the wind and to hunt gazelle and wild ass, mountain goat and hare.

Esau learned about the Sabbath, the day of rest and celebration, time to meet the wildflower and the lizard on equal terms of shared origin. Esau came to respect the day as a time when he would abandon the tools of his trade and contemplate the underlying mystery of Creation. The brothers would sit atop the small rise above the acacias in the dry river bed and greet with songs and blessings the sudden desert dusk— which changed, if only for moments, the dusty landscape into the brilliant shades of a thirsty conflagration.

Esau praised the willow and the lizard. Jacob called upon the tree and the beast to join with him in his praise of the Holy One. Esau spoke with a sun god and Jacob with his one God. However, a passing shepherd, hurrying his flock before him in the gathering darkness, could barely tell the difference between their prayers.

On the eve of the following sunset, they would wait until the three stars of Orion's belt shone clearly in the black sky. Then, greeting the coming week, they burned the fragrant leaves of desert thyme, stared into the flame of a candle of beeswax, and drank dark wine from a cup carved from a wild goat's horn.

Can We Hear the Morning Stars?

Jacob's descendants soon forgot the wisdom of the wilderness and turned their eyes instead to the books, as had Jacob in his youth. In their devotion to a God who lived not on earth, they propagated law after law and lost the taste for wandering in the desert in the light of the festival moon.

Esau's grandson Job repeated the message to Jacob's people who loved a God who watched their every move and was partial to their fate.[4] Through his revelations, Job taught Jacob's heirs—haughty in their righteousness—that they were just one vessel through which God's creativity flowed. Job, like Esau before him, learned from the ostrich and the lion, the raven and the desert grasses. In Job's awe before God, Jacob's descendants were reminded that the wild ass laughs at our cities, and the ostrich, running with outstretched wings, scoffs at the horse and rider.

Have we now forgotten the simple democracy of all beings that pervaded the lives of Esau and Job? Esau's pact with the lizard, the moon, and the limestone cliffs? How Job sang when he saw the desert explode in purple blossoms?

Are the children of Esau still banished to the heathen Red Mountains of Jordan? Have we all become Jacobs, confined to shaded tents, crooked backs hunched over books?

Before crossing the Jabbok River, Jacob became Israel, "the one who wrestled with God." He was no longer Jacob, "the Supplanter." Are we still trying, in his stead, to supplant Esau?

Do we think that in our books, we have already been to the edge of the universe? Or can we, as did Esau, Job, and a middle-aged Jacob, hear the morning stars sing?

In the 1970s, the environmental movement was focused on the individual, on recycling and conscious consumption. The New Age came along and emphasized the need for individual change all the more. Individuals must take responsibility for themselves and for the environment, but individual action alone is not enough. Neither will it sustain us. Environmental problems are too profound for any of us to solve by ourselves. We live in community, in constant relationship with other people. We are as one organism: Jewish tradition teaches that we are all responsible for each other. In the following essay, David Ehrenfeld, in his reading of the *Sh'ma*, the key prayer of the Jewish tradition, underscores the centrality of communal responsibility in Judaism.

28

What Is the Common Wealth?

DAVID EHRENFELD

In his essay "The Gift of Good Land," the gift that Wendell Berry is referring to is the Land of Israel, a gift from God to the Israelites, who have just come out of Egypt. But like so many gifts, even heavenly ones, there are strings attached. In Berry's words, "'The Promised Land' is not a permanent gift. It is given, but only for a time, and only for so long as it is properly used."[1]

If we go back to the story of Eden, the earth and the life it contains is a gift—the original gift, the first wealth. But unlike Eden, the Promised Land of Israel is a gift to a whole people, to an entire *community*. In this story, we see a new element introduced, because Adam and Eve, whatever they were, were not a community. The Adam and Eve story is profound—even more so if we realize that Adam is from the Hebrew, *adamah*, or "earth," and Eve is from *chava*, related to "living." Nevertheless, without any concept of community, the story's significance for our lives is limited. By contrast, the story of the Israelites in the Promised Land is usually thought to be about the relationship between God, the community, and the Land. It places far less emphasis on the individual than does the story of Eden.

Yet four elements, not three, are needed for a whole story: God, community, individual, Land. Where in the Jewish tradition is the necessary connection between God, the community, *and* the individual—in their relationships with the Land—established? To answer this, we can look at the *Sh'ma*, the central prayer of Judaism.

This prayer is named after its first word, which is the command to hear or listen. The *Sh'ma* is the first prayer taught to a Jewish child and the last prayer recited by or in the presence of a dying person. In between, it is recited at least twice a day, morning and evening, by ritually observant Jews. After its opening sentence, "Hear O Israel, the Lord our God, the Lord is One," the prayer from Deut. 6:4–9 continues:

> And you shall love the Lord your God with all your heart, and with all your soul, and with all your might. And these words, which I command you this day, shall be on your heart; and you shall teach them diligently to your children, and shall talk of them when you sit in your house, and rise up. And you shall bind them for a sign on your hand, and they shall be for frontlets between your eyes. And you shall write them on the doorposts of your house, and on your gates.

The second paragraph of the prayer is from Deut. 11:13–21.

> And it shall come to pass, if you shall harken diligently to My commandments which I command you this day, to love the Lord your God, and to serve Him with all your heart and all your soul, then I will give the rain of your land in its season, the former rain and the latter rain, that you may gather in your corn, and your wine, and you shall eat and be satisfied . . .

And you shall teach them to your children, talking of them when you sit in your house, and when you walk by the way, and when you lie down, and when you rise up. And you shall write them on the doorposts of your house, and on your gates; that your days may be multiplied, and the days of your children, on your land which the Lord swore to your fathers to give them, as long as the days of the heavens above the earth.

The Need for Community

How do these passages relate the person to the community and then to the good land? And why did the early rabbis choose to meld these repetitive verses of Deuteronomy together into a single prayer? In the original Hebrew, the answer stands out in absolute clarity. But the problem with the English translation is that the second person pronoun, "you," and its possessive forms, "your" and "yours," are the same in singular and plural. In Hebrew, the singular and plural forms of "you" and "your" are separate and distinct.

All of the first paragraph of the *Sh'ma*, an injunction to love God, to instruct your children in God's law—the code of moral and religious behavior, to bind the injunction on your arm and forehead, and to post it on the doorposts and gates of your house—is written in the singular. You as an individual are responsible for upholding this law, which in its entirety deals with every phase of your private and public life, from the day you are born to the day you die.

The consequences of obeying or not obeying are in the next paragraph of the *Sh'ma*, which is written in the second person *plural*. What a difference! If you, and you, and you, and the majority of other individuals who make up the community live right, then the community reaps the reward: the rain in its season, the grain, the wine, the oil, the grass for your cattle, and the satisfaction of good food. The rabbis who first created the *Sh'ma* as a prayer were farmers or the children of farmers. They knew that the common wealth comes to a community, any community, only when its individual members live just and righteous lives and pass this way of life on to their children. As Wendell Berry writes in *The Unsettling of America*, "The use of the world is finally a personal matter, and the world can be preserved in health only by the forbearance and care of a multitude of persons. . . . One must begin in one's own life the private solutions that can only *in turn* become public solutions."[2]

But what if the majority of individuals live badly? Again, the words of the *Sh'ma* are very clear, and they are in the plural, addressed to the whole community. There will be no rain, and the ground will not yield fruit, and you will perish from off the good land that the Lord gives you. The few good persons will suffer along with the many bad. Thus, common poverty and despair are the alternatives to common wealth.

To make this lesson plain, the last three verses of the second paragraph of the *Sh'ma* switch back and forth in their address, even in mid-sentence, between the second person plural, then the singular, and finally the plural at the end. First, "And you shall teach them to your children": here the text is in the plural and is addressed to the community, because education is partly a communal responsibility. Then, "talking of them, when you sit in your house, and when you walk by the way, and when you lie down, and when you rise up. And you shall write them upon the doorposts of your house, and upon your gates": here, the text is in the singular and is addressed to each individual. Finally, "that your days may be multiplied, and the days of your children, on the land which the Lord swore to your fathers to give them, as long as the days of the heavens above the earth": now, it switches back once again to the plural; the rewards—the common wealth—will come to the community.

The Wealth of the Earth

Throughout the Hebrew Bible, with few exceptions, wealth—the produce of the land, health, and the survival and prospering of the children, who are the next generation—is promised to the deserving *community*, not to the deserving individual. The same is true of punishment. But it is the individual who experiences delight or suffering. There will always be some people in the community who do not merit the common fate. Unmerited delight can be borne easily enough, but unmerited suffering is very hard. The book of Job attempts to deal with this. I'm not even going to try.

So the common wealth is brought about through a ceaseless, positive interaction between the person and the earth, the person and the community, and the community and the earth. Berry writes about this interaction in *The Unsettling of America:*

> Body, soul (or mind or spirit), community, and world are all susceptible to each other's influence, and they are all conductors of each other's influence. The body is damaged by the bewilderment of the spirit, and it conducts the influence of that bewilderment into the earth, the earth conducts it into the community . . .[3]

The complexity of relationships sounds as if achieving the common wealth must be very difficult. I'll let Deut. 30:11–14 have the final word about that:

> For this commandment which I command you this day, is not too hard for you, neither is it far off. It is not in heaven, that you should say: "Who shall go up for us to heaven, and bring it unto us, and make us to hear it, that we may do it?" Neither is it beyond the sea, that you should say: "Who shall go over the sea for us, and bring it unto us, and make us to hear it, that we may do it?" But the word is very nigh unto you, in your mouth, and in your heart, that you may do it.

Each "you" in this passage is written in the singular.

Deuteronomy is named *Devarim* in the original Hebrew, which means "words." The words of this book are words we can stand by as we work for the common wealth.

Fifty years ago, Aldo Leopold, considered by some to be the father of the modern environmental movement, developed the notion of a land ethic. Leopold argued that although our civilization has an unspoken code of proper conduct for humanity and society, there is no ethical system that prescribes the proper relation for humanity and the land. He believed that without a land ethic, Western civilization would slowly destroy itself.

Leopold charged that the "Abrahamic" traditions in particular were negligent with regard to addressing the relation of people to their land. In fact, as we have seen, Jewish tradition does have a land ethic embedded in its way of life. The beauty of the Jewish system is that Jewish law addresses community and land simultaneously. Taking care of community involves taking care of the land and vice versa. In this essay, Victor Raboy probes into the fine points of the terse code of Jewish law, the Mishnah, to uncover an ethical system that would be wise to consider today.

29

Jewish Agricultural Law:
Ethical First Principles and Environmental Justice

VICTOR RABOY

*And when you reap the harvest of your land, do not reap complete-
ly the corner of your field, do not gather the gleaning of the harvest. And do not glean the vineyard and do not gather the fallen
fruit of your vineyard; leave them for the poor and the stranger; I
am the Lord your God.* —LEVITICUS 19:9–10

Farming was the primary occupation of the Jewish people when the Mishnah, the Jewish law code, was compiled in the second century C.E. So it is no surprise that the *first* volume of the Mishnah is called *Zeraim* or "Seeds," and it addresses the obligations of farmers. We can surmise from its place in the Mishnah that the authors believed agriculture was one of the first activities requiring ethical standards. The fundamental agricultural principles expressed in *Zeraim* remain critical tenets today, and they can guide us as we strive to live more ethically with each other and the land.

All eleven books of *Zeraim* pertain to agriculture except the first one, which deals not with agriculture, but with blessings. It was considered appropriate, if not essential, that a uniquely *Jewish* law code begin with the consideration of blessings.[1]

The first book in *Zeraim* after *Berachot*/Blessings is *Peah*. *Peah*, or "Corner," addresses the obligations of the farmer to the poor and the stranger and is so named because it focuses on laws associated with leaving "the corner of the field" for the less fortunate. One explanation for *Peah's* prominent place in the Mishnah is that people's material duties to each other, as described in *Peah*, should directly follow people's spiritual duties to God, as described in *Berachot*.

As the Talmud commentator, S. M. Lehrman, notes, the "two most salient characteristics of the Jewish people receive prominence" in *Peah*: love of the soil of *Eretz Yisrael* and concern for the poor.[2] One acts righteously by showing love for the land and by leaving a generous portion of the harvest for the poor.

Providing Crops for the Poor

As described by the book of *Peah*, the dues owed by the farmer to the poor fall into four categories: the corner crop; gleanings, or grain that has fallen to the ground during harvest; forgotten sheaths, grain collected but misplaced or forgotten; and the "poor man's tithe," which is collected every third and sixth year of the seven-year Sabbatical year cycle. The first four chapters of *Peah* deal with the obligation of *peah* itself, as follows:

> These are the things which have no fixed measure . . . *peah* . . .
> first fruits . . . charity . . . and Talmud Torah [the study of Torah].

These things are the fruits of which man enjoys in this world
. . . honoring one's father and mother, and charity, and making peace between man and his fellow; but Talmud Torah is
equal to them all. (*Peah* 1:1)

In this chapter, the amount of *peah* is not specified. Leviticus 19,
which provides the basis for *peah*, simply commands that the corners
and the gleanings be left for the poor and the stranger, without desig-
nating the amount that must be left. The above chapter from *Peah* 1:1—
so significant it has been incorporated into the daily prayer—lists other
things "which have no fixed measure": giving first fruits, charity, and
study. Nothing is more valuable than study, not even honoring one's parents or making peace. The juxtaposition suggests that just as one should
study Torah as much as possible, one should give *peah* maximally.

The next passage provides details:

One must not give for *peah* less than one-sixtieth. And though
they said there was no fixed limit [no definite amount] for *peah*,
all depends on the size of the field and the number of poor and
the extent of one's generosity. (*Peah* 1:2)

This passage indicates that a literal application of the minimum
rule is not acceptable. Each case must be considered on its own merits.
The proper amount of *peah* depends on the size of the field, the number of poor people, and the generosity of the landowner. For example,
what if a field is large, and the poor are few? Then the minimum rule
makes good sense: one should not give less than one-sixtieth. But what
if the field is small and the poor are many? Or if, in a certain year, rain
floods the crops, or too little rain creates drought, or pests destroy the
harvest? In such cases, one must depend on the generosity of the
landowners. Since such conditions usually affect most of the farmers in
a given area, and since the number of poor is not determined by any
one individual, the proper fulfillment of *peah* calls for a communal
rather than individual approach.

In the study of the Mishnah, variant readings of a given word or
phrase are common. For example, some read the final phrase of *Peah*
1:2 as the "quality or extent of the crop" or the "extent of poverty," rather

than "the extent of one's generosity." Whatever the reading, the intention of the passage is unmistakable: it is to benefit the poor maximally. The first principles of Talmud, then, concern the poor. As Maimonides observed in his study of this portion of Talmud, providing for the poor or less fortunate is the preeminent positive commandment.

As the book continues, more specifics on *peah* are provided. It is crucial to leave a sufficient amount for *peah* regardless of where in the field it is left (*Peah* 1:3). Maimonides insists that no matter how much is left for the poor from sources other than *peah*, the *peah* contribution must still constitute no less than one-sixtieth of the field. In addition, one must designate a portion of the crop specifically as *peah*, for harvest by the poor, and not simply donate it to the public at large. The public includes the entire community, rich and poor, human and animal. In the Sabbatical year, all crops are declared public (*hefker*), free to anyone for the taking. However, declaring one's crop public does not fulfill the obligation of *peah*, the intention of which is give *preferential* treatment to the poor.

The Mishnah continues:

> They laid down a general principle concerning *peah*: Whatever is a food, and is stored, and grows from the ground, and is harvested altogether and is brought in for storage, is liable for *peah*. Grain and pulse fall into this category. (*Peah* 1: 4)

This general principle refers to crops we think of as staples, such as grains, pulses (which include beans, peas, and lentils), and some fruits and vegetables. The five biblical species of grain were wheat, barley, rye, oats, and spelt. Since mushrooms were not viewed as growing from the soil, they were exempt from *peah*, as were certain other vegetables.

The Mishnah goes on to list the kinds of trees that are subject to *peah* and to define the point in the harvest before which the obligation to *peah* must be satisfied (*Peah* 1:5–6). A later chapter deals with *peah* in complex situations: divided fields, fields planted with more than one kind of seed, and fields that have been robbed (*Peah* 2). Details are also provided for special cases such as partial ownership, small plots of grain, and grain harvested in stages (*Peah* 3).

The Poor and the Wealthy
Are Responsible for Creation

The passages concerning how and when *peah* should be distributed in the case of hanging vines and date palms appear contradictory
and have occasioned much discussion (*Peah* 4:1-2). One passage
enjoins the landowner himself to "bring down" the fruit of the date
palm—thereby avoiding any possible injury that may befall a poor person while gathering the fruit—and to distribute it equally to the poor.
In this case, the landowner assumes all risk and is even responsible for
the equitable distribution to the poor. The principle here is that the no
poor persons should be subjected to "occupational" hazards or inequal-
ity on account of their poverty. The next passage seems to contradict the
first; here, the landowner is *not* responsible for "bringing down" the
fruits; that's up to the poor themselves. "Even [if only] one out of a hundred recipients prefer gathering or snatching the fruit" on his or her own,
the method of individual "snatching" should be adopted.

The Mishnah continues this discussion: "*Peah* must not be cut with
scythes or be uprooted with spades, in order that they [the poor and
the stranger] do not strike at one another" (*Peah* 4:4). The intention,
once again, is to protect the poor from injury, either accidental or intentional, including injury from each other, while gathering *peah*. The poor,
too, have obligations, which the Mishnah notes:

> If one took some *peah* and cast it over the remainder, then he
> gets nothing at all. If he threw himself on it, or spread his cloak
> over it, it is taken away from him. (*Peah* 4: 3)

If a person tries to take and hide more than a fair share of *peah*, that
person should get nothing. The poor, too, must act responsibly.

The Mishnah details the procedures for collecting *peah* for the maximum convenience of all concerned. The poor are permitted to come
for *peah* in the morning, at noon, and in the late afternoon. These times
afford ample opportunities for children, women with children, and the
elderly to collect fresh food several times a day. The prescribed times also
enable the owner to be present during the collection periods (*Peah* 4:5).

A concluding passage of the Mishnah, which concerns grain fallen into ant holes during the harvest, is a striking example of the extent to which the rabbis went to make sure a crucial principle would be implemented fairly—and without detriment to the needy.

Ants squirrel away grain in their holes. The Mishnah specifies that if grain is discovered in the *upper* layers of the ant hole, it belongs to the poor. In all likelihood, this grain has fallen *after* the harvest and would be considered "gleanings." However if the grain is found in the *lower* layers of the ant colony, where the ants have stored it for themselves *before* the harvest, the grain belongs to the landowner; it is not considered "gleanings." Rabbi Meir, who argues that "all belong to the poor, for gleanings about which there is any doubt are regarded as gleanings," has the final say in this passage, and his view, that the poor should be given every benefit of the doubt, is accepted by tradition (*Peah* 4:11).

How much of the yield of a field ends up in ant holes? No doubt, not very much. However, the principle is that no matter how minor the concern, it still deserves the same attention as an issue of obvious significance. Seemingly trivial questions may yield profound insights.

To summarize, *Peah* commands us to contribute as much as we can, not less than one-sixtieth of our produce, but up to a maximum amount to be determined by the extent of our harvest, the extent of poverty, and the extent of our own generosity. The community must collectively determine what things are to be distributed as *peah*—and when. Owners must assume the risks associated with harvest, not the poor. The poor, on the other hand, must not cheat the system. Both the wealthy and the less fortunate are responsible for making it work. Finally, each part of Creation, a whole wheat field or a single ant hole, must be given equal consideration.

Peah and Today's World

Grains like barley and wheat were the staples of life in early Middle Eastern communities, as they are today. The central meeting place of our ancestral community was the threshing floor, where grain was separated from chaff. The threshing floor served as the basic institution of early civilization and evolved beyond its agricultural uses into the site of civic, judicial, and religious functions.[3] In effect, many institutions of modern Jewish society evolved out of early agrarian culture and agricultural ethics.

Over time, early agricultural traditions concerning care for the poor, such as *peah*, were replaced by the broader concept of charity. Between the inception of the Mishnah and its codification (circa 200 c.e.), laws concerning charity other than *peah* were dealt with briefly. However, when Maimonides completed his code approximately 1,000 years later (1195 c.e.), he gave the subject of charity a prominent place in the final four chapters of his "Book of Agriculture."

To appreciate the role of *peah* relative to the laws of charity, we must consider Hebrew communities before their dispersal during the Babylonian Exile. We also must distinguish between the local and the transient poor. In these early communities, most people were involved in agriculture, either as workers or landowners. Land tenure was relatively stable, and cultural cohesiveness was relatively undisturbed, certainly compared to subsequent Jewish history. In such an environment, a holistic system, such as *peah*, of caring for the poor could evolve. *Peah* primarily served the local poor, whereas "charity" served the transient poor. While both are important mitzvot, in this system *peah* would play a more central role than occasional charity.

With the Babylonian Exile, Jews found themselves in urban occupations rather than agriculture, and *peah*'s predominance gave way to charity. The cultural cohesiveness and stable landownership and occupancy that characterized the early Palestinian community unraveled in the face of exile and community disruption. The shift from rural to urban living continues to this day in both the Diaspora and Israel, as well as in most other nations throughout the world. As fewer and fewer people in Jewish exile communities were directly involved in farming, the ability to care for the poor via *peah* diminished, and "alms giving"— which originally was a nominal practice—grew in significance.

Two different versions of the Talmud developed, reflecting the shift from rural to urban living. One developed in the urban Jewish community that was in exile in Babylonia; and the other developed in the rural Jewish community that remained in Palestine. Both versions contain essentially the same Mishnah, of which *Zeraim* is the first volume. However, the Gemara—the rabbis' commentary on the Mishnah—differs. The Babylonian Talmud contains (with the exception of *Berachot*) no Gemara concerning *Zeraim*, but the Palestinian Talmud does.

The Babylonian Talmud ultimately gained precedence and is the one best known today. The absence of commentary of *Zeraim* in the Babylonian Talmud indicates these agricultural laws may have lacked relevance to Jewish life during the Babylonian Exile. It further points to the separation of the Jewish people from their own land and, as the Diaspora developed, from land ownership and agriculture in general. The lack of Gemara on *Zeraim* in the Babylonian Talmud assumes a people with a very different world-view from those who placed *Zeraim* first in the Mishnah a few centuries before.

What ethical price have Jews paid for being distanced from agriculture and the land and for abandoning *peah* in favor of charity? Let's consider two principles underlying the tradition of *peah*: the poor should be respected, and they should collect *peah* themselves, with the owner in attendance and responsible for their safety. In a society where such a tradition is observed, respect for the poor is maintained, and the gap between rich and poor is lessened. The wealthy must work directly with the poor, inviting them into their fields.

Contrast this with contemporary American culture, which demeans those in need and separates the haves and have-nots. The well-off pay their dues through taxes, while the poor receive charity through welfare checks. The poor derive no dignity from this system, and the rich are alienated. The wisdom of *peah* is, in part, that it brings the poor and the well-off together in a regular way.

How might we apply the principles of *peah* today? First, we can renew the traditions of *peah* for all involved in agriculture. Jew and non-Jew, small family farm and corporate executive, could invite the less fortunate into their fields to harvest no less than one-sixtieth of the produce. Since the poor should be placed at minimal risk, the farmers must surely avoid the use of agricultural chemicals and pesticides. When the giving of *peah* requires hand harvesting, a sense of connection with nature would be an important side benefit.

Respect the Poor, Respect the Land

The immediate problem is, of course, that in Western society, few people are directly involved in agricultural production. In the United States, less than five percent of the population are farmers. Therefore, we would need to extend *peah* to other forms of production. After all, if agriculture was the main industry for early communities, *peah* can be conceived of as an early form of industrial ethics. What if no less than one-sixtieth of all industrial production was also routinely donated to the poor? What if factory owners were obliged to make such donations?

Perhaps such an approach is not practical. While harvesting crops by hand is possible, even under conditions of corporate farming, there is no immediately obvious way for a poor person to "harvest" automobiles, machine parts, industrial chemicals, and the like. On the other hand, what if all Jewish executives, lawyers, dentists, therapists, store owners, and carpenters took it upon themselves, as a mitzvah, to donate one-sixtieth of their labor? Someone with a $60,000 a year income, for example, would be obliged to offer $1,000 a year of pro bono work, which is probably less than forty hours a year.

Still, judging from *Zeraim*, perhaps the truly ethical society would need to maintain an intimate relationship with agriculture, for only in this way could people literally fulfill the commandments of *peah*. In a primarily urban society, whether in the United States or Israel, people are effectively separated from responsibility for the social and environmental impact of agricultural production. How many of us stop to ask where the groceries came from? How they were grown? What price really was paid for their availability?

One simple way to increase the observation of *peah* today and to increase an understanding of agriculture would be to encourage urban, suburban, and the few rural congregations to grow communal gardens. During harvest time, the needy would be encouraged to gather at least one-sixtieth of the yield. If this sort of activity became widespread, it would simultaneously link people back to nature and to the less fortunate members of the community.

It isn't likely that people will shift their careers—en masse—to become farmers any time soon. In Israel, it has been hard to keep the children of the kibbutz on the kibbutz, even though such a lifestyle can be very satisfying. Yet, young people could be encouraged to pursue careers in agriculture. Agricultural production exacts a heavy price on the environment. There are therefore tremendous opportunities for careers in agricultural research, in seeking ways to lessen this impact. This represents one way of attracting young people to the field.

Whether or not the specific traditions of *peah* may fit well in today's world, the underlying principles have universal importance. A study of *Peah* informs us that the less fortunate should not be viewed as deficient or lazy but should be treated with respect and care. Deut. 15:11 clearly states, "The poor shall never cease from the land." There will always be well-off and less well-off people; one would not exist without the other.

Finally, if the preeminent commandment is to provide for the less fortunate, then a social justice orientation is necessary in the work of Jewish environmentalists. Today, in America, a growing environmental movement focuses attention on the victims of environmental injustice, primarily indigenous people, poor communities, and people of color. It would be appropriate for the Jewish community to add its voice to this movement. As the concluding Mishnah of *Peah* 8:9 admonishes, "Justice, Justice shalt thou pursue."

As the Senegalese conservationist Baba Dioum has said, "In the end, we will conserve only what we love, we will love only what we understand, we will understand only what we are taught."

In Jewish tradition, conservation education begins with the understanding that the earth belongs to God: everything in it is holy. And humans are required to bring this holiness alive by blessing.

In the following piece, Rabbi Lawrence Troster traces the Jewish concept of holiness from biblical to rabbinic times. He shows how the practice of blessing anchors holiness in the routines of daily life and provides the foundation for environmental awareness for the Jewish community.

30

The Blessings of Holiness

LAWRENCE TROSTER

We must keep alive the sense of wonder through deeds of wonder.
—ABRAHAM JOSHUA HESCHEL

In some religious traditions, holiness exists permanently in places, people, and objects. In the Torah, space, time, and life become holy only when God commands it *and* the people respond to the command. For example, God makes Saturday holy, but if the community does not proclaim Shabbat and live it, week after week, its holiness does not exist. Though God has designated Shabbat for holiness, it is the activity of people that actually makes it holy. Holiness, *kedushah*, requires human effort.

In the days of the Jerusalem Temple, certain categories of time, space, people and things were considered more holy than others. On the axis of space, the most holy place was the Holy of Holies, followed by the Temple, Jerusalem, Israel, and finally the whole world. On the axis of time, Yom Kippur and Shabbat came before other holidays and weekdays. Some of these distinctions—especially with regard to time, food, people, and land—continue to the present day.

Because this system of holiness is hierarchical—particular times and places are considered holier than others—it teaches an appreciation of life's distinction and contrasts. Like the *Havdalah* ceremony, for example, which celebrates the distinctions between light and dark, between Shabbat and the rest of the week, this system of *kedushah* honors difference, complexity, and variety. In Temple times, different animals and types of produce—goats, bulls, turtledoves, flour, oil—were designated for different sacrifices. The laws of sacrifice honored the distinctiveness of each life form within the overarching hierarchical arrangement.

This hierarchical model of holiness, in which holiness was graded, was never the only model. In biblical times, two modes of holiness were present simultaneously. In one, holiness was hierarchical; in the other, holiness radiated out toward all existence, and no one place or thing was intrinsically holier than another. Leviticus, for example, is composed of two strands of priestly writing.[1] In one, holiness is restricted to the sanctuary and to the priests; in the other, holiness expands to all the land and people of Israel. Similarly in Torah, the Tabernacle is the focal point of holiness. But the Tabernacle was movable, and wherever it was put down became holy. The whole world has the potential for holiness, if only we realize it.

In the priestly tradition of Torah, there was an evolution of *kedushah* from a hierarchical construct to a more inclusive concept. Such was Zechariah's vision of the Messianic Age. In Zech. 14:16–21, all the nations of the world will go to Jerusalem to celebrate the seven-day festival of Creation, Sukkot. All the pots will be holy. All the animals and horses will have bells saying *"Kadosh L'Adonai,"* "Holy to the Lord." In this vision, holiness has been enlarged beyond the Temple and the Land of Israel and expanded to the entire world.

When the First Temple was destroyed in 586 B.C.E., and Jews began living outside the Holy Land, there was a powerful impetus to make holiness still more mobile. With no central Temple in which to perform sacrifices, local synagogues developed, and holiness became decentralized. Local prayer tended to replace Temple sacrifice. This tendency toward decentralization continued even when the Second Temple was built. A Jew could enter a synagogue anywhere in the world, turn in the direction of Jerusalem, pray to God, and still feel connected to the center of holiness. This new, mobile holiness did not require the presence of a priest; in a sense, it transformed all Jews into priests.

When the Second Temple was destroyed in 70 C.E., holiness devolved still further into the home, and more priestlike functions were developed for individuals and families. This successful adaptation allowed Judaism to survive in a world without a Temple. Food, Shabbat, and the festivals became major concerns. The individual Jew became a priest, the meal a sacrificial offering, and the table an altar. While the rabbis preserved many of the hierarchical aspects of *kedushah* (the regular days as against Shabbat and *Yom Tov*, for example), they extended *kedushah* to all areas of human experience.

This expanded notion of holiness is exemplified in the rules pertaining to eating. All Jews are supposed to wash their hands before the breaking of bread that marks the beginning of a meal. This ritual derives from the priests' practice of washing before participating in sacrifice. Now, the whole community is expected to wash prior to the beginning of a meal. Each of us becomes a priest ready to perform a sacrifice.

The uttering of a blessing or *berachah* further democratizes the priestly function. By reciting a *berachah*, any Jew can bring holiness into the world in a way suited to time, place, and occasion. When we recite blessings, we fulfill the role allotted to humanity in bringing forth, in reaping, holiness.

Pausing for Holiness

By talmudic times, the expanded purview of *kedushah* was clearly delineated in text. *Berachot* 35a of the Talmud reads:

> Our Rabbis taught: It is forbidden for a person to enjoy the things of the world without a *berachah* and anyone who does

enjoy the things of this world without a *berachah* commits sacrilege. . . . Rav Judah said in the name of Samuel: Anyone who enjoys anything of this world without a *berachah* is like eating that which is consecrated to heaven [i.e., the sacrifices] as it is written, "The earth is the Lord's and the fullness thereof" (Ps. 24:1).

Here, the rabbis are teaching us that all food is holy. Eating without first reciting a blessing is equivalent to taking what does not belong to us. In other words, it is stealing from God. The blessing is not a spell that transforms food or injects it with holiness. Rather, it is a daily opportunity to put our lives in perspective: no matter how much we see ourselves as the center of the universe and masters of our destiny, it is truly God who provides for us. When we recite the blessing, we are acknowledging the Divine in everything.

The act of blessing, of making holy, is so important to Judaism that tradition encourages us to make 100 blessings a day. We say *berachot* when we perform traditional commandments such as lighting Shabbat candles and also when we praise God for Creation—for life, rainbows, thunder, people, and even bodily functions.

The language of the *berachah* tells us much about how our ancestors understood blessing, holiness, and God. For example, over bread we say:

Baruch Atah Adonai, Eloheinu Melech ha-olam, ha-motzi lechem min ha-aretz.

Blessed are You, Lord our God, Ruler of the universe, who brings forth bread from the earth.

Like all blessings, this one begins with the standard formulation *Baruch Atah Adonai.* The first word, *baruch,* can be understood as either "praised" or "blessed." We begin by remembering God as the origin of all blessing.

The second word, *Atah,* means "You." It is significant that we talk to God in the second person, just as we would speak to a friend or a loved one. God is close by; the Hebrew God is a personal one.

The third word is *Adonai,* "my Lord." The important point is that the word used is not *Adon,* "Lord," but *Adonai,* "my Lord." This language reinforces the personal relationship to God. Likewise, the next word, *Eloheinu,* means "our God." So while we make our individual prayers, we speak in the plural; our tradition assumes a community.

Yet for all the intimacy of this involvement, God's Name itself is not pronounced. It is held in reserve, replaced in the *berachah* formula by *Adonai*, thus fostering a sense of awe at what we cannot name, cannot know, and cannot control.

In the latter section of the blessing formula, the sense of awe and distance is further accentuated by use of the third rather than the second person. We allude to God more impersonally, saying "who," as in "who brings forth bread from the earth." God is the awesome power that directs the universe and manifests in the forces of nature. By incorporating both the intimate and the awesome aspects of the Divine, the familiar and the remote, the blessing expresses a full range and experience of holiness. In something as mundane as bread, we have an encounter with God.

The simplest blessing resonates; it is part of a system of blessings that leads us back to reverence. We need not wait for the Messiah for "all the pots" to be made holy. All the world is holy now; it is up to us to recognize it and make it so.

Some Jewish mystic traditions assert that when we make a blessing, changes actually occur in the object that we bless. These changes mark the transition from profane to sacred. For us, the issue of whether the bread, say, is transformed by a *berachah* is moot. What is important is that the ritual alters those who perform it. When we are aware that all Creation is connected to us and, in some way, dependent on us for the consummation of its holiness, we become capable of greater reverence and greater respect.

A Jewish environmental ethic must begin with this sense of active communion with all life— concretized in *berachot*. Every moment of our day becomes an opportunity for connection. The environmental writer Bill McKibben has said, ". . . the constant pauses of observance—to say blessings, to touch the mezuzah, and especially to observe the Sabbath— are of profound importance in making people aware of the world around them. We waste the earth because we never stop to think or notice what we are doing."[2]

The blessings are designed to make us pause for holiness.

Blessings in Praise of Life and Its Creator

These blessings are taken from the Mishnah (*Berachot* 6, 8, and 9), the Babylonian Talmud (*Berachot* 54a–59b), and the Palestinian Talmud (*Berachot* 6:1, 9:3).

On tasting fruit for the first time in the season:

Baruch Atah Adonai, Eloheinu Melech ha-olam, she-he-che-yanu, v'ki-y'manu, v'hi-gianu lazman ha-zeh.

Blessed are You, Lord our God, Ruler of the universe, for giving us life, for sustaining us, and for enabling us to reach this season.

On seeing beauties of nature:

Baruch Atah Adonai, Eloheinu Melech ha-olam, she-kachah lo b'olamo.

Blessed are You, Lord our God, Ruler of the universe, whose world is filled with beauty.

On seeing rivers, seas, mountains, and other natural wonders:

Baruch Atah Adonai, Eloheinu Melech ha-olam, oseh ma-asey v'reshit.

Blessed are You, Lord our God, Ruler of the universe, who makes the wonders of creation.

On seeing shooting stars, electrical storms, and earthquakes:

Baruch Atah Adonai, Eloheinu Melech ha-olam, she-kocho u'g'vurato maley olam.

Blessed are You, Lord our God, Ruler of the universe, whose power and might pervade the world.

On seeing trees in blossom:

Baruch Atah Adonai, Eloheinu Melech ha-olam, she-lo chiseyr b'olamo v'ilanot tovim l'ha-not ba-hem davar, u-vara vo briy-ot tovot b'ney adam.

Blessed are You, Lord our God, Ruler of the universe, whose

world lacks nothing needful and who has fashioned goodly creatures and lovely trees that enchant the heart.

On seeing the ocean:

Baruch Atah Adonai, Eloheinu Melech ha-olam, she-asah et ha-yam ha-gadol.
Blessed are You, Lord our God, Ruler of the universe, Maker of the great sea.

On seeing a rainbow:

Baruch Atah Adonai, Eloheinu Melech ha-olam, ocher ha-brit, vane-e-man bi'v'rito, b'kayam b'ma-a-maro.
Blessed are You, Lord our God, Ruler of the universe, who remembers the covenant with Noah and keeps its promise faithfully with all Creation.

For many of us, our relationship to nature is not all that different from our relationship to our bodies. Urban living in a high-tech world demands that we distance ourselves from both. In the process, we have forgotten that our bodies and the land are holy. Life can certainly be easier, more convenient, when we desensitize ourselves to our bodies and nature. But is what we lose—our souls—worth the price? In the following piece, Shira Dicker draws on her own experience to explore these relationships.

31

Nature, Spirit, Body

SHIRA DICKER

At three in the morning, all is silent and dark in the birthing center save for the small candle we have kindled in the room and the primal sounds my friend is making as she slogs her way through a protracted and difficult labor.

Kneeling over the bed in an effort to alleviate the excruciating contractions caused by her back labor, Judy moans and mumbles, breathes deeply and sighs. Periodically, she cries out in despair, "I can't go on!" or "How much longer will this take?!" but for the most part, she is valiant and focused, intent upon birthing her child in an unmedicated, natural state.

I leave my friend for a few minutes to make a cup of red raspberry leaf tea for her in the center's kitchen. The herb is a powerful uterine toner, and I mix a good amount of honey into the drink to give her strength. When I return to the room, she is sitting in the rocking chair, sobbing softly. With eyes closed, head thrown back and lips parted, she rocks back and forth, rubbing her stomach. She looks timeless, ageless, and so beautiful that I briefly imagine myself a valiant knight come to save a lovely maiden from a fire-breathing dragon. Leaning over her, I give her the tea by spoonfuls, and she sips it gratefully. The liquid douses the dragon's flames.

Because I am with my friend, the midwife and labor nurse sleep in an adjoining room. I am grateful for this; it was precisely what I wanted when I volunteered to photograph my friend during childbirth. Her husband and older son, who insisted on being present so they could be involved with the birth, are also sleeping, stretched out on couches in another room. As the hours of the night tick away and everyone else acquiesces to sleep, my role expands, metamorphoses from mere photographer into something larger and inherently grander.

In this room of labor, with its attendant blood, agony, sweat, hope, and tears, I am my friend's coach, partner, sister, mother, nurse, midwife, guide. I make her tea, rub her back, take her on walks up and down the corridors of the silent, darkened birthing center. I lead her through guided visualizations, urge her to summon forth the awesome power of her body, remind her that she is, at this moment, performing the ultimate God-like act: bringing forth the ultimate creation—a human life.

The hour of three gives way to four, to five, to six, to sunrise, and then everyone is suddenly awake. The nurse has wheeled a bassinet into the room, sterilized equipment is laid out, emergency machinery is readied. My friend crouches like a lioness on her birthing bed, rears up suddenly, and then the Red Sea parts and its great waters rush down her legs.

There is mopping and cleaning and assurances that all is going well. Judy's husband has that expectant father expression, and their son, Jason, is rubbing her back. I get my camera ready, poised to capture the imminent birth. My friend gives a mighty roar, there is a sound like a knuckle cracking and then—a miracle!—a tiny human emerges headfirst from my friend's body.

It is astounding. It is overwhelming. It makes me tremble and weep and forget why I'm there. A warm, reassuring presence in the room fills me up and surrounds me. Suddenly, recalling my responsibilities, I begin clicking away while the baby is checked and weighed and measured. I capture images of Judy, smiling, nestling with her new daughter. I tiptoe around the room, photographing father and son, midwife and nurse, mother and child, but I float really, for the ground upon which I stand is holy and God is all around.

Urban Spiritual Poverty

Childbirth is probably the most intense way to experience the beauty and majesty of God's Creation through our bodies. Having given birth three times, twice assisted by midwives, I am intoxicated with the process and frankly puzzled that so many young, healthy women opt instead for high-tech, medicated births where labor can be watched on a computer screen rather than felt, where medications interfere with the body's natural wisdom, where the event is more like a medical procedure and less like a spiritual communion.

The prevalent attitude toward childbirth is a perfect metaphor for our relationship with nature and with our own bodies, which, after all, is part of nature. Just as unnecessary tools, tubes, anesthetics, and machinery distance the laboring woman from the wisdom of her body and the workings of nature, so, too, the urban lives so many of us lead—with its dearth of fresh air, greenery, horizons, and open spaces—results in spiritual poverty and a lessening of our very humanity.

As a reluctant resident of New York City, I spend a disproportionate amount of time feeling orphaned from the earth. Consequently, I feel estranged from my own body. In my urban reincarnation, I fear that I have donned body armor and grown harsher to survive in the city. These days, my credo might as well be Wordsworth's: "Getting and spending we lay waste our powers/Little we see in nature that is ours."

This despondent feeling hits me most intensely in the summer—my favorite season—when the sweet smells I associate with that time of year are replaced by the flatulent winds that blow up from subway gratings; when the cool, clean grass of open fields is replaced by sizzling pavement beneath; when the tempers of those sweating on the city streets rise with the mercury; when relief from the heat comes not from a dip in the lake, pond, or ocean, but from a shower in an air-conditioned apartment or a dash through the spray of an opened fire hydrant.

All the keen bodily pleasures I associate with the season are lost in a swirl of fumes, buildings, cars, buses, noise, filth, concrete, car alarms, hostile gazes, aimless youth, and sooty air. Dark particles wash off my skin when I shower in the evening. In the heat of the day, the very sun seems toxic.

Summer in the city eats away at my spirit, at my humanity. It diminishes me; it diminishes all of us.

Rejuvenation in the Country Air

I moved back to the city on a murderously hot day in July 1994. Having spent seven years living in an old English Tudor home on a quiet, tree-lined street in a suburb north of the city, Manhattan now felt like a punishment for a sin I didn't know I had committed. The contrast between the two places was startling. One day I was running around a lake in the early morning hours, breathing the sweet air, carried by the song of the birds, the geese landing, the turtles sunning, and the beavers burrowing. The next day I was wheezing my way down Riverside Drive, pumping leaden limbs, gulping acrid air, grimacing at the pavement and at the fat rat scuttling his way across a playground, vainly trying to ignore the blaring horns of rush-hour cars, looking for that transcendent oneness with body, spirit, and nature that I had come to expect from my morning runs.

The oneness never came. In fact, the rift widened. By late September, I was pregnant with my third child, and then the splintering really began.

My craving for nature was insatiable throughout the baby's gestation. After passing through the first trimester, I found myself escaping Manhattan at the slightest opportunity, seeking solace, connectedness with the land. I dragged my older children to playgrounds in Westchester and to beaches in Connecticut. I wrangled weekend invitations and vacations out of town as often as possible.

By midwinter, I told my husband that I couldn't spend another summer in the city, particularly with a newborn. Surging with hormones, swelling with new life, I was languishing in my urban prison.

And so, a small cabin in an unassuming summer community in the Catskill Mountains was found. When spring came, I was among the first residents to move up for the season. Weeks away from the baby's delivery, I hiked with my older children through the woods to the lake, lay on a blanket under a tree, and watched the shifting leaves for hours. I slept outdoors, mesmerized by the moon.

With every gulp of country air, my soul was restored to me. I returned to my body as well, just in time to give birth.

In my mind, I gave birth outside my summer cabin, supported by the trunk of the great maple tree. In reality, I gave birth in a friendly birthing room in a New York hospital, surrounded and coached by midwives. During the first two weeks of the baby's life, I endured the heat of the city while my children finished school, shocked that I could find no friendly, clean, safe patch of grass upon which I might spread a blanket and nurse my baby. On one particularly sweltering night, I took my kids on a two-hour cruise around Manhattan, hoping for a little breeze.

When Judah was two weeks old, my entire family moved up to the country for the summer. The two months out of the city were idyllic. We frequented fairs and farms, spent lazy evenings watching the children roll down grassy hills, sat on the banks of a lake and pondered the water.

When I arrived in Manhattan at summer's end, a crane was parked directly outside my apartment and jackhammers were tearing up the pavement. I burst into uncontrollable tears. The furlough was over and the prison sentence reinstated.

Thirteen Ways to Preserve Our Spiritual Well-Being

It is now three years later. My solution to city living is our country cabin and going there as often as possible. Some evenings, I sit in my apartment overlooking the Columbia University campus and fantasize about being a farm woman, raising chickens, goats, and sheep, walking my children to school along country roads, retiring to my farmhouse to spend a few hours writing before tilling the land. Or I devour issues of *Country Living* magazine, gazing at pictures of open fields and pretty gardens. Or I substitute my memory of the cicadas' song in midsummer for a car alarm blasting at 2 A.M.

Just as there is a spiritual lesson in the pain and work of birthing that brings us closer to God, so, too, I believe that our bodies hunger to be connected with nature so we can be fully human. Along with the agony of childbirth comes the euphoria; there is nothing like being able to actually feel your baby moving down the birth canal. So, too, there is nothing like feeling your body in direct contact with the elements, hearing the whisper of God's prayer for humanity in the wind at midnight, tasting the tangy waters of the ocean.

Saying *Kabbalat Shabbat* under the canopy of heaven as the sun goes down on a Friday night is a solace for the spirit. Intoning *"modeh ani"* while running laps around a fog-shrouded lake in the early hours of the morning restores the soul.

We can surely be good Jews and good people if we live out of nature, but we become lopsided. We tend to overdevelop our cerebral senses, or our cynicism, or our fashion sense, or our appetite for culture, or our musculature in an effort to compensate for what can only reach us through nature.

When we live amid God's abundant Creation, we absorb unmediated holiness as effortlessly as a fetus draws nourishment from her mother's placenta in utero. Through nature, God feeds and nurtures our senses, our soul.

Centuries ago, Maimonides created the Thirteen Precepts. They are still a mainstay of Jewish belief. I now propose another set of precepts—the Thirteen Intimate Interactions with Nature that Are Key to Our Spiritual Well-Being:

> I believe, with a deep and abiding faith, that it is a holy act to walk barefoot in the grass and occasionally roll down a soft grassy hill.
> I believe, with a deep and abiding faith, that it is a holy act to sleep outdoors, under the canopy of heaven.
> I believe, with a deep and abiding faith, that it is a holy act to watch the sun come up over the ocean.
> I believe, with a deep and abiding faith, that it is a holy act to bask in the healing rays of the sun.
> I believe, with a deep and abiding faith, that it is a holy act to stand in an open meadow on a clear, starry night.

I believe, with a deep and abiding faith, that it is a holy act to climb a mountain.

I believe, with a deep and abiding faith, that it is a holy act to sit among the branches of a tree.

I believe, with a deep and abiding faith, that it is a holy act to swim in a lake or a river or an ocean or a bay and feel your body supported by water.

I believe, with a deep and abiding faith, that it is a holy act to take a great gulp of country air at night or after a rainfall.

I believe, with a deep and abiding faith, that it is a holy act to jump into great piles of crunchy autumn leaves.

I believe, with a deep and abiding faith, that it is a holy act to build sandcastles and feel the sand run through your fingers and slip between your toes.

I believe, with a deep and abiding faith, that it is a holy act to plant vegetables and herbs or simply dig in dirt.

I believe, with a deep and abiding faith, that it is a holy act to dance barefoot in the moonlight, see the horizon, witness a rainbow, get grass stains on your shorts, smell a barnyard, ride a horse, milk a cow, pet a cat, hug a tree, touch the sky.

Do I have a right to build an incinerator that will foul up your air? How close to your house can I keep my pigeons? Am I permitted to block your view—or build so high that I can see into your private chambers?

Such issues of individual rights versus responsibility to the community are the starting point for a talmudic discussion about what we could call an environmental ethic. It is remarkable, even in our day of heightened ecological concern, how scrupulously such questions were dealt with by the rabbis almost two millennia ago. And it is notable that a thoroughgoing environmental practice can be grounded in issues arising from human community.

Beginning with a discussion of *bal taschit*, the injunction against wanton destruction, Rabbi Barry Freundel examines the rabbinic attitude toward neighborly relations that is, in many ways, exemplary for our own time.

32

Judaism's Environmental Laws

BARRY FREUNDEL

The traditional legal framework of Judaism was meant to structure and direct one's life experiences and perceptions of the world and give them meaning, spirituality, and sanctity. Against that background it is interesting to note how environmental legislation pervades Jewish law, with the consequence that one who follows *halachah*—the Jewish legal system—to the fullest would develop a highly refined environmental consciousness. What follows is a presentation of many of the halachic imperatives that relate to the environment and how they play themselves out in the lives of those who live by them.

Any discussion of Jewish law and the environment must begin with this passage from Deut. 20:19–20:

> When you shall besiege a city a long time, in making war against it to take it, you shall not destroy its trees by forcing an ax against them; for you may eat of them, and you shall not cut them down. For is the tree of the field a man that it should join the siege with you? Only the trees which you know are not trees for food, you shall destroy and cut them down; and you shall build siege works against the city that makes war with you, until it is subdued.

Ancient wars were fought using different materials than those we use today. For armies of the biblical era, wood was crucial for fuel, siege engines, arrows, and spears. While war is a time of great need and great danger and could even determine one's survival, biblical law prohibits using wood from fruit trees even on the battlefield.

If limits are imposed on the use of natural resources in such extreme situations, then clearly ecological concerns are well rooted in Jewish tradition. Wanton environmental destruction is certainly prohibited for anyone if it is prohibited for soldiers during war and battle. In fact, the great twelfth-century sage, philosopher, and physician Maimonides extended the prohibition:

> Rather, anyone who breaks utensils, tears garments, destroys buildings, stops up a stream, or ruins food with destructive intent transgresses the command "Do not destroy."[1]

Thus, Maimonides widened the parameters against using fruit trees during wartime to a variety of objects useful to humans, at *any* time. Not only are direct acts of destruction to a tree precluded, but even indirect acts, such as cutting off water sources necessary for trees to grow. Similarly, when normal human activity does require some destruction of natural resources, decisions must be made in favor of methods that involve less rather than greater destruction, such as destroying a tree that bears less fruit.

Over time, this prohibition, which is now colloquially known as *bal taschit* (from the Aramaic translation of the command, "You shall not destroy"), came to refer to any wasteful or destructive act. All things, living or inanimate, must be treated with respect and not abused or wasted.

Emerging from the negative "you shall not destroy" is the positive "you shall maintain." This affirmative imperative leads to an entire body of laws designed to maintain and improve the general environmental quality of life.

Protecting the Individual's Environmental Quality

Many of the relevant sources appear in a particular tractate of the Mishnah, the earliest codification of the oral law. Tractate *Baba Bathra* (literally, "The Last Gate") deals generally with civil law and monetary matters. Its second chapter makes clear that maintaining an environmentally sound quality of life is an imperative and that damaging that quality is a wrongful act, specifically a physical injury against one's neighbor.

For example, the discussion involving invasion of privacy has environmental implications:

> If a man has a wall running alongside his neighbor's wall . . . if there are windows [in the neighbor's wall], he must leave a clear space of four cubits whether above or below or opposite.[2]

The Mishnah is describing this scenario: Two parties live side by side. The side wall of Party A's dwelling has windows that overlook his neighbor's yard. Party B now wishes to build a wall that will pass in front of the windows of Party A's dwelling. The Mishnah requires that the wall must be either higher or lower than the height of the existing window by a distance of four cubits. This will put the window out of the line of sight, or at least four cubits away.

This four cubit requirement is understood by the Talmud as follows:

> . . . that a space must be left "above" so that he should not be able to peep into the other one's room, and "below" so that he should not stand on tiptoe and look in, and opposite so that he should not take away his light.[3]

Here, concern for privacy is juxtaposed with what we would today call "environmental trespass": not blotting out someone's access to the light. One can, therefore, legitimately suggest that Jewish law views violating and harming someone's environmental well-being as equivalent to trespassing on their privacy. Certainly, the negative impact on health, well-being, and physical functioning that can come with environmental degradation invades the victim's privacy in the most profound way. If my house is assailed by terrible odors or my body is invaded by toxins, I have suffered a serious violation.

The mishnaic statement that precedes the one just discussed deals with noise pollution:

> If a man desires to open a shop in a courtyard, his neighbor may prevent him on the grounds that he will not be able to sleep through the noise of people coming and going. A man, however, may make articles in the courtyard to take out and sell in the market, and his neighbor cannot prevent him on the ground that he cannot sleep from the noise of the hammer or of the mill-stones.[4]

While accommodation must be made, even in residential areas, for people to make a living, limits must be set. Some manufacturing may be allowed, but the noise pollution of crowds and customers cannot be permitted to disturb the peace. Noise, which can penetrate walls and doors, is both an act of pollution and an invasion of privacy. In fact, most environmental violations can be understood in this way. Here, the noise coming from outside invades the intimate space of the home. The same could be said for the toxins of landfills or the sights of billboards and skyscrapers. All of these assault the senses and the body.

Noise Is Another Form of Pollution

Certain occupations, by their very nature, create noise or negatively impact the environment. Limits must be set on the functioning of these occupations to promote good relations between neighbors and maintain a healthy environment:

> A pigeon cote must be kept fifty cubits from a town. A man should not put up a pigeon cote on his own estate unless there is a clear space of fifty cubits all round. R. Judah says, the space

should be sufficient for the sowing of four *kor* [7,500 square cubits, approximately 1,200 to 1,500 square feet], which is as much as a bird flies at a time. If, however, he buys it [from another] with only the space for sowing a quarter of a *kab* [105 square cubits or 300 square feet] round it, he has a right to keep it.[5]

Pigeons make noise and damage crops. Therefore, their owner must have enough land to keep the birds away from a neighbor's land. The optimum distance of four *kor* would prevent any damage to neighboring fields. However, the text included a grandfather clause that allowed for less distance, although a minimum had to be maintained so damage would be small and infrequent.

Concern for noise pollution and potential damage to trees and crops reaches its fullest expression in the discussion in the Gemara, the talmudic analysis of the Mishnah, of the same section of tractate *Baba Bathra*:

R. Joseph had some small date trees under which cuppers [blood letters] used to sit [and let blood], and ravens used to collect to suck up the blood, and they used to fly on to the date trees [with their bloody feathers] and damage them [by bringing the blood in contact with the wood]. So R. Joseph said to the cuppers "Take away your croakers from here." Said Abaye to him, "But they are only the indirect cause?" [The blood is really doing the damage.] He replied: "R. Tobi bar Mattanah has expressly said: "This [the case of the birds with the bloody feathers] is equivalent to saying that it is prohibited to cause damage indirectly." But [R. Joseph] had given them a right [to let blood under the trees]? R. Nahman has said in the name of Rabbah b. Abbuha: "There is no legal title to things causing damage." But are we not told in a gloss on this statement that R. Mari says it refers [for instance] to smoke, and R. Zebid to a privy? [But not to blood.] Said R. Joseph to him, "I am very sensitive, and these ravens are as offensive to me as smoke or a privy."[6]

Rabbi Joseph here insists that even though the damage to the wood is due to the blood and not the ravens, and even though the cuppers had been given the right to work there, the indirect harm caused by the cupper's activity is enough to limit their practice.

It is clear that concern for noise pollution and physical damage to trees was sufficient to significantly alter the lives of anyone who lived according to *halachah* and its principles. Certain activities were severely circumscribed as to where they could be practiced, property rights were curtailed, and individual reactions to environmental violation were held paramount.

Later on in the chapter, the Mishnah reads:

> A fixed threshing-floor must be kept fifty cubits from a town. A man should not fix a threshing-floor on his own estate unless there is a clear space all round of fifty cubits. He must keep it away from the plantation of his neighbor and his plowed fallow field a sufficient distance to prevent damage being caused.[7]

The Gemara's discussion of this Mishnah includes the following comments:

> Why is a fixed threshing-floor kept fifty cubits away from a town? To prevent it doing damage. . . . "A fixed threshing-floor must . . . [also] be kept fifty cubits from a neighbor's cucumber and pumpkin fields, from his plantations and his plowed fallow field, to prevent damage being caused." . . . We can understand [why the threshing-floor must be kept away] from the cucumber and pumpkin fields, because the dust goes and penetrates into them and dries them up but [why should it be kept away] from the plowed fallow field?—R. Abba b. Zebid [or it may be R. Abba b. Zutra] replied: "Because it over-fertilizes it."[8]

The ancient threshing floor produced chaff, which has potential to be airborne and was, therefore, one of the first causes of industrial air pollution. The early Jewish lawmakers were conscious that the chaff would affect not only crops by drying them but also the soil of a field by overfertilizing it. By prescribing zoning regulations, the rabbis acted to mitigate those effects.

Jewish law insisted that one not open a shop in a courtyard if noise from customers would disturb neighbors' sleep, that one must put a pigeon cote at least fifty cubits from town so that the birds would not damage the town's vegetable gardens, and that threshing floors must also be kept at fifty cubits to prevent the chaff from creating an air pollution problem for the city. The rabbis understood that while industry and commerce must be accommodated, they must be located where they will least damage the environment.

Because of the odors and toxins they produce and their potential to cause disease, carcasses, graves, and tanneries—all integral to the functioning of the city—also must obey the fifty-cubit distance requirement:

> Carrion, graves, and tanyards must be kept fifty cubits from a town. A tanyard must only be placed on the east side of the town. R. Akiba, however, says it may be placed on any side except the west [the direction of the prevailing winds in Israel], providing it is kept fifty cubits away.[9]

The rabbis stated that the tannery must be placed on the side of the city opposite the direction of the prevailing winds because toxic tannin fumes carried far. Within these sources is not only concern for the effects of pollution, but also a recognition that action taken in one place may negatively impact the environment somewhere else. Chaff from a threshing floor or fumes from a tannery must be regulated so that they cannot reach and harm another's property some distance away. Many modern parallels to this suggest themselves, from dumping sludge upstream that kills fish and pollutes the water for miles downstream to using chlorofluorocarbons that may widen the hole in the ozone layer. Unfortunately, we are not as quick as the rabbis were to recognize the impact of our actions and to regulate them.

Tradition and Environmental Rights

There is always some debate about what is a destructive activity and what is simply a nuisance. For example, an individual is engaged in an activity that benefits himself, and his neighbors, at first, tolerate the activity. But, after a time, the neighbors feel bothered and start to complain. When the activity is simply a tolerable "nuisance," the individual is not required to stop the activity. In many American jurisdictions, for example, if I have walked across my neighbor's lawn for more than a year to get to work and my neighbor tolerates my action all that time, my neighbor cannot suddenly prevent my passage. American law calls this an "easement."

A similar concept exists in Jewish law. Maimonides' conclusion on the matter reads:

> If one does not keep the proper distance and the other sees it and is silent the latter thereby waives his right to challenge the first and cannot thereafter change his mind and compel him to withdraw to the proper distance.[10]

According to Maimonides, if I remain silent while someone begins a potentially harmful activity, I usually lose my right to protest against it later. This only applies if I *know* about the harmful activity—if, for example, I witness, help, or instruct the person doing the activity. This raises the question, then, of people who band together to protest an incinerator or toxic waste dump *after* it has already been operational. On the other hand, it also insists that workers and the community are entitled to full knowledge of the impact of a local industry before tacitly agreeing to it.

Maimonides goes on to explain that with regard to some "damages" (damaging agents), the right to protest can never be given away. Some activities are considered too harmful to ever be tolerated:

> This [rule] applies only to smoke, the smell of a privy, dust and the like, and the stir of the ground. To these four there is no legal title on grounds of unchallenged practice, and even if he who suffers the damage is silent many years he can change his mind and compel him who causes the damage to withdraw to the proper distance.[11]

Smoke, the odor of a privy, dust, and vibration are assumed to be such great intrusions into a human being's personal ecology that no one can ever be assumed to have truly assented to their presence. Again, we see the strong association between privacy and environmental regulation. Another "intolerable damage" occurs when one is unwittingly "exposed to the view of others." In this case, the exposed person can require a neighbor to build a dividing wall so that the other neighbor cannot see into his or her property. Being "exposed to the view of others," an issue of privacy, is equivalent to ecological intrusion.

The aggrieved party may, however, sell his right to protest a nuisance: "if he has bound himself by a *Kinyan* [a halachic symbol of sale] when he waived his right he cannot retract [even] in case of those damages."[12] If I engage in work that produces pollution, I can protect myself only by purchasing rights to produce these nuisances from those affected. In Jewish law, then, the cost of doing work that causes "nuisances" is born by the producer. This, too, serves to limit and control the production of such pollutants and is conceptually similar to a Bush Administration plan—never implemented—to regulate industry through a system of violation points and corresponding taxation. An environmental taxation system would be a modern equivalent of the general ethical principle underlying these Jewish laws, which is that business not be completely hampered but that it be regulated by and respectful of the surrounding community.

Even simple environmental amenities that improve the quality of life are subject to halachic concern. The Mishnah requires that cities in Israel be surrounded by a *migrash*, an area between 1,500 and 2,000 feet wide left for public enjoyment, into which nothing may intrude. These were park-like areas kept free from cultivation so that city inhabitants could enjoy nature when visiting them. Trees were kept about 50 to 100 feet from the city wall so people would get the full benefit of the *migrash* and so they would not block the cool breezes from reaching the city streets.

The city is made beautiful by the presence of the *migrash*, and the rabbis, therefore, do not allow the *migrash* to be turned into a field. To maintain balance, a field may not be made into a *migrash*, as it will diminish the crops. The principle of balance between environmental and other needs is again at work here. Today, parks and wilderness areas serve similar needs. However, preserving these areas can be challenging. Wilderness areas are disappearing under encroaching development, logging, and mining. City parks often do not have the resources necessary for maintenance.

A more absolutist position, but one that still retains at least some balance, is taken by Jewish law in regard to what farmers call the "woolly locusts." This refers to sheep that could not be raised in Israel because their grazing defoliates the land and destroys its crops. But they could "be bred in Suria or in the deserts of the land of Israel."[13] Relatively unimportant in talmudic times, Suria was under Jewish control but had a small population. There environmental damage would be of less consequence. The writers of the Talmud apparently understood that while environmentally damaging activities may be necessary, they must be minimized as much as possible.

Special laws apply to preserving the unique environment of Jerusalem. One states: "No dunghills should be made there."[14] Accumulated garbage had to be removed from Jerusalem on the day it was created. The Dung Gate in the Old City walls of Jerusalem near the Temple Mount is testimony to Jewish compliance with this ordinance.

Another claims: "No kilns should be kept there."[15] Kilns produce two things: pottery and smoke. In Jerusalem, the former is not worth the price of the latter. This concern is so deep-seated that leniency in some *kashrut* laws is permitted within a fifteen-mile radius of Jerusalem to help preserve its environment.

An interesting law promoting positive development of the environment in Israel comes from the case of a farmer whose olive trees were swept away and then found rooted in another farmer's field.

> If the river swept away a man's olive trees and deposited them in his neighbor's field [and there they produced olives] [and] one maintains, "my olive trees produced them," whereas the other claims, "my land caused the yield," they divide [the value of the fruit].[16]

The Gemara adds a statement that if the farmer says he wants his olive trees back, he cannot have them because it is most important that Israel be "well cultivated." Though this discussion begins with the question of who owns the transplanted olive trees and the olives, it ends with the conclusion that the trees are not to be returned to their original spot. The primary concern of the rabbis was that Israel be "well cultivated" and settled. Presumably, the new owner will farm his serendipitously acquired trees, while the original farmer will, in all likelihood, replace his loss. In this way, two sets of trees will grow in the Land where only one set had existed before.

Jewish Ecological Wisdom

Environmental concerns have continued to affect contemporary rituals in small ways. Traditionally, when you see someone wearing a new garment, you say, "May it wear out and you acquire another one." This, however, is not said for leather garments, as an animal must be killed for the wish to come true. So, too, one who slaughters for the first time, unlike one who performs other ritually significant acts for the first time, does not say a *Shehecheyanu* (the blessing recited when one reaches or achieves an important milestone in one's life), as an animal must be killed in the process.

These symbols of concern are elements of a complicated system of environmental ethics, sensibilities, and controls. Many people say that modern living and production require loose environmental standards. In response, let us return to the laws of war:

> When you go out to encamp against your enemies. . . you shall have a place outside the camp, where you shall go. And you shall have a spade among your weapons; and it shall be, when you will ease yourself outside, you shall dig with it, and shall turn back and cover your excrement. (Deut. 23:10, 13–14)

Even in the great urgency of war, the small details of maintaining a proper environment remain a priority. Therefore, it is this type of spiritual and environmental sensitivity that can be developed by living a halachic lifestyle. If our professional, ritual, and military lives are ecologically controlled, if our cities are environmentally planned, if we are prohibited from engaging in wanton destruction, if we are asked to develop an environmental sense of privacy, then an environmental consciousness can develop that will influence all of our activities. Regardless of our level of religious observance, the ecological wisdom and morality of the law should become part of every Jew's knowledge and identity.

Since the beginning of time, people have used nature—it goes without saying. We depend on nature for all of our needs. Pollution is an inevitable byproduct of our use of nature. In the days when rabbis were the authorities over all kinds of community affairs, they had to address pollution issues—particularly pollutants that obviously affected people's health. In the following essay, Rabbi Philip Bentley explores the rabbis' approach.

33

Business and Environment: A Case Study

PHILIP J. BENTLEY

Whether we are dealing with a nuclear waste dump in New Mexico, logging in Oregon, or a paper mill in Georgia, the issue often comes down to jobs versus the environment. Jewish law has much to teach about resolving the conflict between economic well-being and environmental quality: Can a confrontation be avoided through advance planning? Can conflicting claims be resolved? The Torah, the Talmud, and the literature of rabbinic case law all deal with this subject. The following case is based on several different cases that actually occurred over the course of many centuries in many locations.

A leather dealer builds a tannery just outside of a small town that has no major business. Tanneries use chemicals and other materials that have unpleasant and penetrating odors, and the fumes can be irritating and dangerous to health. Following both law and common sense, the tannery was located downwind, to the east of town. The tannery became very successful and helped the town prosper. Eventually, as the town grew, houses were built to the east of the tannery, and the people who moved in found themselves breathing foul air. They brought a suit against the tannery, demanding that it either modify its operations or move further east. The tannery owner claimed that doing either would be too expensive and might force him to close his facility and move to another town. How can the town keep the source of its prosperity and also improve its residents' quality of life? What are the rights and responsibilities of the business community and the public?

A Delicate Balance of Interests

Lenny Bruce used to say that law was first introduced to the world when somebody in a cave announced, "We eat here, sleep there, and throw the garbage over there." One primary reason for setting up laws and a social structure is to keep people who live near each other from infringing on each other's safety and comfort. We allow the community to make rules and limit our personal freedom so all of us can stay out of each other's way. Zoning laws, which tell us that we cannot do everything we want anywhere we want, are essential to a community.

Jewish zoning regulations address all kinds of pollution—air, water, land, and noise.[1] For example, according to the Talmud, in order to avoid vermin, no dunghills or garbage heaps are allowed inside a city.[2] Even ashes from the Temple sacrifices had to be taken outside of the city.[3] Several laws address air pollution by demanding that industries and other facilities with noxious odors be sited outside and downwind of inhabited areas, as illustrated in the case of the tannery. Jewish law restricts the kinds of commercial activities that could go on in residential areas or near certain business facilities. For example, the Mishnah states:

> No one may open a baker's shop or a dyer's shop under his fellow's storehouse, nor may he keep a cattle-stall nearby. [The sages] have allowed a baker's shop and a dyer's shop under a wine store, but not a cattle stall. A man may protest against a shop within a courtyard and say to the shopkeeper, "I cannot sleep because of the noise of those that go in and out." He that

makes utensils should go to the market to sell. But no one may protest to another and say, "I cannot sleep because of the noise of the hammer, or because of the millstones, or because of the noise of children."[4]

It was believed that the warmth of the bakery would improve wine but that the stench of a cattle-stall would spoil it. Note also that only certain kinds of noise that might be judged "unreasonable" are prohibited.

The strongest indication that Jewish law is concerned about zoning is the description of the Levitical cities to be established throughout the Land of Israel.

> The town pasture that you are to assign to the Levites shall extend a thousand cubits outside the town wall all around. You shall measure off two thousand cubits outside the town on the east side, two thousand on the south side, two thousand on the west side, and two thousand on the north side, with the town in the center. That shall be the pasture for their towns. (Numbers 35:4–5)

The case of the tannery is called an "external cost" case in economic theory, a case where one party suffers an economic loss due to another. The suffering party could be a producer or merchant, labor, the government, consumers, or the public in general. In this kind of case, the law should determine what the costs or losses are, who is responsible, and who must pay whom. This might be done through mediation, arbitration, legislation, or the courts. If this does not happen, then the losses will eventually cause a disruption in the economy.

In considering this kind of case, many people just want to look at a simple "how much money is involved" analysis. However, there are many other factors to consider. For example, suppose a developer wants to build a shopping mall in a town. The mall will provide jobs and a convenient place for people to shop, obtain services, and meet for a meal or a movie. However, it will also take business away from the older commercial areas and bring traffic and possibly strangers into the area. It will use local resources and create waste and pollution. A wise community will balance all these considerations before deciding whether to allow the developer to go ahead. One community might demand that the developer modify the plans, while another might create incentives to encourage the developer. Some communities will do both in an effort to reap the greatest benefits and avoid the disadvantages. Of course, changing conditions in the community over time may cause unforeseen problems that will need to be addressed after the project is completed; this was the situation in our tannery case.

In Jewish law, the external cost case is called *gira delei*, which literally means "his arrow." *Gira delei* is a case in which one party sues another for damages caused directly by someone else's actions or property. In other words, damages caused "by the other's arrow." The damage may be actual or potential, and it may affect quality of life as well as cause physical damage. Whoever makes such a complaint must prove that the damage results from or may result directly from something the accused party has done, is doing, or plans to do.

In some cases of *gira delei*, such as a dispute between neighboring homeowners, an arbitration process is usually followed. Each side chooses one member of a panel of three, and these two choose a third panelist acceptable to both of them. If the case goes to court, the panel of three judges will seek a solution to the dispute that will give the best result for all parties.

Working for the Good of the Whole

The communal authorities are obligated to work for the good of the total community. In a case like that of our tannery, they will have to balance the economic benefits this factory brings to the town against the quality of life of the people living in the town.[5] The judges or arbitrators are not bound by law codes alone but may consult the entire literature of case law (*tshuvot*) as well as take into consideration any special factors in the case at hand. If there is an aspect of the case to which the judges cannot respond, they will write to an expert for a *tshuvah*, a legal opinion, on that aspect of the case.

The first issue in such a case is to determine that the unpleasant air is coming from the tannery. This is almost certainly the case, as this is a problem with all tanneries. Then the judges must determine whether the fumes are an actual health hazard or whether they are simply unpleasant. Having clarified these issues, the judges will want to know what the alternatives are. Can the fumes be reduced or made less dangerous? Can the tannery change the way it operates or alter its physical plant so that the fumes will affect the neighbors less? If not, must the tannery relocate further from town? If so, will the tannery be able to stay in business?

If the fumes are merely unpleasant or only a minor health hazard, they may charge the tannery a pollution tax as an indemnity to those whose lives are being made unpleasant. If this indemnity is too expensive, the tannery will have to do something about the emissions problem. If the health hazard is serious, another principle of Jewish law is brought to bear: *hoveyl b'atzmo*, the self-inflicted wound. Jewish law forbids us from damaging our health. The judges would then issue a restraining order against the tannery and demand that it take whatever action necessary to protect the health of the townspeople.[6]

In brief, the judges will seek a solution for the greatest good of all. They will try to keep the owners and operators of the tannery in business. The employees should still have their jobs. The tannery might have to pay damages to the victims of the pollution. Only if absolutely necessary will action be taken to shut the business down. Those who built, purchased, or rented homes in the areas downwind of the tannery will not have the right to dictate any of this. The court and communal authority must arrive at the best solution for all, even if some are unhappy with the final outcome. Jewish law and ethics attempt to consider all the factors needed for a clean and safe environment and a healthy business climate. The health of the total community is the highest priority. Our tradition teaches that potential conflicts—such as jobs versus environment—can be resolved through thoughtful stewardship.

The word *anthropocentrism*, whose roots are *anthropo*, or "human," and *centrism*, or "center," is a buzzword in environmental thinking. It expresses the notion that the world was made expressly for humanity. Many think that as long as we see ourselves as center (and master) of the universe, there will be no end to the environmental crisis. In such a world, the rest of Creation exists to satisfy ever-increasing human needs, and the exploitation of resources becomes habitual. In today's environmental debate, the strongest arguments against anthropocentrism come from the Deep Ecologists, who call for a "biocentric" world-view. In fact, their debate is not new. It has been going on in a different guise in religious circles for centuries. In the following piece, Rabbi Dan Fink explores one such debate that took place several hundred years ago.

34

Between Dust and Divinity:
Maimonides and Jewish Environmental Ethics

DAN FINK

Keep two truths in your pocket, and take them out according to the need of the moment.
Let one be: "For my sake was the world created."
And the other: "I am dust and ashes."　　　—HASIDIC SAYING

The Babylonian Talmud recounts a debate over why God created humanity last of all the living beings. One rabbi suggested that people were the pinnacle of Creation. He compared God to a king who prepared a fantastic feast and, after all was readied, invited the guest of honor. Thus, God made the entire natural world for the sustenance and enjoyment of humanity.

A second sage offered a very different response: "Adam was created at the end of the sixth day so that if human beings should grow too arrogant, they may be reminded that even the gnats preceded them in the order of Creation."[1] According to this perspective, humanity is more or less a divine afterthought.

Today, the question that underlies this discussion confronts us still: How important are we? Are we the measure of all things, created to master nature? Or are we an insignificant blip in the earth's enormous history? The answer to this question has a tremendous impact on how we relate to nature.

One intriguing discussion of this issue is found in the writings of Moses Maimonides. In his *Guide to the Perplexed*, Maimonides explores the question of humanity's centrality and challenges his readers to examine their relationship with the rest of Creation. The context for Maimonides' discussion is not environmental; rather, he arrives at his insights on human nature from his observations of human suffering. Today, his thinking can help to pave the way for all who seek to formulate a Jewish environmental ethic.

The Origin of Evil

In the third section of the *Guide to the Perplexed*, Maimonides considers why evil exists in such abundance. He introduces his readers to Mohammed Ibn Zakariyya al Razi, a highly esteemed physician and philosopher, who was frequently praised as one of the most original minds in the history of Islam. Maimonides, however, views him as shallow and misguided.

Razi claimed that there is more evil than good in the world and that existence is a punishment. He maintained that anyone who compares the quantity of human suffering with the quantity of goodness and joy will inevitably conclude that "the pains, infirmities, afflictions, wretchedness, sorrows and calamities that befall us" clearly outweigh our pleasures.[2]

Maimonides concedes that most people share this perspective. He even understands its popularity among the uneducated masses, for whom this life is a mere proving ground for the rewards of the world to come. However, while this notion may be tolerable for the average person, Maimonides takes umbrage when it is expressed by those like Razi who "deem that they know something." Therefore, when Maimonides argues for the prevalence of goodness in this world, he addresses Razi and his followers with unmitigated scorn.

Maimonides begins with the observation that when Razi speaks about the preponderance of evil on earth, he means that humanity endures more sorrow than joy. This is the root of Razi's error: he equates evil with human suffering. People may experience more pain than pleasure, but still, notes Maimonides, it does not follow that whatever appears to be bad to Razi is intrinsically evil. To Maimonides, Razi errs because he cannot escape his self-referential bias:

> The reason for this whole mistake [Razi's assertion that evil outweighs good] lies in the fact that this ignoramus and those like him . . . consider that which exists only with reference to a human individual. Every ignoramus imagines that all that exists, exists with a view to his individual sake; it is as if there were nothing that exists except him. And if something happens to him that is contrary to what he wishes, he makes the trenchant judgment that all that exists is an evil. However, if humans considered all that exists and knew the smallness of their part in it, the truth would become clear and manifest to them.[3]

A Prescription for Humility

Maimonides does not merely dismiss those whose narrow-mindedness leads them to see human beings as the measure of all things. Rather, he insists that those who wish to achieve the true perspective on humanity's place in the world can do so by studying the two great sources of revelation: Scripture and nature.

Regarding Scripture, he acknowledges that some misreadings of biblical texts imply that the rest of the Creation exists for the sake of humanity. However, Maimonides asserts that when interpreted properly, the Torah affirms that "all the other beings, too, have been created for their own sakes, and not for the sake of something else [i.e., humanity]."[4]

For instance, upon first consideration, the Creation account seems to support an anthropocentric perspective: God gives humanity dominion over other creatures and urges us to "fill the earth and master it" (Gen. 1:28). Yet Maimonides insists this narrative merely describes humanity's great power and concurrent responsibility; it does not endorse the view that the entire natural world exists for our sake. Rather, Creation exists for its own sake. This is why the Torah tells us that after each day's creation, ". . . God saw that it was good."[5] Indeed the Creation story ends with the statement, "God saw all of the works of Creation and behold, they were very good" (Gen. 1:31). The text goes out of its way to emphasize the value of each plant and animal.

Passages from the Prophets and Writings further emphasize humanity's proper place in the scheme of things. Maimonides cites examples from Psalms and Isaiah, which teach that "humanity is like a breath; our days are like a passing shadow . . ." and "the nations are but a drop in a bucket, reckoned as dust on a balance. . . ."[6] He also refers to Job, which more than any other book in the Hebrew Scriptures consistently accentuates humanity's smallness. Maimonides urges his readers to study these sources, for they are "most useful in giving human beings knowledge of our true value."[7]

While, for Maimonides, studying Scripture provides one path to reach the ultimate goal of humility, contemplating nature provides another.

What people ought to consider in order to know what their own souls are worth and to make no mistake regarding this point, is what has been made clear concerning the dimensions of the spheres and the stars and the measures of the distances separating us from them.[8]

The rest of the chapter offers a detailed description of the workings of the universe according to the Ptolemaic system that was accepted in Maimonides' time. By today's standard, this geocentric model of the universe is, of course, all wrong. Nonetheless, our contemporary cosmology emphasizes Maimonides' central point even more than the science of his own day: we are a relatively insignificant part of the universe. Maimonides speaks of the vast distance between the earth and the other heavenly bodies. Today, with our knowledge of a rapidly expanding cosmos of almost infinite proportions, Maimonides' appreciation of these vast distances is exceptional. Anyone who would see humanity as the measure of all things need only contemplate the night sky to see the absurdity of this perspective. Thus, Maimonides concludes:

> If the whole of the earth would not constitute even the smallest part of the sphere of the fixed stars, what is the relation of the human species to all these created things, and how can one of us imagine that they exist for our sake and because of us and that they are instruments for our benefit?[9]

For Maimonides, then, both Scripture and nature teach that humans are not the ultimate arbiters of good and evil. We may suffer a great deal, yet we err when we assume that whatever brings us sorrow is intrinsically bad. The world is bigger than we are, and it does not revolve around us. Like the teacher in the Talmud, Maimonides reminds us that even the gnat preceded us in the order of Creation.

The World Pursues Its Natural Course

Maimonides' view on divine providence further clarifies his perspective on the human place in nature. To explain his position, he presents two opposite conceptions of God's role in earthly events.

On the one extreme is the attitude articulated by Epicurus, the Greek philosopher, who denied the existence of any sort of providence and insisted that the world is governed entirely by chance. The antithesis of this position is represented by Ashariyya, an Islamic sect, which maintained that "nothing . . . is in any respect due to chance, for everything comes about through [God's] will, purpose, and governance." God is directly responsible for every breeze that blows and leaf that falls.[10]

Maimonides seems to seek the middle ground. He clearly rejects the Asharite claim that God watches over particular plants and animals, though he believes there is Divine providence for entire species. He cites biblical texts to show that God cares about the existence of lions, for example, but does not intervene—for good or bad—in the life of any individual lion. Maimonides asserts that while the Eternal One provides an ecological niche for every type of creature, when "this spider has devoured this fly" it is an act of pure chance.[11]

Maimonides' view on divine providence for human individuals is more complicated. Initially, he appears to reject those who put humanity on a par with the other animal species. He points out that the Torah makes explicit statements that God watches over certain people. However, when he elaborates on this discussion, Maimonides indicates that his notion of divine providence for human individuals is quite different from the traditional understanding of a beneficent and omnipotent God who rewards and punishes each of us according to our merits.[12]

Instead, Maimonides believes that human beings receive the benefits of providence in proportion to their knowledge. The more learning we attain, the more benefits we are granted. Providence is not the graceful gift of a God who watches over your ship at sea during a storm. It is, rather, the wisdom not to get on a rickety boat when the weather bodes to turn ill. Therefore, human beings who are ignorant of God's (and nature's) ways are just like individual animals—entirely lacking providence.[13] In short, while perhaps it "would not be proper for us to say that [for humans] providence watches over the species and not the individuals," Maimonides concedes that nature cares nothing for us. The best we can do is use our God-given intellects to protect ourselves from what, according to our perspective, are some of nature's more dangerous expressions. As the Talmud teaches, "the world pursues its natural course," oblivious of human needs and desires. Once again, we see that we are just a small part of the cosmos.[14]

Is There Comfort in Our Insignificance?

Significantly, for Maimonides, humanity's relative smallness is not only true but also satisfying. He notes, "When a person knows his own soul . . . and understands every being according to what it is, he becomes calm and his thoughts are not troubled."[15]

This perspective echoes that of Job, who responds to the ultimate divine demonstration of humanity's insignificance by saying, "I am comforted, for now I know that I am dust and ashes" (Job 42:6).[16] In both cases, a heightened awareness of our finitude creates an abiding sense of peace.

Many others have shared this experience. Mystics and transcendentalists seek to lose themselves in the infinite, finding God's presence in the magnificence of the creation. Biologists, paleontologists, and astronomers understand our insignificance and sometimes rejoice in it; so does anyone who has ever looked up from the bottom of a deep canyon or high mountain peak and felt awe and ecstasy.

Yet, for many people, this perspective is disconcerting. We *want* to believe that we matter as individuals, even if nature's evidence points to the contrary. On the human level, we struggle with the possibility of a brutally amoral world. We treasure the individual above all—our friends, parents, children—thereby defying the law of the jungle. Our rage and shock at the pain and death of loved ones may be futile, but these feelings are at the core of our humanity. Parents whose child dies from a snakebite may rationally understand that snakes are not an evil, that they, too, have their ecological niche. Perhaps these parents *might* even concede that if they had possessed more providence—i.e., knowledge—they may have been able to protect their child from poisonous snakes. Still, it is unlikely that all of this reasoning would console the grieving parents. Philosophically and scientifically, Maimonides may be right, but emotionally, I, for one, am drawn back to Razi.

Between Conceit and Self-Loathing

Maimonides and Razi lived centuries ago. The world as we know it today is, paradoxically, at the same time more Razian and more Maimonidean. On the one hand, we humans are more central than ever before, albeit too frequently in using our power in negative ways. We are capable of wiping out tens of thousands of species and of creating new ones through genetic engineering. Modern technology has lengthened the reach of our dominion.

On the other hand, contemporary science accentuates our insignificance. James Hutton's eighteenth-century discovery of geological "deep time," the notion that the earth is millions of years old, not 5,000 years old, taught us that humanity's sojourn on earth has lasted little more than the blink of an eye, and Darwin's theory of evolution postulated that we owe our existence largely to chance. We really are last in the order of Creation, long after the gnats, needless to say the trilobites and dinosaurs.

So, like the rabbis of old, we, too, ask: what is our place in the scheme of things? Now, as then, one answer lies in maintaining a sense of scale and balance. In his essay, "The Golden Rule," paleontologist Stephen Jay Gould reminds us that the vastness of geological time and the long-run inevitability of every species' extinction do not relieve us from our short-term responsibilities to the rest of the Creation.[17] It is probably true that, in the end, human life will have almost no measurable lasting impact on the universe. Still, we have a legitimately parochial interest in our own lives, the happiness and prosperity of our children, the suffering of our fellows.

Similarly, Maimonides warns that the proper sense of humility that follows from knowing our true place in the world should not deteriorate into self-deprecation. In the neo-Aristotelian tradition, he speaks of the ideal mean—the balance—that lies between the excesses of conceit and self-loathing. While he clearly castigates those who consider humanity to be the measure of all things, he also cautions against overreacting by denying the worth of human existence. For all of our failings, we are still "the noblest thing that is composed of the elements . . . singled out and perfected by God."[18] This echoes the words of Psalm 8, which first asks, "What is humanity, that You should take notice of us?" then asserts, "Yet You have made us little lower than the angels, and crowned us with honor and glory."[19]

Two Environmental Movements: Stewardship and Deep Ecology

This same tension between our smallness and our power defines two competing schools of contemporary environmental thought. The "Stewardship" model emphasizes our capacity to affect the rest of the Creation, for good or ill. Our challenge is to be loving caretakers of the earth. This position is grounded in God's commandment to Adam to work the soil and watch over the world (Gen. 2:15).

By contrast, the "Deep Ecology" model portrays humanity as just another transient species, of no greater significance than any other creature. We are simply one tiny strand in the web of life. Therefore, it is both arrogant and nonsensical to assume that our planet needs any stewards. It did fine before our arrival, and it will undoubtedly thrive when we are gone. We find echoes of this position in the Voice that speaks to Job from the whirlwind: "Where were you when I laid the earth's foundation? . . . Who set its cornerstone when the morning stars sang together and all the divine beings shouted for joy?" (Job 38:4, 6–7).[20]

Each of these two perspectives has its own strengths and weaknesses. Deep Ecology arose as a twentieth-century response to humanity's history of environmental degradation. The movement's founders have criticized the anthropocentrism of Stewardship, pointing to its poor record on ecological issues as proof of our failure to protect the planet from exploitation. Their critique reminds us of the danger and foolishness of appraising Creation by our own human standards. They powerfully reaffirm the intrinsic value of every species, not just those that are useful to people. Like Maimonides reprimanding Razi, they declare that "all the other beings, too, have been created for their own sakes."

Yet if it is true that the life of a human being has no greater intrinsic value than that of a flower or a frog, why should we bother to try to change our ways and repair the damage we have done? If we really are insignificant, why worry about conserving water, writing our congresspeople, and recycling waste? Deep Ecology successfully punctures our arrogance but, taken to its logical end, can easily lead to apathy.

Stewardship asserts that our actions make a measurable difference. Its advocates recognize that, at the very least, humans are in a unique position due to our power over and responsibility for the welfare of the natural world. They provide us with genuine incentives to live in a fashion that is ecologically sound.

However, as the past has often shown, the noble ideal of stewardship has frequently deteriorated into domination and despoliation. People claiming to be earth's caretakers have done horrendous things to it. The line between use and abuse is a fine one.

This is why, in the end, we need both of these movements. Together, they provide the balance that calls us to action while keeping us humble. Like Razi, the disciples of Stewardship emphasize humanity's centrality, urging us to choose environmental responsibility and restraint. Like Maimonides, the Deep Ecologists remind us that we are a tiny speck in a vast cosmos. They help us appreciate the significance of those aspects of Creation we overlook or misunderstand.

"Let Us Examine Our Deeds"

Our sages taught that for two and a half years, the school of Shammai and the school of Hillel disputed. The school of Shammai argued that it would have been better if humanity had not been created. The school of Hillel insisted that it was better for humanity to have been created. Finally, a vote was taken, and it was decided: "It would have been better if humanity had not been created, but now that we are here, let us examine our deeds."[21]

Perhaps the earth does not need us to tend it. The planet might have been better off without us. Maybe just vanity and inflated self-importance lead us to believe that we, who were created just a geological instant ago, should bear any responsibility for a world that has been evolving for 4.5 billion years. Still, for the duration that we are here, we would do well to heed the prevailing talmudic majority and, aware of our finitude, weigh our actions and do our best for ourselves, our descendants, and the rest of God's extraordinary creations.

At the age of forty-eight, A. D. Gordon, a frail Ukrainian Jew with no experience working the land, set out to become a farmer in Israel. Out of his experiences, he developed a philosophy of the relationship between land and people. While many Zionists believed that the land belonged to the people and they had a mandate to develop it, Gordon believed that the people belonged to the land. Gordon also differed from other Zionists who sought political solutions to societal ills. He called instead for a revolution of the spirit, a revolution in which people cultivate a healthy relationship to their own work and to their land. He believed that healthy individuals would develop viable communities and ultimately produce an enlightened nation. Ideas like this which were articulated by Gordon seventy years ago, are expressed today in the thinking of many modern eco-philosophers. In this essay, Rabbi David Gedzelman emphasizes the spiritual dimensions of Gordon's philosophy and its implications for the individual and ultimately for the community.

35

What Does the Hour Demand?
Environmentalism As Self-Realization

DAVID GEDZELMAN

A. D. Gordon was convinced that humanity's hope lay in the joint realization of nation and individual. National fulfillment could not be achieved at the expense of personal realization. The two processes, that of a people and that of an individual becoming whole, had to occur hand in hand, and both depended on reconnecting with nature. The way to that reconnection lay in the experience of work.

Gordon challenged the pervasive Victorian world-view in which humanity was detached from nature and urged his readers and those who looked up to him to think of their relationship to nature in a fresh and compelling way: that they were an integral expression of nature, while also set apart from it. Gordon expressed these two ways of being with the words *hacarah* and *chavayah*. *Hacarah* means "perception," "recognition," "consciousness." It is that aspect of human life that sets us apart from nature, that objectifies the natural world. *Chavayah*, on the other hand, is a term Gordon invented to express how humans are a part of nature; it means "immediate life experience." The term combines the words *chai*, "life," and *havayah*, "being."

In the healthy individual, the energy of the *chavayah*, the immediate life experience, feeds the power of the *hacarah*, perception. Using the metaphor of oil and lamp, Gordon wrote that immediate life experience—experience in nature—fuels the light of perception. Yet Gordon found that most people sacrifice *chavayah* in favor of *hacarah*. This imbalance is reflected in the way people treat nature as an object and use it for their shortsighted ends. Gordon proposed that the two ways of experiencing the world—*hacarah* and *chavayah*—need not be severed from one another.

Work and Change

Gordon believed that the individual can become rerooted in nature and fulfilled through "work." Work is that "way of being" that links people to their natural source and to themselves. Through work, perception and experience meet, becoming integrated parts of a whole; then the oil flows to the lamp. Gordon's "work" is not just any kind of physical labor. Rather, it is a way of living imbued with a profound respect for the relationship between humanity and nature, between part and the whole. As the constituent parts of the individual become integrated, so too does humanity become integrated in nature. When we work the soil in a way that lets it flourish, when we build houses in a way that settles us firmly in the world, we are moving and breathing in time with nature. When our work helps nature to realize herself, we become open to *chavayah*, and human intelligence can realize itself as an expression of the divine intellect.

Gordon wrote:

> And on that day you shall open your eyes, son of man, and you shall peek directly into the eyes of nature and you shall see in them your own image. And you shall know that you have returned to yourself, for in your hiding from nature you have hidden from yourself. . . .
>
> And you will understand on that day, that everything has not been according to your real measure and that you must invent everything anew: the way you eat and drink, your dress and your habitation, the way you work and the way you learn, everything. . . .
>
> And you will feel every slightest separation which separates your soul from the cosmic expense, from cosmic life. . . .
>
> And when you build yourself a house you will make sure not to build too many rooms and chambers, you will make sure that there will not be anything in it to block out the cosmic expanse, the cosmic life. . . .
>
> And on that day, your construction will no longer be, son of man, that which destroys the majesty of the world's own construction, and the beauty of your building a blemish in the sphere of cosmic beauty. . . . And you shall learn torah from the mouth of nature, the torah of building and creating, and you shall learn to do as nature does in everything you build and in everything you create. And so in all your ways and in all your life you will learn to be a partner in creation.[1]

Renewing the Jewish People

An individual does not become connected to "cosmic life" alone. One's connection grows along with other people's. Together, a common soul is reawakened. "The revival of the people," wrote Gordon, "its renewal as a working and creating people, will not come except through work in nature."[2] For the Jew, this connection to "cosmic life" and nature happens as the Jewish people returns to its land. According to Gordon, work is redemptive not only for humanity but for nature as well: "The redemption of the land will not come except through work. One only acquires the land through work. . . . "[3]

As Gordon saw it, the Jewish People—divorced from its natural environment, the Land of Israel—must reconnect with its homeland, not just for themselves but for all peoples. Jews were a model of a people exiled from nature, and all nations need to renew their relationship to nature.

Gordon was not a political Zionist. Rather for him, Zionism demanded

a fundamental revolution in spirit, in the patterns of life, in one's relation to life. . . . There is no war between labor and property, but rather the war is between creativity and parasitism. Property is not the key to power or happiness or the essence of life. The key is creativity.[4]

Gordon was uneasy with certain Marxist assumptions. Although an active member of Degania, Israel's first kibbutz, and enthusiastic about collective life, Gordon refuted Marxist claims that change would only emerge from conflict between classes, between property and labor, between ruling class and proletariat.

Gordon believed the "state" had created unhealthy conditions for collective life. As long as the state encouraged a mechanized society in which each individual was valued according to the needs of the state, individuals would have no choice but to experience each other and nature as something to be exploited for gain. To aspire toward a Jewish "state" was to aspire toward the same social structure that plagued the world.

Gordon believed that the essential and natural units of family and community life had atrophied under the mechanistic influences of the state and must be revived. Only when the individual was reintegrated with family and community and revitalized by work could a healthy Jewish enterprise be forged.

Gordon understood the relationship between people and nature and between the Jewish people and the Land of Israel as a religious relationship. The healing of individual and nation could only occur as people opened to the Divine. "Work" was the means by which this could happen. In the end, building a new life for the Jewish people depended on the relationship between humanity and nature.

While Deep Ecologists claim that anthropocentrism is the basis of our environmental crisis and that the solution to the crisis is a biocentric world-view, religious thinkers claim that anthropocentrism is the root of all of our problems—not just environmental—and that the solution is a theocentric, or a God-centered, world-view. Abraham Joshua Heschel, one of the most important Jewish thinkers and more eloquent writers of the twentieth century, argued that we must abandon our anthropocentric ways and substitute a God-centered vision for the sake of ourselves, for the sake of Creation, and for the sake of God. In the following essay, Marc Swetlitz explores Heschel's vision.

36

Living As If God Mattered: Heschel's View of Nature and Humanity

MARC SWETLITZ

Our age is one in which usefulness is thought to be the chief merit of nature; in which the attainment of power, the utilization of its resources is taken to be the chief purpose of man in God's creation. Man has indeed become primarily a tool-making animal, and the world is now a gigantic tool-box for the satisfaction of his needs.

—ABRAHAM JOSHUA HESCHEL, *God in Search of Man*

Today's environmental crisis will not be solved by lawyers, environmentalists, and superior technologies alone. The problems we face point to deeper problems of the human condition. They strike at the heart of what it means to live a Jewish life: to have a sense of the sacred; to see the world, as it were, through God's eyes.

A.J. Heschel, one of the most important Jewish theologians of the mid-twentieth century, confronted these deeper problems years before environmentalism became popular. Heschel was concerned with the growth and pervasiveness of "technical civilization"—its detrimental impact on humanity's relationship with God and with the material world.

Heschel argued that "technical civilization" exists to harness nature for the fulfillment of human need. Essential to "technical civilization" is a utilitarian view of humanity, a humanity seeking to fill itself with the products and artifacts of nature.

In a world dominated by the utilitarian ethic, a sense of wonder dissolves. There is little time for appreciation and reverence, since the value of utility transcends all our interactions, including those with neighbors and community. By reducing the world to an instrument, we lose our own value, and we become instruments of productivity. Eventually, we relate to others as similar instruments of productivity. The qualities of compassion and empathy are lost, leading invariably to the "disintegration of man."[1]

Heschel believed that a society oriented toward utility develops when we see ourselves as the center of the universe, when we view nature and others in terms of our needs and desires. The alternative to such a universe is one in which *God* is at the center, in which we view nature and others as part of God's Creation. In a universe where we endeavor to see the sacred in everything, we are unlikely to practice utilitarianism. In a God-centered universe, all life becomes a source of wonder.

Throughout his writings, Heschel contrasts the human-centered view of nature associated with our technical civilization with the Creation-centered view represented by the prophets in the Bible:

> Modern man dwells upon the order and power of nature; the prophets dwell upon the grandeur and creation of nature. The former directs his attention to the manageable and intelligible aspect of the universe; the latter to its mystery and marvel. . . . The Biblical man does not see nature in isolation but in relation to God.[2]

The way out of this crisis of technical civilization—out of utilitari-anism—is by recovering our ability to experience God and to see nature as God's creation. According to Heschel, we need to break old patterns of thinking and behavior and adopt a radically different way of life, an authentically Jewish way.

The Path of Prayer

How can we acquire this new way of seeing? We are habituated to think-ing of nature solely in terms of ourselves. What could shake us out of our self-centeredness and the illusion that we are the masters of our uni-verse? Changing attitudes and world-views takes a serious, concerted effort, especially when we are enveloped by a culture that is constantly marketing products it wants us to "need."

Heschel argues that "prayer" is the way back to wonder. Whether or not we sense God's presence when we encounter some aspect of nature, we are commanded to utter prayers at such moments. This prac-tice reminds us of the sacred in the mundane aspects of everyday living and points us to the mystery of God.

> We are trained in our sense of wonder by uttering a prayer before the enjoyment of food. Each time we are about to drink a glass of water, we remind ourselves of the eternal mystery of creation, "Blessed be Thou . . . by Whose word all things come into being." . . . Wishing to eat bread or fruit, or enjoy a pleas-ant fragrance or a cup of wine; on tasting fruit in season for the first time; on seeing a rainbow, or the ocean; on noticing trees when they blossom . . . we are taught to invoke His great name and our awareness of Him.[3]

It will do no good to seek rational and logical answers to accept or reject God. In Judaism, we are required to act as if God exists, as if the sacred is alive in everything. Judaism requires a "leap of action": we act *before* we believe. Indeed, "right living is a way to right thinking."[4] Prayer is not the mindless repetition of a credo. True prayer begins only when we *cultivate* an awareness that reality points to something beyond itself.

Experiences in nature can have a similar effect on our attitudes and perceptions as prayer does.

> It is only when we suddenly come up against things obviously
> beyond the scope of human domination . . . such as mountains
> or oceans, . . . that we are somewhat shaken out of our illu-
> sions. . . . Confined in our own study rooms, we may entertain
> any idea that comes to our mind. . . .[5]

We must get out of our offices, out of artificially constructed environments, and encounter natural phenomena over which we have no
control.

Both experiences of prayer and nature have a similar effect: They
draw us out of "the narrowness of self-interest and enable us to see the
world in the mirror of the holy. We do not step out of the world when we
pray; we merely see the world in a different setting. . . . In prayer we
shift the center of living from self-consciousness to self-surrender."[6]
Through prayer, we become aware of nature as an object of God's love
and compassion.

> The world that we nurture through an attitude of prayer, God's
> world, is a very different one from the one that we have become
> habituated to in our technical civilization. What we consider
> inanimate is alive from God's point of view: "What is a *thing*
> to us is a concern to God."[7]

The appropriate response to God's world is "reverence," the attitude
that assumes that all is "precious" and "valuable." We express reverence
when we are eager to find a trace of the Divine everywhere, when we lose
interest in how the world can be used and instead appreciate the world
for what it is.

A Path to Follow

If nature does not belong to us, Heschel asked, "By what right, do we
exploit, consume and enjoy the fruits of the trees, the blessings of the
earth?"[8] God granted us the right to transform nature to satisfy our
needs. "The duty to work for six days is just as much a part of God's
covenant with man as the duty to abstain from work on the seventh
day."[9] It is precisely this duty that constitutes the legitimate impulse
behind our technical civilization.

However, the danger in our technical civilization is that the satisfaction of needs is paramount. The more we have, the more we want, and we soon lose the ability to distinguish what we "want" from what we "need." "Acquiring things, [we] become enslaved to them."[10] How can we break our infatuation with things, which leads to the exploitation of nature and our fellow human beings?

The Jewish way of living rejects both the renunciation of technical civilization and our infatuation with it. Judaism offers a middle way. The Sabbath provides an archetype for living with the artifacts of the material world, without becoming dependent on them for fulfillment.

On the Sabbath, we are independent of technical civilization not because we renounce technology, but because we turn our souls away from our mundane human needs and toward God. During the Sabbath, we escape the grip of technical civilization and express our supreme love for God rather than for things.

The importance of the Sabbath, for Heschel, lies not simply in the day itself, but in the effect of that day on the rest of our lives. The Sabbath needs "the companionship of all other days."[11] Our actions throughout the week must be shaped by our deep attachment to God forged on the Sabbath. The Sabbath invigorates us with the energy necessary to bring a Sabbath consciousness to the rest of the week, to bring a taste of the sacred to what is ordinarily profane.

A life with a Sabbath practice at its core is a life of piety. Piety involves constant awareness of the nearness of God. It is the antithesis of the idolatry at the heart of our technical civilization, an idolatry that places things, the satisfaction of needs, and the value of utility at the center of life. The pious life involves asceticism and sacrifice, for it is this practice that frees us from the illusion that humans are the rightful owners of nature. In sacrificing, we return to God what belongs to God. This expresses our awareness that nature and the things we create from it are, ultimately, gifts from God.

However, asceticism and sacrifice do not point to a life of poverty. Poverty can be a hindrance to the life of the spirit. Indeed, the inability to satisfy our basic physical needs may interfere with developing a life of reverence. "Judaism," Heschel wrote, "does not despise the carnal. It does not urge us to desert the flesh but to control and to counsel it."[12]

In the end, how do we live? Jewish living, for Heschel, involves "checks and balances." Aware that God created the world and that all of nature exists in continual relationship to God, we respond in reverence and prayer. Aware that we are permitted by God to subdue the earth for six days a week, we labor to transform nature to satisfy our needs while maintaining a constant awareness of God's presence. We produce and purchase things, but we also prevent our enslavement to them by attaching our souls to God. How do we balance reverence and use in our relationship to nature? Is it possible to have too many things, such that it becomes impossible to keep God's concerns uppermost in our minds? To begin to ask such questions is to break the mental habits created by our technical civilization and to take a significant step toward a Jewish way of living in the material world.

You don't have to live far off in wilderness to experience nature on a regular basis. Nature is alive in the city if we take the time to notice. The most important thing is to love wherever we are. That's the beginning of stewardship. A Jewish community can help us walk the stewardship path.

37

How Community Forms a Jew

ELLEN BERNSTEIN

I grew up in Haverhill, Massachusetts, a small depressed city on the Merrimac River. It had neither the cultural advantages of the city nor the aesthetic pleasures of the country. My entire extended family on both sides was in the shoe business. My parents moved from Newburyport—where my grandfather's factory was located—to Haverhill the year I was born because of the "Jewish" community there. For us kids, my parents' decision backfired. We found nothing in the Jewish community to attract us. Hebrew School was boring, and the High Holy Days were a fashion show. And that was the extent of my *Jewish* life in the 1950s. Life in Haverhill was hardly any better: *the* place to be was Tic Toc, a greasy spoon downtown. By the time we were old enough to drive, my Catholic friends and I fled town every weekend and took to the mountains for skiing adventures.

Throughout high school and college, I had been disheartened by our culture's ungrateful attitude toward nature. I longed to live close to nature. I still remember a story in the *New York Times* one Sunday by a student who was among the first women admitted to Yale. Her one ambition was to move to the country and live simply on the earth. She spoke my mind. I dreamed of spending my entire life on a large rambling farm in Vermont with an extended family of friends.

After college, I moved to Northern California and Oregon and for many years guided wilderness trips. I read every book I could find by nature and science writers. My friends and I found solace and joy in mountains and birds. We were more interested in nature than in people.

Ultimately, my single-mindedness led to isolation and misanthropy. At the same time, my romance with guiding white-water trips was fading. For too long, I had internalized *other* people's glamorous fantasies of the life of a river guide. On the inside I felt empty, lonely, and tired of being on the road all the time. I longed for stability and a more balanced life.

The year I turned 30, I moved from the mountains of southern Oregon to Philadelphia, ostensibly to pursue a career in physical therapy. Physical therapy never really inspired me, but I wasn't sure that I would ever find a career that would express who I was.

Living my parochial life in the country, I had developed misconceptions about cities and people. Cities were devoid of nature and without beauty. They were nasty places full of violence and crime, where everyone was swept up in the "rat race." I planned to move to Philadelphia, get a quick education, and escape back to the country.

In fact, it was moving to Philadelphia—not being in school—that changed my life. I remember my first visit there in the spring of 1982. The azaleas were blooming in dazzling shades of fuchsia, peach, and purple, the brilliant and intoxicating colors of the tropics. I was completely overwhelmed—and still am—at how beautiful it was. The summer I began school, the humidity was overbearing, but I didn't mind. Compared to the dusty, dry summers in California and Oregon, Philadelphia seemed like a tropical rain forest. It was as though I had been reborn. My eyes were wide with the delight of seeing the world for the first time.

I graduated school, but I never left Philadelphia.

My greatest lessons really came from living in community, rather than living on the river or far off in the mountains, where I had expected all my dreams would be fulfilled.

Finding My Place

Upon arriving in Philadelphia, I settled in Mount Airy because of the proximity of the Wissahickon River Valley— which continues to take my breath away every day—and because I had heard there was an "interesting"—read: "alternative"—Jewish community there. I tiptoed around the Jewish community for a while, trying to avoid it. But before long, I found myself thrust headlong into a variety of its activities. Eventually, I founded *Shomrei Adamah*—Keepers of the Earth, the nation's first Jewish environmental organization. From then on, I headed unwittingly in a community-oriented direction. Running an organization is much more about people and community-building than about nature and environment. I had never pictured myself working in the Jewish community. Yet, it was the communal nature of the work that affected me most deeply.

Even though I understood the need for Jewish community in my work, I did not, at first, see its value in my personal life. I assumed—from my childhood experience—that synagogues were cold and empty buildings, void of any spiritual substance. One day several years ago, Rabbi Joseph Glaser *z"l*, the late leader of the Reform movement and one of my favorite mentors, sat me down and demanded to know why I didn't belong to a synagogue. I reminded him that I was single and childless and cynically questioned what synagogue life might possibly offer me. I was involved in informal Jewish learning and regularly visited many *havurot*. I could do all this without belonging to any *institution*. He suggested I drop my judgment and see what I might discover. I was more content to keep my distance and remain the outsider.

But I always held onto a vision of the "ideal" synagogue: a place where all stripes and all ages of Jews—anyone who chose to follow a Jewish path—gathered for conversation, comfort, friendship, skill swapping, learning, and genuine spiritual direction. I had always thought that if synagogues (and other religious institutions) did what they were intended to—give people the tools to find/create meaning in their lives—there wouldn't be the preponderance of therapies, self-help techniques, and New Age alternatives that overwhelm us today. Still, I couldn't imagine that the synagogue of my dreams could actually exist.

On the other hand, the "alternative" Jewish options did not really provide what I was looking for, either. I was not moved by the experimental, interpersonal prayer services that are popular in Mount Airy. My intellectual curiosity, my drive to do what needs to be done, and my new interest in community were motivating me. Then Lenny Gordon become the rabbi at Germantown Jewish Center—the neighborhood shul—and my friend and mentor Neil Gillman said to me, "*Now* you will have a home." I took Neil's words as a challenge, met Lenny, and instantly knew that Neil was right. Lenny prodded me along; he invited me to help build the Friday night service, positioned me as co-chair of the Outreach committee, and nourished me at our Center City "Lunch and Learns."

Today, Germantown Jewish Center provides much of the context of my life. Besides offering friendship, intellectual stimulation, and a connection to the larger world, living a Jewish life reinforces all the ecological lessons that I have tried to live and promote for so long. I have always felt that a future for people and for our planet requires integrating ecological awareness and practices into our daily lives. One of the greatest obstacles to our meeting the environmental challenge is that we often *forget* that nature matters. We may have momentary glimpses of the value of nature when we travel to mountain retreats and tropical resorts, but how do we consistently maintain a sense that the earth is sacred so that stewarding the earth becomes habitual and normal? What can keep us remembering, acting? That's where community comes in. In my case, that's where Jewish community comes in.

Living in Community

My most regular connection to the Jewish community comes on Friday night. Only recently did I begin to grasp what the Friday night service was about, but I still went to shul because I enjoyed the routine, and the service provided a context for a weekly meditation. Now that I have actually studied the prayer book (which for so many years I found offputting), my experience of the service is deeper. The single most important theme of the *Kabbalat Shabbat* service—the first half of the Friday night service—is nature, or in the religious vocabulary, Creation. *Kab-*

balat Shabbat is composed of psalms that are linked together by their universality and their orientation toward nature as a manifestation of God:

> For in His hands are the hidden mysteries of the earth. . . (94:5)
> Tremble before Him, all the earth. . . (96:9)
> When the Lord reigns, the earth will exult. . . (97:1)
> His lightnings lighten the world; the earth sees and trembles; the mountains melt like wax at the presence of the Lord, at the presence of the Lord of the whole earth. . . (97:4–5)
> Let the sea roar. . . the rivers clap their hands. . . the mountains sing for joy (98:7–8)
> Let the earth be moved. (99:1)

The psalms not only offer a heightened vision of nature; they also call us to examine ourselves and, in particular, our arrogance. This is in keeping with the meaning of the Hebrew word "to pray," *l'hitpalel*, which can also be translated "to judge." Because the verb is reflexive, it means to judge *ourselves*, to examine *ourselves*.

In Ps. 95:8, we are told: "Do not harden your hearts like you did at Meribah, and like you did in the day of Massah in the wilderness." God pleads with the Jews not to grow hardhearted like Moses did when, in his one self-centered act, he struck the rock instead of talking to it, believing that *he* had the power to make water. For this moment of hardheartedness, of not listening to God, of believing he knew better than God, Moses was punished and never allowed to enter the Land of Israel. Hardheartedness can be the ruin of us all. It can ruin nature as well. The metaphor itself is telling. We can't appreciate nature if our hearts are closed; if we don't see or experience the blessings of nature, it's easy to exploit nature. But if our hearts are open enough to recognize the life that's there—the holiness of place and creatures—then stewardship flows naturally. Opening our hearts requires abandoning the idea that we control the universe and we are its master. This could be our greatest spiritual challenge.

Judaism, then, offers us perceptual tools—the idea of God as Creator, of nature as a manifestation of God, of personal responsibility and renewal—that we can use each day to remind ourselves how magnificent the world is and that we have a profound responsibility toward nature. It

also offers us a discipline of learning that has environmental implications. Learning in the Jewish sense is not to be equated with weighty
classroom study. Traditional Jewish learning involves exploring a few
lines of the Bible or a Jewish text. What does it mean to me, to you, to
our many ancestors? The learning begins as a focused conversation and
turns into a stream of consciousness. Learning becomes a journey into
the soul—the individual soul and the collective communal soul. In
Mount Airy on any Shabbat afternoon (particularly between Passover
and Shavuot, when it is traditional to study *Pirke Avot*), neighbors often
gather in the late afternoon to learn together. In fact, nearly every night
of the week throughout the year, study sessions take place in homes
throughout the neighborhood. Such "entertainment" requires no amuse-
ment parks, no home entertainment centers, no fancy clothes, no great
expense of money. It is beautiful in its utter simplicity. The centrality of
learning in Jewish life is another way that Judaism teaches that we don't
need to exploit nature to nourish our souls.

There are also practical dimensions of living in a synagogue community that can contribute to a more environmentally oriented way of
life. Last year, Lyndal and Chuck Miller installed a biblical garden at the
synagogue. They planted a fig tree, a grape arbor, flax, wheat, barley,
and many other plants that reflect the biblical landscape of Israel; Lyndal
uses the garden to give her students from the Jewish Center a hands-on
appreciation of the plants they read about in Jewish texts. I am delighted that people recognize the synagogue's potential for bringing nature
into the lives of their children and their families. The garden project
offers a powerful vision of what might be possible if *every* synagogue
developed a garden—be it for teaching purposes, for meditation, for raising food for the disadvantaged, or purely for aesthetics.

The synagogue and other Jewish institutions also serve as labora-
tories for organizing environmental change. I now participate on the synagogue's board and work with a variety of Jewish institutions. At another time, I would have thought board meetings and organizational design
tiresome and unproductive. But today, the problems of synagogues and
Jewish institutions interest me. They reflect the sort of generational and
lifestyle differences that invariably interfere with change. For example, I
take the garden idea quite seriously. Gardens—planned properly—pro-

vide the perfect opportunity to teach environmental awareness and Jewish values. They can also transform synagogues or Jewish institutions into more welcoming and sacred places. After all, the first Temple was traditionally associated with the Garden of Eden. But my idea is not particularly fashionable—yet. At least as much organizational work must go into developing and selling such a simple idea as a synagogue garden as the implementation of the garden itself. First you need to research and formulate plans for the project, then try to convince all the appropriate individuals and committees that the idea is a sound one, then secure funding for the design and the plants, then rouse volunteers and identify possible staff. There's always a multiplicity of decisions to be made, and progress is sometimes unbearably slow. That is the nature of institutional change. It is frustrating, but the rewards on the other side may be great: organizations working for you, not against you.

I have often thought that the most radical thing I could do would be to fully live a Jewish way of life. Growing up with no Jewish education or practice, in an assimilated, secular family, in a culture that doesn't value religion, I have no *outside* motivation to be Jewish. Rather, I *choose* to be Jewish, and I have to make this choice over and over again. Judaism doesn't tell me how to live my life, but it does *keep* me oriented in the direction I want to go. It reinforces the values that I want to stay true to but am constantly being seduced away from. Life is a narrow bridge. It's easy to fall. Being Jewish—living in a Jewish community—helps to keep me focused on the path.

Notes

Sacred Place

1. *Adam, Adamah,* and *Adonai:* The Relationship between Humans, Nature, and God in the Bible

1. Brigitte Kahl, "Human Culture and the Integrity of Creation: Biblical Reflections on Genesis 1–11," *The Ecumenical Review* 39 (April 1987): 130.
2. For a fuller discussion of this concept, see Tikva Frymer-Kensky, *In the Wake of the Goddesses* (New York: The Free Press, 1992), chaps. 3, 9.
3. Charles F. Melchert, "Creation and Justice Among the Sages," *Religious Education* 85 (summer 1990): 372.

3. (Mis)reading Genesis: A Response to Environmentalist Critiques of Judaism

1. Lynn White Jr., "The Historical Roots of our Ecological Crisis," *Science* 155 (10 March 1967).
2. For an overview of the debate and an extensive bibliography, see Elspeth Whitney, "Lynn White, Ecotheory and History," *Environmental Ethics* 15 (summer 1993). Whitney reviews various Christian responses to White, and she points out that they often want to debate over what the Bible means in some objective sense, rather than what it *has meant* through history.
3. Ian McHarg, "The Place of Nature in the City of Man," in *Western Man and Environmental Ethics,* ed. Ian Barbour (Reading, Mass.: Addison-Wesley, 1973), p. 175.
4. For development of this idea in depth, see John Passmore, *Man's Responsibility for Nature: Ecological Problems and Western Traditions* (London: Duckworth, 1974), pp. 28–40.
5. This is the theme of much of the biblical book of Deuteronomy and specifically of Deut. 28:63–68.
6. Elinor Gadon, "Metaphors of Birthing: Toward a New Creation Story for

the Age of Ecology," in *After Earth Day*, ed. Max Oelschlager (Denton, Tex.: University of North Texas Press, 1992), pp. 187–191. Gadon's ideas appear to be influenced by or are at least strikingly similar to the views of the late Joseph Campbell, who wrote extensively on myth. Campbell was also hostile to both historical and contemporary Judaism; for a critique of Campbell's treatment of Judaism in his work, see Tamar Frankiel, "New Age Mythology: A Jewish Response to Joseph Campbell," *Tikkun* 4, no. 3 (May/June 1989). For documentation of his social anti-Semitism, see *What Did They Think of the Jews?*, ed. Allan Gould (Toronto: Stewart House, 1991), pp. 356–358.

7. Thomas Berry, *The Dream of the Earth* (San Francisco: Sierra Club Books, 1988), pp. 80–81, 148–152.

8. Moses Maimonides (also known as Rambam), *Mishneh Torah, Hilchot Yesodeh Torah* 1:8–9. trans. Philip Birnbaum (New York: Hebrew Publishing Company, 1989), p. 7.

9. Arnold Toynbee, "The Religious Background of the Present Environmental Crisis," in *Ecology and Religion in History*, ed. David and Eileen Spring (New York: Harper and Row, 1974), p. 141.

10. Warwick Fox, *Toward a Transpersonal Ecology* (Boston: Shambhala, 1990).

4. Is There Only One Holy Land?

1. See T. H. Gaster, "Earth," in *Interpreter's Dictionary of the Bible (IDB)*, (Nashville: Abingdon Press, 1962), vol. 2, pp. 2–3.

2. *Midrash Ha-Gadol, Bereshit*; and E. A. Speiser, *Genesis*, The Anchor Bible (New York: Doubleday, 1982), p. 16, n. 5.

3. See S. Talmon, "Wilderness," in *IDB Supplement* (Nashville: Abingdon Press, 1984), pp. 946–948; and Exod. 4:22 f, 33:12; Deut. 27:9, 1 Kings 19:4–8; Hos. 2:14–15; Jer. 2:1, 31:2 f.

4. M. *Berachot* 6:3.

5. Harry Orlinski, "The Biblical Concept of the Land of Israel," in *The Land of Israel: Jewish Perspectives*, ed. Lawrence A. Hoffman (Notre Dame: University of Notre Dame Press, 1986), p. 53. This observation was made in the *Mekhilta, Pisha*, 1: "Before the Land had been especially chosen, all lands were suitable for divine revelation; after the Land had been chosen, all other lands were eliminated."

6. *Webster's Unabridged Dictionary*, 1989, p. 1574.

7. Lev. 19:9, 10; Deut. 24:19–21; M. *Peah*.

8. Lev. 19:23–25; M. *Orlah*.

9. Lev. 19:19; Deut. 22:9–11; M. *Kilayim*.

10. Num. 18:8, 12, 24–26; Deut. 18:4; M. *Terumot*.

11. Exod. 23:19; Deut. 26:1–11; M. *Bikkurim*.

12. *Rosh Hashanah* 31a.

13. M. *Kelim* 1:6.

14. Charles Primus, "The Borders of Judaism: The Land of Israel in Early Rabbinic Judaism," in *The Land of Israel: Jewish Perspectives*, ed. Lawrence A. Hoffman (Notre Dame: University of Notre Dame Press, 1986), p. 102.

15. M. *Orlah* 3:9; T. *Terumah* 2:13; T. *Orlah* 1:8; T. *Kiddushin* 1:9–10, 12.

16. See M. *Mikva'ot* 8:1.

17. M. *Oholot* 2:3, 17:5, 18:6–7; M. *Tohorot* 4:5, 5:1; M. *Nazir* 3:6, 7:3; T. *Mikva'ot* 6:1; T. *Oholot* 17:7–18:11.

18. Richard S. Sarason, "The Significance of the Land of Israel in the Mishnah," in *The Land of Israel: Jewish Perspectives*, ed. Lawrence A. Hoffman (Notre Dame: University of Notre Dame Press, 1986), p. 123.

19. *Ketubbot* 110b.

20. *Sotah* 14a (see also M. *Kelim* 1:6).

21. See Arnold A. Lasker and Damiel J. Lasker, "The Strange Case of December 4: A Liturgical Problem," *Conservative Judaism* XXXVIII:1 (fall 1985): 91–96; and "The Jewish Prayer for Rain in Babylonia," *The Journal for the Study of Judaism*, (June 1984): 123–144.

22. For the history of the Ben Meir calendar controversy, see Henry Malter, *Life and Works of Saadia Gaon* (Philadelphia: Jewish Publication Society, 1921).

23. Jacob Neusner, "Map without Territory: Mishnah's System of Sacrifice and Sanctuary," *History of Religions* XIX (November 1979): 125.

24. *Berachot* 35a.

25. For a few examples, see Lev. 18:24–30, 20:22–26; Num. 25:34; Deut. 4:40, 21:6–9; Ps. 106:38 f.

26. W. D. Davies, *The Territorial Dimension of Judaism* (Berkeley: University of California Press, 1982), p. 134.

5. How Wilderness Forms a Jew

1. Chaim Potok, *Wanderings* (New York: Fawcett Crest Books, 1980), p. 81.

2. Samson Raphael Hirsch, *The Hirsch Haggadah* (New York: Feldheim, 1988), pp. 124–128.

3. Bruce Chatwin, *The Songlines* (New York: Viking, 1987), p. 193.

6. A Sentient Universe

1. Thomas Nagel, *Mortal Questions* (Cambridge: Cambridge University Press, 1979), p. 181.

2. Johannes Pederson, *Israel: Its Life and Culture* (London & Copenhagen: Oxford University Press, 1959), I–II, p. 479

3. Ibid.

4. Ibid.

5. Monford Harris, "Ecology: A Covenantal Approach," *CCAR Journal*, (summer 1976): 103–104.

6. For example, Ps. 19, 96:11–12, 98:7–9; Isa. 44:23, 55:12; Job 38:7.

7. Nahum M. Sarna, *Songs of the Heart* (New York: Schocken Books, 1993), p. 78.

8. Ibid.

9. Cf. "All that is either spatial or conscious. . . . What is spatial is not conscious; what is conscious is not spatial. . . . All things are either bodies or minds; substances are either spatial or conscious. . . . The world falls thus into two completely different and completely separated realms: that of bodies and that of minds" (W. Windelband; *A History of Philosophy* [New York: Macmillan, 1901], p. 405).

10. *Soncino Talmud* (London: Soncino Press, 1936), *Shabbat* 63a; cf. *Yebamot* 116, 24a.

11. Z. H. Chajes, *The Student's Guide through the Talmud* (New York: Philip Feldheim, 1960), p. 177.

12. Ibid.

13. Ibid., 148:5.

14. *Encyclopedia Judaica*, vol. 13, pp. 273–275, s.v. "Perek Shirah"; Barry Holtz, "A Chapter of Song: Perek Shira," *The Jewish Almanac*, eds. Richard Siegel and Carl Rheins (New York: Bantam Books, 1982), p. 324.

15. For example, *Otzar Hatefilot*, *Siddur Bet-Yaakov*, and *Siddur Tefilah l'Moshe*.

16. Ibid., p. 324.

17. Pedersen, op. cit., p. 155.

18. John B. Cobb Jr. and David Ray Griffin, *Process Theology: An Introductory Exposition* (Philadelphia: Westminster Press, 1976), p. 77; cf. especially chap. 4, "A Theology of Nature."

19. Cited in Jay B. McDaniel, *Earth, Sky, Gods, Mortals* (Mystic, Conn.: Twenty-Third Publications, 1990), p. 87.

20. Ibid., p. 91.

21. *Maggid Sichot*, p. 8.

22. *New Union Prayerbook*, p. 8; paraphrase by Rabbi Dr. Aaron Opher of Hebrew original in *Badereck*, vol. 1, p. 47.

7. Practical Kabbalah: A Family History

1. Professor Miles Krassen translated the *Peri 'Ez Hadar* into English, for the first time, in 1991.

8. Jewish Perspectives on Limiting Consumption

1. *Genesis Rabbah* 9:7.

2. Babylonian Talmud, *Berachot* 35a.

3. Babylonian Talmud, Tractate *Hullin* 109b.

4. *Genesis Rabbah* 16:5.

5. *Mishnah Avot* 4:1.

6. See Moses Maimonides, *Laws of Gifts to the Poor* 7:5.

7. Cited in J. R. Marcus, *The Jew in the Medieval World* (Athenaeum: New York, 1983), p. 195.
8. Moses Maimonides, *Laws of the Scroll of Esther* 2:17.
9. Jerusalem Talmud, *Demai* 1:3.
10. Moses Maimonides, *Laws of Opinions*, chap. 5.
11. Babylonian Talmud, *Sukkah* 52b.
12. Nahmanides' commentary on the Torah, Deut. 22:6, s.v. "if you chance upon a bird's nest."
13. Abravanel's commentary on the Torah, Deut. 22:6, s.v. "if you chance upon a bird's nest."
14. Ibid.
15. Babylonian Talmud, *Baba Kamma* 91b.
16. *Shabbat* 67b.
17. See, for example, Rashi on *Baba Kamma* 91b, s.v. "and if its value was great."
18. See Smith, *The Wealth of Nations*, bk. II, chap. I.
19. *Responsa Hatam Sofer, Yoreh Deah*, no. 102.

Sacred Time

1. Abraham Joshua Heschel, *Between God and Man* (New York: Free Press, 1965), p. 215.
2. Stephen Jay Gould, *Time's Arrow, Time's Cycle* (Cambridge, Mass.: Harvard University Press, 1987).
3. D. H. Lawrence, "A Propos of Lady Chatterly's Lover," in *Phoenix II: Uncollected, Unpublished, and Other Prose Works by D. H. Lawrence*, eds. Warren Roberts and Harry T. Moore (New York: Viking Press, 1968), p. 504.

10. The Sun, the Moon, and the Seasons: Ecological Implications of the Hebrew Calendar

1. Nahum Sarna, *Exploring Exodus* (New York: Schocken Books, 1986), p. 81.
2. Nogah Hareuveni, *Nature in Our Biblical Heritage* (Israel: Neot Kedumim, 1980), p. 49.
3. Solomon Gandz, "Studies in the Hebrew Calendar," *Jewish Quarterly Review* 39 (1948–49): 259 and 40 (1949–50): 251.
4. Historians conclude that Gezer was a city fortified by Solomon, which survived only a short time before it was destroyed in 918 B.C.E. The Gezer Calendar was probably written during the brief period of Israelite occupancy between 950 and 918 B.C.E.
5. W. F. Albright, "The Gezer Calendar," *BASOR* 92 (1943): 16–26.
6. Ibid. p. 25.

7. Ben Zion Wacholder and David B. Weisberg, "Visibility of the New Moon, in Cuneiform and Rabbinic Sources," *Hebrew Union College Annual* XLII (1971).
8. *Mishnah Rosh Hashanah* 2:5.
9. *Mishnah Rosh Hashanah* 1:9.
10. *Mishnah Rosh Hashanah* 1:8.
11. *Mishnah Rosh Hashanah* 2:7.
12. *Mishnah Rosh Hashanah* 2:3.
13. *B. Erubin* 56a.
14. *B. Hullin* and *B. Rosh Hashanah* 20b.
15. *Encyclopedia Judaica*, vol. 8, p. 486, s.v. "Hillel II."

11. "In Your Goodness, You Renew Creation": The Creation Cycles of the Jewish Liturgy

1. Cf. Jon Levenson, *Sinai and Zion: An Entry into the Jewish Bible* (San Francisco: Harper and Row, 1987).
2. Richard Morris, *Time's Arrows: Scientific Attitudes Toward Time* (New York: Simon and Schuster, 1984), p. 23. Cf. also Mircea Eliade, *The Myth of the Eternal Return* (Princeton, N.J.: Princeton University Press, 1991).
3. Yoseph Hayim Yerushalmi, *Zachor: Jewish History and Jewish Memory* (Seattle: University of Washington Press, 1982), pp. 7–8.
4. Cf. Northrop Frye, *The Great Code* (Toronto: Academic Press, 1982), p. 169 f.
5. Gershom Scholem, *Kabbalah* (New York: Quadrangle/The New York Times Book Co., 1974), pp. 118–122.
6. Cf. Lawrence Troster, "Journey to the Center of the Earth: *Birkat Ha-Mazon* and the Quest for Holiness," *Conservative Judaism* XLVII, no. 2 (winter 1995): 3–16.
7. Cf. I Sam. 20, where the new moon is celebrated by a sacred feast that requires all its participants to be in a state of ritual purity.
8. Cf. Jon Levenson, *Creation and the Persistence of Evil* (San Francisco: Harper and Row, 1988), pp. 66–77; Raphael Patai, *Man and Temple* (London: Thomas Nelson and Sons, 1947).
9. Cf. Baruch Levine, *The JPS Torah Commentary: Leviticus* (Philadelphia: The Jewish Publication Society, 1989), pp. 263–265. Theodore Gaster, *Festivals of the Jewish Year* (New York: William Sloane Associates Publishers, 1953), pp. 31–32.

12. Shabbat and the Sabbatical Year

1. Babylonian Talmud, *Shabbat* 49b.
2. *Shabbat* 119a.

3. *Shulchan Aruch shel ha-Ari*, as cited in *Encyclopedia Judaica*, vol. 14, p. 569.
4. *Exodus Rabbah* 12:5.

13. The Land of Your Soul

1. TB *Bezah* 16a.
2. *Zohar* 2:204a.
3. Rashi on *Bereshit* 2:2.
4. *Tikkune ha-Zohar* 21 (45b).
5. *Ra'aya Meheimna* 3:29.
6. Moses Maimonides, *Mishneh Torah, Hilchot Shabbat* 29:29.

14. Rain and the Calendar

1. Deut. 11:10–12. The second paragraph of the *Sh'ma* derives from Deut. 11:13–21.
2. *Rosh Hashanah* 17b.
3. Rashi's commentary on *Talmud Rosh Hashanah* 14a.

15. Sukkot: Holiday of Joy

1. Philip Goodman, *The Sukkot/Simchat Torah Anthology* (Philadelphia: Jewish Publication Society, 1988).
2. Ibid.
3. Ibid.

17. A History of Tu B'Sh'vat

1. *Mishnah Rosh Hashanah*.

18. The Tu B'Sh'vat Seder

1. In 1989, Dr. Miles Krassen was commissioned by *Shomrei Adamah*—Keepers of the Earth to translate the *Peri 'Ez Hadar (The Fruit of the Goodly Tree)*. This essay draws largely from his translation.
2. This piece draws from an article written by Hannah Ashley, "Fruit of the Goodly Tree," for *Shomrei Adamah*'s newspaper, *Voice of the Trees*.
3. *Zohar Exodus* 23b.

24. In Search of the Omer

1. Maimonides' commentary on *Mishnah Menachot*, chap. 6, *Mishnah 6*.
2. *Sefer HaChinuch* on the Torah portion *Emor*, Mitzvah 303 and 307.
3. *Pesachim* 7b.
4. *Rosh Hashanah* 16a.
5. Rashi's commentary on *Talmud Rosh Hashanah* 16a.
6. Cf. Rabbi Shmuel Eidels on *Talmud Rosh Hashanah* 16b.

Sacred Community

26. Cosmos and Chaos: Biblical Views of Creation

Due to limitations of space as determined by editorial considerations, this essay is an abridged and somewhat simplified version of a significantly longer and more extensive treatment of the subject, as yet unpublished. For a comprehensive and masterful overview of many of the issues considered here, consult Jon D. Levenson, *Creation and the Persistence of Evil* (San Francisco: Harper and Row, 1988).

1. Clifford Geertz, "Religion as a Cultural System" in *The Interpretation of Cultures* (New York: Basic Books, 1973), p. 99. This seminal paper is devoted to a systematic discussion of Geertz's definition of religion. Note also Geertz's quotation of a definition of religion by Salvador de Madariaga: "The relatively modest dogma that God is not mad." Idem.

2. See, *inter alia*, E. A. Speiser's commentary to *Genesis*, The Anchor Bible (New York: Doubleday, 1985), pp. 8–13, 18–20; and Richard Elliot Friedman, *Who Wrote the Bible?* (New York: Summit Books, 1987), pp. 50–51.

3. Note that Creation 2 uses the Hebrew form *ytzr* (JPS translation: "form") to describe what God does to produce human beings (Gen. 2:7) and beasts and birds (Gen. 2:19), whereas Creation 1 uses the Hebrew *br'* (JPS: "create") throughout. The first suggests a preexistent matter out of which God "forms" creatures. The second suggests a more *ex nihilo* process at each stage of the process, though not, as noted above, for the process as a whole.

4. On the role of religion in structuring space, see Mircea Eliade, *The Sacred and the Profane* (San Diego: Harcourt Brace Jovanovich, 1959). See in particular Eliade's views on "the Center of the World," chap. 1 *passim*. In Judaism, that place is occupied by the Temple, which 2 Chron. 3:1 identifies with Moriah, the site where Abraham prepared to sacrifice his son Isaac (Gen. 22:14). Adopting Eliade's perspective, it is tempting to suggest that the tradition would identify Eden and Jerusalem. There are a number of texts that do imply such an identification, e.g., that locate Adam in Jerusalem. Adam is portrayed as sacrificing on Moriah and as having been buried in "the center of the earth," which is the site of the altar in the Jerusalem Temple. Other traditions teach that the site of the Temple, i.e., the center of the earth, was the place for the beginning of Creation. See Louis Ginsberg, *Legends of the Jews* (Philadelphia: The Jewish Publication Society of America, 1909), vol. 1, pp. 12, 89 and the endnotes in vol. 5, p. 14, n. 39; p. 117, n. 109; and pp. 125–126, n. 137.

5. This is a significant anticipation of the notion, central to the later Jewish

mystical tradition, that exile is as much a metaphysical condition as it is a historical condition.

6. Though in an ironic way, ultimate responsibility even for human evil can be attributed to God, for it is God who, according to Ps. 103:14, "formed" us "out of the dust," clearly an allusion to Gen. 2:7. That's why, according to this psalm, God must have compassion over us and not treat us according to our sinfulness.

7. On the relation of Creation and eschatology (the doctrine of the "end of days"), see my *Sacred Fragments: Recovering Theology for the Modern Jew* (Philadelphia: The Jewish Publication Society, 1990), chap. 10; and my *The Death of Death: Resurrection and Immortality in Jewish Thought* (Woodstock, Vt.: Jewish Lights Publishing, 1997), chap. 1. I understand Creation and eschatology as the parentheses that bracket the age of history in which, according to the Bible, we now find ourselves.

8. For an elaboration of this perspective on the relationship of history and eschatology, see Will Herberg, *Judaism and Modern Man: An Interpretation of Jewish Religion* (New York: Farrar, Straus and Young, 1951; Woodstock, Vt.: Jewish Lights Publishing, 1997), chap. 16.

9. On these genealogies as an ordering device, see Susan Niditch, *Chaos to Cosmos: Studies in Biblical Patterns of Creation* (Chico, Calif.: Scholars Press, 1985), pp. 55–56.

10. The claims that "God is the source of cosmos" and that ". . . humanity is the source of chaos," are clearly oversimplifications. They may reflect the thrust of the Genesis Creation narratives, but they seem to be contradicted by other versions of God's role in Creation scattered throughout the rest of the Bible. See Levenson's study of some of these passages and his conclusions, first, that God's control of the chaotic forces of nature is far more tenuous than the Genesis stories would have us believe and, second, that many biblical passages (e.g., Psalms 44 and 74) decry God's apparent inability to control the chaotic forces of history (Levenson op. cit. pp. 14 ff and *passim*).

11. *Mechilta* to Exod. 31:17.

12. *Mishnah Tamid* 7:4.

27. Restoring a Blessing

1. All the plants and animals alluded to are native to the deserts of Israel and are mentioned in the Bible.

2. Louis Ginsberg, *Legends of the Bible* (Philadelphia: Jewish Publication Society, 1956), p. 162.

3. Genesis 3:18, Job 31:40.

4. Ginsberg, p. 266.

28. What Is the Common Wealth?

1. Wendell Berry, *The Gift of Good Land* (San Francisco: Northpoint Press, 1981), p. 271.
2. Wendell Berry, *The Unsettling of America* (San Francisco: Sierra Club Books, 1977).
3. Ibid.

29. Jewish Agricultural Law: Ethical First Principles and Environmental Justice

1. P. Blackkman, *Mishnayot Volume 1, Order Zerayim* (New York: The Judaica Press, 1964).
2. S. M. Lehrman, *Seder Zera'im: Hebrew-English Edition of the Babylonian Talmud* (New York: MP Press).
3. Maurice Moshe Aranov, "The Biblical Threshing Floor in the Light of Ancient New Eastern Evidence: Evolution of an Institution," (Ph.D diss., New York University, 1977).

30. The Blessings of Holiness

1. Jacob Milgrom, *Leviticus 1–16*, The Anchor Bible (New York: Doubleday, 1991).
2. Private communication, October 1994.

32. Judaism's Environmental Laws

1. Moses Maimonides, *Law of Kings* 6:10.
2. *Mishnah Baba Bathra* 2:4.
3. Ibid., 22b.
4. Ibid., 2:3.
5. Ibid., 2:5.
6. Ibid., 22b–23a.
7. Ibid., 2:8.
8. Ibid., 23a.
9. *Mishnah* 2:9.
10. Moses Maimonides, *Laws of Neighbors* 11:4.
11. Ibid.
12. Ibid.
13. *Baba Kamma* 79b.
14. Ibid., 82b.
15. Ibid.
16. *Mishnah Baba Metziah* 8:5.

33. Business and Environment: A Case Study

1. Eric Freudenstein, "Ecology and the Jewish Tradition," *Judaism* 19 (1970): 406–14.
2. *Baba Kamma* 82a.
3. Lev. 6:4; *Pesahim* 27b; Moses Maimonides, *Mishneh Torah, Laws of Tamid and Musaf Offerings* 2:15.
4. *Baba Batra* 2:3.
5. Aaron Levine, "External Costs" in *Free Enterprise and Jewish Law* (New York: KTAV/Yeshiva University Press, 1980), pp. 58–77.
6. *Baba Kamma* 91b.

34. Between Dust and Divinity: Maimonides and Jewish Environmental Ethics

1. *Sanhedrin* 38a.
2. Moses Maimonides, *Guide to the Perplexed* III:12. Translated from the Arabic by Shlomo Pines (Chicago: University of Chicago Press, 1963). All quotations from the *Guide* are my gender-inclusive adaptation of the Pines translation.
3. *Guide to the Perplexed* III:12.
4. Ibid., III:13.
5. *Guide to the Perplexed* III:13; Gen. 1:1–31.
6. Ps. 144:4 and Isa. 40:15 as cited in *Guide to the Perplexed* III:12.
7. *Guide to the Perplexed* III:12.
8. Ibid., III:14.
9. Ibid.
10. Ibid., III:17.
11. Ibid.
12. Ibid.
13. Ibid.
14. Ibid., III:17 and III:18.
15. Ibid., III:18 and *Avodah Zarah* 54b.
16. Following the translation of Stephen Mitchell and others who read Job's statement *nechamti* as "I am comforted" rather than the traditional "I repent."
17. Stephen Jay Gould, "The Golden Rule," in *Eight Little Piggies* (New York: Norton, 1993), p. 49.
18. *Guide to the Perplexed* III:12. See also Maimonides' works on ethics such as *Shemonah Perakim*.
19. This paradoxical emphasis on humanity's smallness yet ultimate significance pervades many of the psalms and much of our liturgy, especially during the Days of Awe.

20. The entire speech coming from the Voice in the whirlwind is a magnificent poetic expression of humanity's smallness amid the terrible grandeur of Creation.

21. *Eruvin* 13b.

35. What Does the Hour Demand? Environmentalism As Self-Realization

1. Aaron David Gordon, "The Human and Nature," in *Mivhar Ketavim (Selected Writings)* (Jerusalem: Hassifiria Haziyonit: Publishing House of the World Zionist Organizations, 1982), pp. 57–58. Gordon's writings first appeared in many different journals, newspapers and sources. Gordon's collected writings were edited by S. H. Bergman and published in three volumes by Hassifiria Haziyonit from 1951 to 1954. Those volumes are now out of print. For that reason, all references will be made to this latest selection of Gordon's writings, which is only available in Hebrew. All translations are mine.

2. A. D. Gordon, "A Human People," in *Mivhar Ketavim (Selected Writings)* (Jerusalem: Hassifiria Haziyonit: Publishing House of the World Zionist Organizations, 1982), p. 264.

3. Ibid., p. 264.

4. Ibid., p. 265.

36. Living As If God Mattered: Heschel's View of Nature and Humanity

1. A. J. Heschel, *God in Search of Man* (New York: Farrar, Straus and Giroux, 1955), pp. 34, 285.

2. Ibid., p. 97

3. Ibid., p. 49.

4. Ibid., p. 283; A. J. Heschel, *Quest for God* (New York: Crossroads, 1982), p. 106.

5. A. J. Heschel, *Man Is Not Alone* (New York: Farrar, Straus and Giroux, 1951), p 290; *God in Search of Man*, pp. 105–106.

6. *Quest for God*, p. 7.

7. *Man Is Not Alone*, p. 145; *God in Search of Man*, p. 74.

8. *God in Search of Man*, p. 286.

9. A. J. Heschel, *The Sabbath* (New York: Farrar, Straus and Giroux, 1951), p. 28.

10. *Man Is Not Alone*, p. 189.

11. *The Sabbath*, p. 89.

12. *Man Is Not Alone*, p. 263.

About the Contributors

EILEEN ABRAMS is a writer and teacher and lover of trees. She lives in a Philadelphia suburb with her partner, their dog, two cats, and numerous fish. She is a member of Mishkan Shalom, a progressive Reconstructionist community.

BRADLEY SHAVIT ARTSON is rabbi of Congregation Eilat in Mission Viejo, California, and is author of *It's a Mitzvah! Step-by Step to Jewish Living.*

PHILIP J. BENTLEY is rabbi of Temple Shalom in Floral Park, Queens, New York. He has been a Jewish environmentalist for so long that when he first raised the subject in rabbinical school, he was told, "The environment? That's just a distraction from the real issue—Vietnam."

ELLEN BERNSTEIN, the editor of *Ecology & the Jewish Spirit,* is the founder of *Shomrei Adamah*—Keepers of the Earth, the first institution dedicated to cultivating the ecological thinking and practices integral to Jewish life. Her books include *Let the Earth Teach You Torah* and *A Celebration of Nature.* She currently works as Director of Community Building at the Jewish Federation of Greater Philadelphia.

ELLEN COHN is a Jewish Family Educator. She holds master's degrees in Talmud from The Jewish Theological Seminary of America and in Jewish Communal Service from Brandeis University, and she has been a fellow at the Drisha Institute in Manhattan. An environmentalist since childhood, she studies rabbinic texts to explore their sensitivity to nature. She grooms horses in her spare time.

ELIEZER DIAMOND acquired a love for nature from summers spent in bungalow colonies and a religious Zionist summer camp. An assistant professor of Talmud and rabbinics at The Jewish Theological Seminary of

America, he has written and taught on Judaism and the environment. He is married to Rabbi Shelly Kniaz and is the proud father of Aviva, David, Tova, and Yoni.

SHIRA DICKER writes for a variety of publications, both national and local, religious and secular, obscure and well-known. She has recently left her job at The Jewish Theological Seminary of America to spend a year in Israel with her family researching a book that will be published by Jewish Lights. On summer nights, she can be found in a small cabin in upstate New York meditating upon the moon.

DAVID EHRENFELD is professor of biology at Rutgers University in New Brunswick, New Jersey, where he teaches undergraduate and graduate courses in ecology. His books include *The Arrogance of Humanism* and *Beginning Again: People and Nature in the New Millennium*; he was the founding editor of the international journal *Conservation Biology*. He is married to Joan Gardner Ehrenfeld, who is also an ecologist. They have four children.

CHARLES FENYVESI writes a weekly column on gardening for *The Washington Post* and is a writer for U.S. News & World Report. His book chronicling his family history, *When the World Was Whole*, was published by Viking in 1990.

SHAMU FENYVESI teaches environmental studies and Judaism and ecology at the Teva Learning Center—cosponsored by *Shomrei Adamah*, Yitziah/Jewish Wilderness Journeys, and the Wild Rockies Field Institute. The inspiration for his stories comes from his work exploring the landscape of tradition and creation, his desert treks in Israel, and his family's stories. He grew up editing and being edited by his writer father and gardening in a front lawn–turned–vegetable garden in Washington, D.C.

DAN FINK is the twelfth in an uninterrupted line of rabbis. He has served in many rural congregations across America and is currently the first rabbi in Idaho. He is the co-author of *Let the Earth Teach You Torah*, and the primary contributor to *Judaism and Ecology*. He has hiked 1,000 miles of the Appalachian trail.

BARRY FREUNDEL is rabbi of Kesher Israel, a Modern Orthodox synagogue in Washington, D.C. He is an adjunct professor at Georgetown University Law Center and chairs the ethics committee of the Rabbinical Council of America.

DAVID GEDZELMAN was ordained as a rabbi at the Reconstructionist Rabbinical College, and is the creative and spiritual director of the Partnership for Jewish Life, a community of New Yorkers in their twenties and thirties. He is an avid outdoor enthusiast and has enjoyed many wilderness experiences in the western United States. He is also a musician and poet.

EVERETT GENDLER, a native of Iowa, studied at the University of Chicago and was ordained at The Jewish Theological Seminary of America. He served congregations in Mexico, Brazil, Cuba, and Princeton, New Jersey before spending the past 25 years as rabbi of Temple Emanuel in Lowell, Massachusetts. For most of that time, he was also Jewish Chaplain in Philosophy and Religious Studies at Phillips Academy, Andover. He and his wife, Mary, have lived for the last two and a half decades on a small acreage in Andover, where they have tended and tilled the soil.

NEIL GILLMAN was ordained as a rabbi at The Jewish Theological Seminary of America, where he is Professor of Jewish Philosophy. His books include *The Death of Death: Resurrection and Immortality in Jewish Thought* and *The Way Into Encountering God in Judaism* (both Jewish Lights).

NEAL JOSEPH LOEVINGER has been an outdoor and environmental educator for many years and holds a master's degree in environmental studies from York University. He spent several years studying for the rabbinate at the Reconstructionist Rabbinical College and is completing his rabbinical degree at the University of Judaism in Los Angeles.

VICTOR RABOY is a Research Geneticist working in the USDA's Agricultural Research Service in Aberdeen, Idaho. He studies the genetics of grains and investigates the nutritional quality of corn, wheat, barley, rice, and soybeans. His interest in agriculture was encouraged by his family and by his participation in the youth branch of the kibbutz movement Dror.

DEBRA J. ROBBINS is associate rabbi at Temple Emanu-El in Dallas, Texas and was ordained by the Hebrew Union College–Jewish Institute of Religion. Debra is married to Larry S. Robbins and is the mother of Samuel Norman Robbins, and they enjoy their summer vacations outdoors in New England.

ROBERT SAND lives in Los Angeles, California and writes screenplays and short stories.

MARC SIRINSKY is rabbi of Temple Emek Shalom in Ashland, Oregon. He is an avid white-water kayaker, and uses the proximity of the natural beauty in Southern Oregon to create innovative programs that link traditional Jewish teachings and practices with the natural world.

JEFF SULTAR is a graduate of the Reconstructionist Rabbinical College and is the rabbi at Choate Rosemary Hall in Wallingford, Connecticut. He founded the Natural Security Program at the Center for Common Security in Williamstown, Massachusetts, and has taught on environmental issues at Williams College. He is the author of *Little Miracles*, which traces the spiritual side of a 27-month, 16,000-mile, 46-state, solo bicycle journey across the United States.

MARC SWETLITZ was educated at M.I.T., The Jewish Theological Seminary of America, and the University of Chicago. He has published articles on the responses of nineteenth-century American Jews to evolutionary theory. Marc has a long-standing interest in Judaism, ecology, and Heschel. He edited *Shomrei Adamah*'s first publication, *Judaism and Ecology*.

LAWRENCE TROSTER is rabbi of Oheb Shalom Congregation in South Orange, New Jersey. He is a graduate of The Jewish Theological Seminary of America and has also served in pulpits in Toronto, Canada. Rabbi Troster has been active in the Jewish environmental movement through his writing, teaching, and his involvement with several organizations including the Partners for Environmental Quality, an interfaith environmental coalition in New Jersey.

Indexes

Index of Concepts

acid rain, 111

agriculture, 12, 72, 101, 146, 191, 196–205

angels, 29, 73–74, 142, 237

asceticism, 144, 145

balance, 67, 82–84, 97, 226–29, 237–39

Berachot, 43, 47, 148, 149, 150, 202, 203, 204, 205, 206

blessing, 202–6

business, 72, 119, 135, 222, 225, 227, 229

chaos, 175, 177, 184–85

childbirth, 208, 209, 212

community, 13–14, 22–23, 29, 32, 39, 55–56, 60–61, 68, 83, 97–98, 104–6, 110, 112, 114, 123, 125, 134, 143, 171–72, 177–78, 185–89, 190, 193, 195–96, 198–200, 202, 204, 211, 214, 221, 225–29, 240, 245, 250–56

consumption, 80–87

cosmos, 175, 177, 184–85

Creation, 27–28, 33, 35, 41, 44–45, 61–62, 64–68, 70, 74, 75–77, 87, 111–16, 118–19, 121, 123, 125, 128, 148, 179–83, 185, 189, 207, 209, 212, 230–31, 236–37, 242, 244, 253

Deep Ecology, 11, 18, 25, 28–31, 37–39, 42, 50–56, 65, 66, 101, 122–24, 162, 183, 222, 230, 238–39, 244, 250, 251, 254

desert, 25, 28, 29–30, 55–56, 99, 107

dominion debate, 20, 31, 33, 113, 233, 234, 236

Lynn White, 32, 33, 36, 39

Eden, 17, 20, 21, 82, 110, 143, 165, 175, 176, 185, 186, 256

environment

  assumptions related to, 26

  awareness of, 97

  concern of Sabbatical year for, 117–19

  cycling of elements in, 57

  halachic imperatives related to, 215–23

  implications of community for, 14

  implications of Shabbat for, 113, 115

  importance of Jubilee year for, 119–20

  maintaining healthy, 217–20

  protecting quality of, 216–17

  sense of place in, 172

  sustainability of, 85–86, 171

  taking responsibility for, 185, 198

environment *cont.*
  treatment with shift
    of perception, 68
  variation in customs
    related to, 154
  worsening crisis of,
    116
  See also ethic,
  environmental;
  laws, environmental
environmental thought
  Deep Ecology
    model, 37–39, 66,
    230, 238–39, 244
  stewardship model,
    237
ethic, environmental
  concept of holiness
    in, 13
  conventional
    Western, 38
  of Deep Ecology,
    38–39, 230
  effect on contempo-
    rary rituals, 224
  of Judaism, 39–40
  related to land, 190
ethics, 38, 114, 139,
  196, 198, 224, 229,
  231
four worlds, 144–45
freedom
  for the Israelites, 53,
    99
  symbolized in the
    Omer period, 165
Gaia
  defined, 57
  earth as living
    system, 57
goodness
  (Maimonides), 232
holidays, 22, 101–2,

104, 113, 123, 125–
  26, 129, 132, 159
kedushah (holiness),
  14, 200–2, 204,
  231, 232, 233, 235
law, 11–12, 22–23, 36–
  38, 44, 46, 48, 55,
  71, 85, 114, 135,
  143, 171, 181, 188,
  190–91, 214–19,
  221–23, 236
laws, environmental
  Jewish zoning
    regulations,
    226–29
  of Judaism, 214–23
  specific to
    Jerusalem, 223
liturgy, 46, 109–11,
  139, 179
moon
  dates determined by
    cycle of, 100,
    104–5, 113
  in determining the
    calendar, 104
  special blessing and
    fast day for, 111
  as unit of time, 99
  witnessing new
    moon, 104–6, 111
  yerach in Hebrew, 100
Omer, the, 167–71
panpsychism.
  See sentience, or
    panpsychism.
pilgrimages
  to gather sukkah
    branches, 137–38
  historical and
    present-day, 53
  Jewish festivals
    related to, 56

of Job, 29–30
place
  biblical sense of,
    172
  concept of sacred,
    13–14
  creating sense of,
    173–74
  of humans in the
    world, 237
  linked to order,
    177–78
  loss of, 175–76
  of man in Garden of
    Eden, 174–75
  Noah's ark as safe
    place, 177
pollution, 218, 219,
  220, 225–29
prayer, 61, 63, 65–68,
  107, 109–10, 117,
  127–28, 130–31,
  137, 139–40,
  185–87, 192, 202,
  212, 246–48, 253
rain
  beginning at Sukkot,
    130–31
  controlled by God,
    22, 25
  cycle in Israel of,
    128–29
  in the desert, 25, 28,
    30
  Passover heralds end
    of, 131–32
  praying for, 99
seven species, 129, 140
  barley, 99, 101, 106,
    111, 129, 147, 157,
    158, 162, 163, 164,
    165, 166, 182, 193
  wheat, 70, 74, 75, 76,

wheat cont.
106, 111, 129, 147,
162, 163, 164, 165,
166, 193, 195, 255
Sh'ma: prayer about,
127, 129, 186–88
See also
acid rain
sentience, or
panpsychism
of all Creation, 64
defined, 58
distinction within
sentient creation,
66–67
Jewish acceptance
of, 65–66
universal, 61
stewardship, 237–39,
250
of the earth, 136,
172
goal to be a good
steward, 77
perspective of Deep
Ecology, 238
in resolving poten-
tial conflicts, 229
tikkun, 75, 77, 140,
143, 158
time, 13–14, 39, 46,
97–99, 100–3,
107–8, 109–10,
113, 117, 121, 123,
151, 160, 200–2
utilitarianism, 245–46
wilderness, 11, 18, 25,
28–31, 42, 50–56,
65, 101, 122–24,
162, 183, 222,
250–51, 254
Wisdom literature, 19,
23, 25–27

work, 20–21, 31, 45,
54, 59, 78, 82, 88,
94, 113, 115–18,
120, 122, 136, 189,
197–98, 222, 228,
235, 241–42, 247
Zionism, 39, 243

Index to Jewish Sources

The Bible

Genesis
1   110
1–2:4a   173
1–11   21, 257
1:14   98
1:21   64
1:26   20
1:27–28   33
1:28   233
1:31   233
2:1–3   176
2:3   114
2:4b   174
2:4b–3:24   173
2:5–6   184
2:7   264
2:8   174
2:9   20
2:15   20, 174,
                 237
2:17   175
2:19   21, 264
2:23   175
3:17   22
3:18   265
3:19   21, 176
4:2   21
4:4–5   176

4:12   176
4:12–13   176
4:14   176
4:16–5:32   177
4:17   21
4:21–22   21
6:1–4   176
6:5   176
6:5–13   38
6:8   177
6:13   176
7:11   177
8:21   21, 177
8:23   177
9:1   177
9:2   21
9:8–17   59
9:9–17   177
9:20–27   177
10:1–32   177
11:10–32   177
12:1   177
22:14   264

Exodus
3:5   42, 58
4:22f   258
12:2   100
13:4   100
20:8–11   114, 178
20:14   84
23:1–10   118
23:15   100
23:19   258
24:10   36
31:7   265
31:13–14   178
31:13–17   115
31:18   36
33:12   258
34:21   114
34:22   163
35:1–3   115

Leviticus

1–16	266
6:4	267
18:24–30	259
18:26–28	22
19:9–10	190, 258
19:19	258
19:23–25	258
20:22–26	259
23:22	83
23:40	136
25:2–7	117
25:8–12	23, 119
25:23	43

Numbers

15:37–41	110
18:8, 12, 24–26	258
25:34	259
35:4–5	227

Deuteronomy

4:39	35
4:40	259
5:18	84
6:4–9	110, 186
8:7–10	47
8:8	129, 140
8:8–9	147
11:10–12	129, 263
11:13–14	22
11:13–21	110, 186, 263
14:27–29	83
15:11	199
16:11	136
16:14	136
16:15	136
17:16–17	84
18:4	258
20:5–7	81
20:19	85
20:19–20	86, 215

21:6–9	259
22:6	261
22:6–7	85
22:9–11	258
23:10, 13–14	224
24:19–21	258
26:1–11	258
27:9	258
28:63–68	257
30:11–14	189

1 Samuel

20	262

1 Kings

6:1, 37	101
6:38	101
8:2	101
12:32–33	102
19:4–8	258

2 Kings

23:22–23	103

2 Chronicles

3:1	264
30	102
35:17–19	103

Joshua

2:11	35
24:13	43

Ruth

1:16–17	160

Esther

9:22	151

Job

12:7–9	25
31:40	265
38:4, 6–7	238
38:7	259
38:26	25
39:9–12	25

42:6	235

Psalms

8	237
19	259
19:1–2	65
19:2	64
24:1	203
24:1–2	42
44	265
74	265
95:4	268
95:8	254
96:9	268
96:11–12	259
97:1	268
97:4–5	268
98:7–8	268
98:7–9	259
98:8	65
99:1	268
103:14	265
104:24	42
105:44–45	43
106:38f	259
144:4	267
148	61–64
148:7	64

Proverbs

6:6–9	24
16:4	64
104:13–16	140

Ecclesiastes

1:4, 9	137
1:4–7	24
2:1, 11	81

Song of Songs

2:10–13	155

Isaiah

35:1	65
40:15	267

Isaiah *cont.*
44:23   259
52:11   43
55:12   259

Jeremiah
2:1   258
8:7   38
31:2f   258

Lamentations
1:1   167
5:21   167

Ezekiel
4:13   43

Daniel
1, 3   64

Song of Three
23–40   65

Hosea
2:14–15   258
9:3   43

Amos
7:17   43

Micah
6:8   84

Zechariah
14:16–21   201

The Mishnah
44, 45, 83, 104, 162,
191, 192, 193, 194,
195, 199, 205, 216,
217, 218, 219, 220,
223, 227

*The Babylonian
Talmud*
44, 45, 46, 47, 58, 63,
81, 82, 84, 87, 104,
106, 111, 115, 117, 122,
129, 131, 164, 166,
202, 205, 216, 218,
223, 226, 229, 231, 268

*The Jerusalem
Talmud*
44, 45, 84, 205

The Midrash
42, 44, 162, 163

Maimonides
35–36, 84, 104, 123,
137, 163, 215, 221–22,
226, 231, 232, 233,
234, 235, 237

The Zohar
122, 144

About Jewish Lights

People of all faiths and backgrounds yearn for books that attract, engage, educate, and spiritually inspire.

Our principal goal is to stimulate thought and help all people learn about who the Jewish People are, where they come from, and what the future can be made to hold. While people of our diverse Jewish heritage are the primary audience, our books speak to people in the Christian world as well and will broaden their understanding of Judaism and the roots of their own faith.

We bring to you authors who are at the forefront of spiritual thought and experience. While each has something different to say, they all say it in a voice that you can hear.

Our books are designed to welcome you and then to engage, stimulate, and inspire. We judge our success not only by whether or not our books are beautiful and commercially successful, but by whether or not they make a difference in your life.

For your information and convenience, at the back of this book we have provided a list of other Jewish Lights books you might find interesting and useful. They cover all the categories of your life:

Bar/Bat Mitzvah
Bible Study / Midrash
Children's Books
Congregation Resources
Current Events / History
Ecology/ Environment
Fiction: Mystery, Science Fiction
Grief / Healing
Holidays / Holy Days
Inspiration
Kabbalah / Mysticism / Enneagram

Life Cycle
Meditation
Parenting
Prayer
Ritual / Sacred Practice
Spirituality
Theology / Philosophy
Travel
12-Step
Women's Interest

ELLEN BERNSTEIN is the founder of *Shomrei Adamah*—
Keepers of the Earth, the first institution dedicated to cultivating the ecological thinking and practices integral to
Jewish life. She currently works as director of community
building at the Jewish Federation of Greater Philadelphia.

"This timely collection, bringing out the ecological soul of Judaism, is a cause for
celebration. Its many refreshing voices call Jewish spirituality to reawaken to its own
glad reverence for Earth." —JOANNA MACY, author, *World As Lover, World As Self*

"Ellen Bernstein's pathbreaking work helps us to rethink the meanings of Judaism's
ancient texts as we struggle to find new ways of resolving today's ecological dilemmas."
—CAROLYN MERCHANT, professor of environmental history, philosophy,
and ethics, University of California at Berkeley; author, *Earthcare*

Also Available from Jewish Lights

The Way Into Judaism and the Environment
By Jeremy Benstein, PhD

An accessible introduction to the Jewish understanding of the
natural world and the key concepts central to Jewish environmentalism.

6 x 9, 288 pp, Hardcover
ISBN-13: 978-1-58023-268-5, ISBN-10: 1-58023-268-X

Torah of the Earth, Volumes 1 and 2
Exploring 4,000 Years of Ecology in Jewish Thought
Edited by Arthur Waskow

In two volumes, serves as an invaluable key to understanding the intersection of ecology and Judaism, and
offers the wisdom of Judaism in dealing with the present
environmental crisis.

Vol. 1: Biblical/Rabbinic, 6 x 9, 272 pp, Quality PB Original
ISBN-13: 978-1-58023-086-5, ISBN-10: 1-58023-086-5
Vol. 2: Zionism/Eco-Judaism, 6 x 9, 336 pp, Quality PB Original
ISBN-13: 978-1-58023-087-2, ISBN-10: 1-58023-087-3

For People of All Faiths, All Backgrounds

JEWISH LIGHTS Publishing
www.jewishlights.com

Printed in the USA
CPSIA information can be obtained
at www.ICGtesting.com
JSHW012021140824
68134JS00033B/2816